Independent Living with Autism

Your Roadmap to Success

Wendela Whitcomb Marsh, MA, BCBA, RSD

INDEPENDENT LIVING WITH AUTISM
Your Roadmap to Success

All marketing and publishing rights guaranteed to and reserved by:

FUTURE HORIZONS INC.

(800) 489-0727
(817) 277-0727
(817) 277-2270 (fax)
E-mail: info@fhautism.com
www.fhautism.com

ISBN: 9781949177046

This book is for

Anne Caitlin Robinson Marsh
Siobhan Eleanor Wise Marsh
Noel Maebh Whitcomb Marsh
and always
David Scott Marsh

ACKNOWLEDGMENTS

So many people along the road have helped this book come to be.

My beloved David Scott Marsh, and my parents, Drs. David and Susanne Whitcomb, whose unconditional love and support live on though they have gone.

My three brilliant and talented daughters, Anne, Siobhan, Noel. I am so proud of you and grateful to have you in my life. Your loving support, your courage, and your unique perspectives have helped make this book, and me, better.

My siblings, authors Jonathan David Whitcomb, Cynthia Susanne Whitcomb, Laura Louise Whitcomb. You inspire me.

Writers Support Group members Linda Leslie, Kristi Negri, Cherie Walters, Cynthia Whitcomb, Laura Whitcomb;

"Chez" authors who lunch Pamela Smith Hill and the Whitcomb sisters;

Diane Hagood, for her encouragement, insights, and recreation.

Early readers and personal editors, Cynthia Whitcomb, who read every word and would not let this book be less than its best, and Siobhan Marsh, whose eye for what's important helped take a much-too-long book and make it work.

Autistic authors and bloggers who have inspired me: Sean Barron, Gavin Bollard, Chris Bonello, Temple Grandin, Naoki Hagashida, Anita Lesko, Morgan Marie, Jerry Newport, Mary Newport, Ron Sandison, Amythest Schaber, Stephen Shore, Daniel Tammet, Diane Holliday Willey, and so many more.

INDEPENDENT LIVING WITH AUTISM

Many thanks to autistic adult contributors to *Speaking For Ourselves*: Cat, Kato Foxx, Morgan Marie, Noel, and Scott. Special thanks to The Doubleclicks for permission to use their lyrics in Part IV.

I am so very grateful to the outstanding team at Future Horizons, Inc, especially president Jennifer Gilpin Yacio and editor Rose Heredia-Bechtel. Thank you for your encouragement and support, and for making this book happen. I'm proud and honored to be on the Future Horizons team.

Finally, I owe a debt of gratitude to the many autistic adults I have met along the road, those whom I have known, loved, lived with, and worked with. You have each taught me something valuable I needed to learn, and this book would not have been possible without you.

CONTENTS

PART I
SOLUTIONS

———— ❦ ————

Navigating the Road Trip of Your Life

"Different ... not less."

— *Temple Grandin*

CHAPTER 1
INTRO TO ADULTING

———◄►●◄———

(Unfolding the Road Map)

I f you're reading this book, you may have received special education services as a student with autism when you were in school. Or perhaps you went through school without being identified, but now you, or people who know you well, wonder if you might be on the spectrum. Many "high functioning" individuals are not diagnosed until much later in life. Either way, now that you're an adult, you may be facing some challenges and looking for solutions. If only adulting came with a road map to help you avoid blind alleys, dangerous destinations, and precarious precipices.

If you're just out of school, your new status as a graduate may come with a sticker price. The services and supports you received in high school disappear the moment you walk across that stage and accept your diploma. Suddenly, you're expected to be an adult with all the rights and responsibilities that go along with adulthood. You can vote, but do you know how to find your own apartment, or land a job? In high school, your day was laid out for you by others; your class schedule told you where to go and what to do. Now that you're at home, the days stretch out and you may find yourself doing nothing, or doing the same things for long periods of time, with no one to tell you when to switch subjects. Maybe no one taught you how to schedule your own time or plan for independence.

Or maybe you went through school always knowing there was something different about you, but never knowing why. You may have been diagnosed with ASD as an adult, or you may have diagnosed yourself after reading about it and taking online tests. It doesn't matter if you have a formal diagnosis or not. (No one knows you better than you know yourself.) Now, you realize that knowing you're on the spectrum answers so many questions you had or things you wondered about. This book is for you, too, no matter your age or diagnosis.

The important thing to know is, you are not alone. There are a lot of people on the spectrum who experience the same kinds of challenges that you do: challenges related to social communication, relationships, unusual sensory responses, and intense interests.

Having challenges doesn't mean you can't live the life of your dreams. While there are no guarantees of anyone getting everything their heart desires, it's possible to have a life filled with meaning, fulfillment, and joy. You need the right solutions for your particular challenges.

Plenty of other people share your experience. If you're a young adult, then at last, after years of having your teachers and parents make up goals for you, you are now in charge of setting your own goals. If you are an older adult, understanding autism may be like turning on a light and suddenly seeing your life through a new lens. Armed with self-knowledge, you are ready to take your life in the direction that you want to go. All you need is a road map.

CHAPTER 1

You hold that road map in your hands. This book can be your guide to use as you see fit. It goes in depth into four main areas of living that many autistic adults find challenging: housing, independence, recreation, and employability, with potential solutions for each. If you don't have challenges in all of the areas the book covers, you can pick and choose what you want to work on. I suggest that you read the whole book first, and then go back down the roads that lead to your personal solutions.

One thing you may notice is that I often use identity-first language, "autistic adult," rather than person-first language, "adult with autism." This is because most of the autistic adults I know prefer it, and I want to honor this. Anne Marsh wrote, "Autism is rooted in the very way my brain is structured, which is a big part of why I prefer identity-first language. You don't need to say, 'Dorian is a person with autism,' any more than you would say, 'Billy is a person with gayness,' or 'Becky is a person with Jewishness,' or 'John is a person with blackness.' People who fit into these groups often choose identity-first language because our identities come with a fundamental way that experiences are shaped and shared." That said, since not everyone feels the same way about any issue, you will also find instances where I use person-first language. It is never my intention to disrespect anyone who prefers one or the other, but rather to honor diversity of expression.

Throughout this book you'll meet and get to know five fictional adults on the autism spectrum, of various ages and situations. Each one is working on becoming more independent and living their best life. You may see something you can relate to in one or all of them. Now, let's meet our five examples.

JACOB, 18

Jacob, a high school senior, just had his eighteenth birthday. He was diagnosed with what they called "high-functioning" autism at age four and has had an individualized education program (IEP) in school since then. Preschool through first grade he was in a small special day class (SDC) with other children who had autism and other learning disabilities. During the rest of his elementary school years, he spent most of his days in general education classes and was pulled out part of every day to receive resource specialist program (RSP) services and social skills training. Since middle school, his education has been almost entirely in general education courses with minimal support services. He is proud to be on track to graduate with a diploma rather than a special education "certificate of completion." He only needs to go to school half days this year because he has enough credits, but he's not sure what to do with his life after he graduates. Jacob loves video games and watching cartoons on television, but the afternoons are long while his parents are at work all day and he has nothing in particular to occupy himself with. He's bored and feels "up in the air," but he doesn't know what to do. The students he goes to school with are not really close friends, he realizes, but merely acquaintances. He never sees them outside of school. As for his future, Jacob would like to graduate and move into an apartment where friends could hang out. He would like to have a job he loves, a cool car, and a girlfriend. He wants solutions to get him started on his adult life.

CHAPTER 1

EMILY, 22

Emily, who just turned twenty-two, was diagnosed with autism spectrum disorder (ASD) at age eight and received special services in small special day classes throughout school. Although she did well on individually administered academic and IQ tests, she was considered too fragile or vulnerable to succeed in general education. She graduated from high school and has taken a few community college classes. Eventually, she wants to transfer to a four-year college in another state, far away from her parents. She realizes she has been coddled and infantilized in special education and by her parents, and that the people closest to her don't believe that she could live alone successfully. Her parents discourage her from trying to move out because they fear that she will be hurt or that she will fail. She wonders if they want to keep her at home because of the social security check that comes to them as representative payees every month, or if they have too much anxiety to let her out of their control. Whether they want her to stay home for financial reasons or because they worry too much, Emily would like to prove that she can get out and make it on her own. It's scary, but she really wants to do this.

ZACH, 33

Zach has not been formally diagnosed with any autism spectrum disorder, but he has always struggled with social communication. He graduated from college with a BA from the state university near his parents' home, where he lives. He did receive minimal special education services in elementary school, but when he asked his parents why, they said that he had a minor "social learning disability" but it was no big deal.

College was difficult for Zach, but his mother helped him organize his assignments and reminded him which classes he had on which days and times. He did not make friends in college, which he attributed to the fact that he lived at home rather than in the dorms. Now, just after his thirty-third birthday, he still has no idea what he wants to do with his life, or how to go about even trying. He spends much of his time on the computer, and his search for solutions led him to websites that described Asperger's syndrome (AS). The characteristics of AS sound familiar to him, and he is convinced that he has this syndrome, even though he has not been formally diagnosed. He would love to get out of his parents' home, if only to get away from their constant bickering and nagging, but he recognizes that he needs help to get on with his life.

MARIA, 45

Maria was a shy, quiet student in school with few friends. After graduation she married the first boy who paid attention to her and they had two children, twin girls. She enjoyed the life of a stay-at-home mom. Her husband divorced her because he said that she was "distant" and that she did not respond or relate to him as he expected a wife should. She chalked this up to jealousy, since as a full-time mom the twins were her primary job. Now they are off in college, and she has not yet decided what she wants to do "when she grows up." She

CHAPTER 1

is increasingly alone as her friends from before the divorce (wives of her husband's friends) have drifted away. Her sister and parents can't understand why she doesn't pull herself up by the bootstraps and get into a career of some kind. She has a nephew with autism, and as she learns more about him, she sees herself and her own life challenges. Her sister accuses her of being a hypochondriac, but the more Maria learns about autism and Asperger's, the more convinced she becomes that she has it. Maria's forty-fifth birthday served as a wake-up call for her to figure out what she wants the rest of her life to be like. She wants solutions to get her act together and to create the future she wants for herself.

ROBERT, 62

Robert lives with his wife, their adult daughter, and her son, Bobby. He had a career as a television repairman, which he loved. Then the world changed; there were no more cathode ray tubes that he knew and loved. People went out and bought a new flat screen set when their old TV broke. There was no place for an old-school TV repairman in the new century.

When his grandson, Bobby, was diagnosed with autism, Robert became fascinated with learning about the subject. Because he had been pushed into an early retirement before his sixty-second birthday, he had plenty of time to help his daughter and grandson. Robert attended every IEP meeting, and the more he learned, the more he realized that he himself was probably on the autism spectrum. He found a psychologist with experience evaluating autism in adults and learned that he does, indeed, have autism spectrum disorder. Now that he is around the house most of every day, he drives his wife and daughter crazy. Robert wants solutions to improve communication with his wife and family, and to live his best life.

None of these fictional characters will be exactly like you, but each of them has at least some problems in the areas of housing, independence, recreation or employability. Some are major problems and others are minor issues, but these challenges are shared by many. Maybe you can relate to some of them. As you go through the chapters of this book, you will see how each of these five characters learned to manage each challenge.

In addition, each chapter contains a section called "Speaking for Ourselves." These short essays are written by real people with ASD, unlike the fictional characters we just met. They share their own personal journeys in the hopes that you might find encouragement and support to map out your own journey.

SPEAKING FOR OURSELVES

"I was in college when I first received a diagnosis on the autism spectrum. There wasn't a whole lot it seemed this could do for me at that point—I was out of primary and secondary school, where a more accurate IEP might have made a difference; the college didn't have specific accommodations for ASD—and yet at the same time, it was incredibly helpful to have just for myself. Being able to read up on the diagnosis gave me a better understanding of myself and let me know that for someone on the autism spectrum, I was normal and doing well in many areas.

CHAPTER 1

"Having this diagnosis also gave me another way of interacting with the world, of finding other people online who related to this part of my life and who could share their experiences, commiserate with mine, and trade tips on managing life.

"The process of receiving a diagnosis as an adult can be difficult. I had had other diagnoses in the past, which didn't cover the whole picture but which I was accustomed to. It's not easy to reformat your identity when you've been carrying a whole different set of labels for fifteen years, or twenty. It's not all unmixed relief. If the face of autism had been different when I was a child, I might have grown up with a diagnosis on the autism spectrum.

"I first self-diagnosed with autism around second grade, after reading an article in *Reader's Digest*, back during a time when autism was seen as presenting with a more rigid set of signs, among them being non- or low-verbal and having a low IQ and intolerance for touch. After accepting that I 'couldn't be autistic,' it was difficult to later find that I was. However, the greater self-understanding and sense of community both helped as I came to embrace what makes me, me. I wouldn't want anyone else's brain. It took me a long time to learn just what made mine what it is, and it's a part of me that's worth knowing."

— *Cat, autistic adult*

CHAPTER 2
INTRO TO COMMUNICATION

➤❖⬟❖◄

(He Said, She Said)

In the world of communication, there is a lot more going on than a simple "he said, she said." How did he say it? What did she mean by it? What is the subtext? There are hidden messages, things people communicate nonverbally, and meaning behind the face value of the spoken words. Everyone has misunderstandings sometimes, but communication is an area of particular challenge for most people on the autism spectrum. That's partly because communication includes a lot more than words. It includes tone of voice, inflection, facial expression, gestures, and underlying context, all rolled up together. Sarcasm, for example, is difficult to understand for some autistic people. Why would someone say one thing, like, "That's just great," and mean the opposite? It doesn't make sense. But when you get the full context, you can figure it out.

Suppose you told your significant other that you got a promotion at work, and they say, "That's just great." On face value, you would assume they were happy for you. But check out the nonverbal cues to be certain. Are they smiling? Does their smile appear to be genuine and fairly symmetrical, rather than lopsided or with one corner of their mouth tensed up? Are they making eye contact (if this is something they usually do)? Is their forehead as smooth or unwrinkled as usual? Do they have both eyebrows fairly straight across rather than raised or lowered, and are both eyebrows in the same position? Is their body in a relaxed state with no visible tension, shoulders down and hands resting in a naturally open position? Are they turned toward you more than away from you? You might not see all these things, but if most of them are true you should assume they are really happy for you and your promotion.

Words alone don't tell the whole story, though. There is usually an unspoken subtext, the hidden meaning behind their words. They might be using sarcasm and mean the opposite when they say, "That's just great." Check out their facial expression. Are they frowning? If they are smiling, does their smile appear to be pinched or twisted, lopsided, or pulled up on one side? Are they looking away from you, looking up or down, or rolling their eyes? Is one eyebrow raised higher than the other? Are their shoulders raised up, hands fisted, body turned away from you? Any one of these could be a sign that the phrase was meant sarcastically, and they don't really think your promotion is great at all.

Think also about context, or other facts related to your message about getting a job promotion. Will this promotion mean you will be working longer hours, or traveling farther away, or even moving to another city? Will it be more stressful for you? Your significant other might be worried that you will be overworked or overwhelmed, that you won't be there for companionship, or that you'll be unable to handle your share of the household chores. If a longer commute is involved, they may worry that any raise in pay associated with the promotion will be eaten up by gasoline and automobile maintenance, plus even more time away from home. If you need to move for this job, they may be wondering what will happen to your relationship. Will they be expected to leave everything behind and follow you, or will the relationship break up?

Don't assume that your partner is thinking any of these things, but definitely do ask them how they feel about what you shared. Maybe their nonverbal communication means they are preoccupied by stress in their own life, unrelated to the news about your promotion. If they really are happy for you, but they have other worries, this may be a good time for you to listen to them. If they have concerns about your job, talk it out calmly. If it's not a good time to have a longer conversation about it, set a date to talk about it later.

When it's time to talk about a serious issue, it's important to start calm and stay calm. Try not to be critical or defensive, or say things like, "You never ___!" or "You always ___!" Instead, stick with your own feelings and needs, not your partner's. State your position with phrases like "I feel ___" and "I need ___." (Don't be sneaky with this by saying "I feel that you never ___!" or "I need you to stop always ___!" That's not starting calm and staying calm.)

Take turns listening to each other, and I mean really listening, not thinking about what you're going to say when it's your turn to talk. To show that you were listening, repeat back your partner's ideas in your own words and check with them that you understood correctly. Then switch, and let your partner listen to you and rephrase your words to show they understand you. This is active listening (or reflective listening). Stick with it until you can each understand and describe your partner's position.

Read how our five example characters dealt with communication challenges in their lives.

JACOB, 18

When Jacob started half-days at school, his parents asked him to get a part-time job. Every day when Jacob's father got home from work, he asked Jacob questions like, "Do you have any jobs lined up yet?" "Why not?" "What are you doing about it?" "Where have you applied?" He also made comments such as, "You'll be out of school soon. You can't waste your life playing games all day. You're not a kid any more, you need to start pulling your weight." The more questions he asked, and the more critical remarks he made, the more stressed out Jacob felt. After a few questions the pressure got to be too much, until he couldn't think of what to say. He usually ended up yelling at his father to "get off my back!" and shut himself up in his room.

Jacob knew that this argumentative cycle wasn't good for his relationship with his dad, and it wasn't helping him, either. Every negative comment or question seemed to fill up his brain with numbing anxiety so that he couldn't respond calmly. When he retreated to his room, he played video games to help relieve his stress, even though he realized that only supported his father's position about "wasting his life on video games." Jacob needed to find a way to communicate with his father to stop the toxic pattern that was not working for either one of them.

CHAPTER 2

In school, when Jacob gets stressed out, his teachers write him a note. They knew it was easier for him to communicate in writing when things got to be too much and his verbal communication systems started to shut down. He decided to try writing instead of talking.

He also tried to see things from his father's point of view. What did his father really want? What was he trying to communicate? Was he actually trying to stress Jacob out and purposefully push him over the edge into escape mode? Was his motivation to harm Jacob, or was he trying (unsuccessfully) to help him? Jacob recognized that his father really did love him and worry about his future, and all the overwhelming questions and comments come from a place of wanting to help but not knowing how. Jacob decided to write his father a letter:

Dear Dad,

I know you love and worry about me, and I want you to know that I am worried, too. I understand I can't spend the rest of my life living here and playing video games, and I do want to get a job and get on with my life. It is painful for me to admit that I don't know what to do. When you ask me questions about my future, I freeze up, panic, and run away to hide in my video games. I know you ask me these questions because you love me, but it's not helping.

Here is what I already do to try to get an after-school job: I search for jobs online and fill out applications online. I never hear back from any of them. I don't know what else I can do. I worry that I will never find a job. I worry that if I do get called in, I will make a mess of the interview and no one will hire me. I worry that I will be homeless one day. All of these worries fill up my brain and I can't think, so I play video games. I win at video games, but I suck at life.

Instead of asking me questions when you get home from work, can you help me figure out what I can do next? I'm sorry for this long note but I find it difficult to talk about it. I love you and Mom very much and I hate to be a burden to you.

Love, Jacob

When Jacob's father read the note, he shared it with Jacob's mom, and then all three of them sat down to talk. His father apologized for not seeing how his questions affected Jacob, and said he'd try to change. Both parents assured him that they loved him and wanted the best for him, that he was not a burden, and that they would never kick him out to make him homeless. They agreed to help him with his job search, and his father said he'd look into to some possible connections he had at work. This helped Jacob relax about the future, and he felt encouraged that his father would help him with his job search.

Writing down all of the difficult things he had to say, so that he could take his time and state his ideas calmly, was the solution for Jacob's communication challenge.

EMILY, 22

Emily was tired of being babied by her parents, and of being in the dark about her social security money. She had no idea how

CHAPTER 2

much money came in, where it went, or what it paid for. Whenever she asked her parents about money, they told her she didn't need to worry about it and offered to buy her whatever she wanted. In the past she used to whine and cry that she wanted to be the boss of her own money, but they said her childish attitude proved she was not grown up enough to handle it. They always responded to reasonable requests for books or clothes and bought her what she asked for, but she still didn't have any idea about the government money that helped support her as a disabled person. Could she use that money to live on her own in an apartment instead of living with her parents? She decided to find out.

Emily had a case management meeting coming up, so she emailed her social worker in advance to let her know she had a lot of questions about becoming more independent and taking control of her own money. Her social worker encouraged her to speak up at the meeting and said she would support Emily. She also let her know that often when she spoke her voice was quiet, high-pitched, and raised up at the end of sentences so that they sounded like questions. She told Emily that many people had one or more of these vocal qualities, but when all three were put together they gave the impression that Emily was uncertain, and she sounded younger than her age. Emily practiced using a calm voice, not too high, and loud enough to be heard. She also tried not to let her voice raise up at the end of sentences. She practiced in her bathroom with the fan on so her parents wouldn't hear her, and eventually felt confident in her ability to speak in a calm, confident voice, not too soft, and not too high or childish.

When the day of the meeting came, the social worker asked if she had any questions. Emily took a deep, relaxing breath and tried to keep her voice steady and firm, not high, whiny or childish. She calmly asked how much money was in her monthly check, and if she could control that money herself instead of her parents. She learned that, because of her disability (autism spectrum disorder), someone in authority had decided that she could not control her own money but had to have a representative payee, which was her father. He repeated his usual statement he would take care of her and she would never have to worry about money. Her parents were shocked when she asked, "What about when you die? Do you think you are going to live forever?" Her mother started to cry quietly, which upset Emily, but she felt strongly about this and pushed on. "I want to take care of myself and my own money. I'm not a baby anymore, and I'm not stupid. How will I learn how to survive after you die if you don't let me start learning now?" Her case manager supported her, and together they developed a plan for her to show that she was capable of independence. Even if it was not possible for her to have complete control of her money, her father agreed to share with her the decisions about how the money got spent. She felt bad about making her mother cry, but at the end of the meeting both her parents hugged her. They said they only wanted her to be protected and taken care of, and they would help her learn to take care of herself.

When she spoke up for herself calmly in a voice that was not too high or too quiet, with a support person (her social worker) to back her up, Emily found that her parents really listened.

CHAPTER 2

ZACH, 33

Zach went online daily and searched, "Why can't I find a job?" He scrolled down to read all the comments on every post. He spent hours bogged down in angry, negative complaints about the failing economy, the dismal job market, and how American jobs are outsourced or taken over by computers. It seemed impossible for anyone to get a job these days. Why even try?

Every day when his parents got home from work, he talked to them nonstop about the bleak outlook for anyone trying to find work in today's economy. He quoted statistics and theories he found online, without even giving them a chance to respond. Eventually, they gave up trying to reason with him and asked him to be quiet and let them have a quiet dinner. It was hardly quiet the way they bickered back and forth, but apparently, they wanted to talk to each other without his lectures. He found this frustrating and discouraging. Why wouldn't they listen and help him?

One day he decided to try something different. Instead of, "Why can't I get a job?" he searched, "How can I get a job?" He read the content only and didn't scroll down to read the comments. They were usually negative and depressing, anyway.

That night when his parents came home from work, Zach didn't say much beyond, "Hi, how was your day?" He waited until they were seated around the dinner table and his parents had chatted about their days. Then he told them about one of the articles he read online. After sharing the main points, he asked them what they thought about it. They were surprised and pleased by this different approach, and it opened the door for an interesting and enjoyable conversation over the dinner table. They also gave Zach some new ideas to try in his job search.

When Zach focused on the positive rather than the negative, shared a small amount of information rather than lecturing, and asked his parents' opinion, their communication improved.

MARIA, 45

Maria wanted to be in better communication with her daughters in college, but she didn't know how to connect. She hated talking on the phone, and she didn't know how to text or tweet. While she had an email account, she rarely remembered to check her emails for messages, and her children were often angry with her because she didn't respond when they emailed her. Maria found it stressful to open her email and see dozens of messages, most of them advertisements wanting something from her. She couldn't face it, so she shut it down.

Maria preferred writing longhand rather than typing. She wondered how she could find a way to be in touch using her strength rather than her stressor, and at the same time improve her responsiveness to her children.

Maria decided that every month she would write a letter to each of her girls and mail the letter to them at college. Each letter would be short and would include a memory of something they had done together during that month when the kids were younger, such as remembering their first day of kindergarten, a family vacation, or a holiday memory. There would also be a simple statement that she was fine, hoped they were too, and that she loved them. She bought attractive stationery and

CHAPTER 2

stamps, and wrote on her calendar to write letters every Sunday. She knew they wouldn't write letters in return, so she had two more parts to her plan.

Maria made an appointment with herself, and wrote it on her calendar, to check her emails at five o'clock every evening. This would not be a huge chore, because she determined to skip over all emails that were not from her children or close family or friends, and only respond to those she knew personally and cared about.

She also made a separate appointment with herself to delete old emails from her account every Wednesday at noon. When she saw repeated messages from the same company, she went in and found the place to unsubscribe to avoid getting those in the future. After fifteen minutes of working on deleting emails, no matter how many were left, she would close the computer and do something she enjoyed, such as reading.

Maria found a solution to her problem communicating with her daughters in two ways. First, she focused on her strength, writing longhand and using "snail mail." Second, she made plans to manage her email accounts to avoid being overwhelmed. These two steps helped her feel more connected to her girls while they were at college.

ROBERT, 62

Robert made a point of attending Bobby's IEP meeting with his daughter because he loved his grandson and wanted to learn more about autism. He had plenty of questions, and as soon as an idea or question popped into his head, he put it out there.

The IEP lasted two and a half hours and had to be held over for a second meeting. He didn't notice that his interruptions prolonged the process. At the end of the meeting, he felt exhilarated by everything he had learned. He didn't notice that his daughter and the IEP team were weary and exasperated with him.

On the way home, his daughter told him that she was embarrassed that he dominated the meeting, talking over people and getting in the way of the work they were trying to do for Bobby. If he couldn't sit quietly and listen to the team, he could stay home next time.

Robert was devastated. He hadn't realized that his many questions about autism bogged everything down. He loved getting a personal education from the experts at the table, but his daughter told him he shouldn't expect his grandson's IEP team to be his teachers. This meeting was not about him. Robert didn't want to be cut out. He'd need to change his behavior drastically.

With his daughter's permission, Robert attended the follow-up IEP, this time as a silent team member. He brought a small notebook and whenever he thought of a question, he wrote it down. Often, the question was answered later in the meeting, so he jotted down the answer and checked it off his list. His other questions he saved, and he either asked his daughter when they got home or he searched online for answers.

At first it was difficult for Robert not to blurt out everything that popped into his head, because he wasn't used to stifling his impulses, but he worked on it. Having his notebook right in front of him on the table was a visual reminder for him to write it down instead of interrupting. Learning that his grandson also struggled to raise his hand instead of calling out answers in class made him try even harder to avoid interrupting.

CHAPTER 2

Robert found a solution to his communication problem by writing down his questions and curbing his impulse to interrupt. This made him a welcome member of his grandson's IEP team.

SPEAKING FOR OURSELVES

"One of my biggest frustrations in communicating and socializing with groups of neurotypicals is how fast the conversation moves, and how some neurotypicals are no better than we are at spotting cues. I often find myself talked over, even when I feel like I've made it clear that I have something to say. It can really dampen my enthusiasm socially to feel ignored and overlooked, and I used to just withdraw from group conversations after having this happen once or twice. It can feel like the whole conversation has passed me by.

"I've discovered that most people actually don't think it's too strange or bothersome if you take advantage of a lull to bring things back to an earlier topic. While there are times that it doesn't feel natural, when there is a pause, people often accept returning to an earlier point to add something new. I can say, 'Going back to ____,' or 'You know, I just remembered ___.' Then I still have the chance to contribute, even when the initial moment went by too quickly. It's led to my feeling more confident, not just about joining in with those thoughts, but more confident engaging in verbal communication, period."

— *Cat, autistic adult*

CHAPTER 3
INTRO TO SOCIAL NAVIGATION

(Avoiding the Road Blocks)

R oad trips are fun until you run into a road block. Social events can be like a journey into uncharted territory. It isn't easy finding your way through a social world that seems designed by and for neurotypicals. It can be especially difficult if the people around you believe that their idea of a healthy social life should be yours, too. But we know people and paths are different, and the best route for you will not be identical to someone else's. You may need to advocate for yourself and tell the people who love you that you appreciate that they care, but sometimes their suggestions for socializing don't fit with the person you are.

Like many people on the autism spectrum, you may find that you have a strong desire for predictability. Not knowing what to expect can increase your stress and decrease your ability to cope. Unfortunately, social situations are seldom predictable and often fraught with potential pitfalls. You can create a road map for yourself, though, to make navigation more manageable. There are two important steps you can take before any social activity that will help keep you on the right road: make yourself a Plan A, and a Plan B.

PLAN A: First, think about what you believe the social event will be like. Ask some basic questions to get a feel for what to expect.

Where will it be held? Have you been there before? If not, see if you can make an advance trip to the location. Even if it's a quick drive-by, it will be somewhat familiar when you return. If you can't do that, many public buildings have images online so you can see what the place looks like. Having a mental picture of where you're going can give you confidence.

Who will be there? Relatives and long-time family friends? People from work? Strangers? Knowing up front who you are likely to see can help you feel prepared.

What will happen? Is this an audience type of event such as a movie, play, lecture, or concert? If so, there will be less demand for conversation. Is it an unstructured party? Then be prepared to make small talk, and create a mental list of potential topics.

What should you talk about? Avoid anything controversial, such as politics or religion. If you have an interest that you love to discuss, consider keeping it to yourself at social events, particularly with people you don't know well. Hold off until you find out if others are also interested in your topic. Then, pay attention to how much you are talking as compared to your conversation partner or group. If you seem to be doing most of the talking, take a breather. Try asking someone else a question, or pause and allow someone else to change the subject.

Having a plan will ease your way. However, if Plan A falls through, you need ...

CHAPTER 3

PLAN B: Things have changed. Maybe the party moved to a new location, or maybe people you don't know show up unexpectedly, or maybe you thought you were going to a lecture but it turned out to be a discussion group. Everything is different from what you prepared yourself for. Now what? This is when Plan B goes into effect. Before the event, after familiarizing yourself with Plan A, think about what you could do if things change.

You might have an affirmation you can repeat silently to yourself, something that helps you cope, such as, "This is different, and that's okay." You don't need to say it out loud, but keep thinking about it to remind yourself that everything is going to be all right.

When you first arrive, look for a safe space where you can retreat if you need to regroup. You might step outside for a breath of fresh air, weather permitting. In someone's home, you might go to a den or guest room. If you know your hosts well, especially if they are aware that you're on the autism spectrum, let them know up front that you might need a quiet place to go and ask them for suggestions. In a public place, such as a restaurant, church, or concert hall, look for a lounge, foyer, or restroom. Plan where you could go if you needed to calm down.

Have an exit strategy in mind before you arrive, especially if you suspect you may not be able to handle the entire social event. If you drove yourself, try to park in a place where you can easily leave. If you came with someone else, plan your exit strategy if they don't want to leave as soon as you do. Do you wait in the car? Do you call a taxi or use a rideshare app? Do you have a relative or close friend who is prepared to come pick you up? Be sure to get their agreement to be your backup transportation in advance. If you have the safety valve of an exit strategy in place you may find you don't need to use it, but it's wise to plan for detours just in case.

Let's see how each of our five characters dealt with social challenges in their lives.

JACOB, 18

Jacob had the feeling that his mother was often mad at him, but he didn't know why. She always denied it when he asked her. When she came home from work, she usually looked around and sighed with a small frown on her face. Jacob felt something was wrong but had no clue what it might be. Finally he decided to write her a note, because that worked with his dad. He wrote:

> Dear Mom,
> When you come home from work, I feel like you are mad at me but I don't know why. You say nothing is wrong, but you don't seem happy. This is confusing. Is it me? Have I done something you don't like? Please tell me, even if it's something bad, because I worry that something terrible must be wrong. I have trouble figuring out stuff like this on my own, and the confusion makes me anxious.
>
> Love, Jacob

His mother read the note and asked him to sit down for a talk. She told him that she wasn't mad at him, but she was disappointed that he never did the things she asked him to do around the house. Jacob was surprised.

"When did you ever ask me to do anything?"

CHAPTER 3

"Just this morning. Before I left for work, I asked you to pick up the books and newspapers scattered around the living room, but they're all still here."

"You never told me to do it. I remember, you said, 'There are too many books and newspapers all over the place, those need to be put away,' which was true. That's a statement, Mom. You never asked me to pick them up."

"I assumed you would know you were the one I wanted to put them away," she said. "Your father and I are at work, and you're home all afternoon. You're old enough to start pulling some weight around the house like an adult."

The social glitch was because of Jacob's literal way of thinking. His mother assumed that by pointing out a job that needed to be done, he would realize she wanted him to do it. He would have been happy to help out if he had understood what she wanted. He didn't get it, though, and then he felt embarrassed about missing the message.

Jacob's mother agreed to leave him a list of jobs to do around the house before she left for work in the morning. That was their Plan A, because having a physical list on paper was something Jacob could easily respond to.

But sometimes she was in too much of a hurry to write things down, and she would mention something else for him to do as she was going out the door to work. The problem was, she was used to phrasing things gently, such as, "Dinner's over. Don't you want to load the dishwasher now?" Jacob saw this as a literal question about whether or not he actually wanted to do the job, not as a request for him to do it. He was an honest person, and would truthfully answer, "No," if he didn't want to, but he had no problem doing it if he knew it was his job.

Plan B was that if his mother thought of something else she wanted him to do at the last minute and she couldn't write it down, she would put it in the form of a direct, non-ambiguous request, such as, "Please unload the dishwasher before I get home." He agreed to do jobs around the house while his parents were at work, as long they told him what they needed.

Jacob solved his social-emotional problem of misunderstanding his mother's feelings by writing her a letter and then talking with her about it. They came up with a Plan A (making a list of chores) and Plan B (using direct language rather than hinting when she couldn't make a list). Being clear by making lists and using literal language was a good solution for them.

EMILY, 22

Sometimes Emily's parents had dinner parties for their friends or colleagues from work. Emily always found these difficult. She ate quickly with her head down and then ran to her room to escape as soon as the meal was over. Her parents were disappointed. They thought that their guests felt snubbed or unwelcome when Emily failed to look at anyone when they talked to her, and then rushed off to her room as soon as she was done eating. Because she wanted to become more independent, Emily knew she would have to find a way to handle social events gracefully.

Emily understood that most people expect eye contact during conversations. She didn't want to be rude, but she found eye contact extremely uncomfortable and sometimes painful. She couldn't stand the weird feeling she got when looking at

CHAPTER 3

eyeballs. She decided to train herself to lift her head as if she were making eye contact, and then to look at a spot between the person's eyes on the bridge of their nose, or at their glasses. She thought that if she did this while smiling and occasionally nodding, they might not realize she wasn't actually making eye contact.

Emily also knew that she probably couldn't manage an entire social evening with her parents' guests, but that running away suddenly made other people feel awkward. They might wonder if they had said or done something to offend her and drive her away. So, Emily had an escape route with a Plan A, the set-up, and Plan B, the escape.

Emily wanted to set up her escape so that it wouldn't seem so abrupt and the guests would realize she wasn't avoiding them. This would be her Plan A. She was a student at the community college, so she decided to use studying as an excuse. During the dinner, if anyone asked her how she was doing, she would tell them what course she was taking and that she enjoyed it. Having an idea of what to say in advance made her more comfortable.

Emily's Plan B was the actual escape. She wrote a script for what she would say to the group before going upstairs, and practiced it: "This has been great, but I'm afraid I have to go study. It was wonderful to see you all again." She could modify it to, "It was lovely to meet you," in the case of new guests she didn't know. Then, as soon as everyone stood up from the table to move to the living room, she smiled, gave her rehearsed statement, and left.

Planning alternate ways to get her own needs met without being socially awkward, such as approximating eye contact, having scripts of things she might say, and having an exit strategy, helped solve Emily's social dinner party problems.

ZACH, 33

Zach has always had a hard time making friends. In school, the other kids never seemed to share his interests. Eventually, they started blocking empty seats when he approached their cafeteria table and he ended up eating alone or going to the library. He had strong opinions about politics and current events, and they didn't want to hear about it. As an adult, he assumed everyone should share these interests, but people often walked away while he was talking. It hurt.

He decided to analyze what went on right before people left. It seemed like each time he had been talking excitedly about something in the news that he felt strongly about, giving his own interpretation and suggestions of what should be done about the political problem. He realized that when he was excited, he talked nonstop and no one else had a chance to get a word in. He liked being able to finish a string of thoughts without being interrupted, so he talked quickly with few pauses to allow others to offer their ideas or try to change the subject. He didn't want the subject to change. Now he saw that this was putting people off.

Zach decided to practice letting others lead the conversation rather than always taking over. This was his Plan A. Wednesday night, his temple hosted a social event for "thirty-somethings." He had attended in the past, but people avoided him. Maybe they were fed up with his lectures. This time, he was determined to be a conversation follower rather than a conversation hijacker. He sat down with some people he had known since they were teens. They were talking about some boring TV show he hadn't seen. This time, though, instead of interrupting and turning the conversation to something he wanted to talk about, he just listened. After a while, the conversation turned to movies, including one that he had seen. He made a statement about what he liked about the movie, and then stopped talking. Someone asked him a question, and he answered briefly, and then asked them what they thought of the movie. He spent much more time listening than talking, which felt different, but he also felt accepted by the group. Once they saw that he wasn't trying to take over the conversation, they were much more open to him, and he didn't get those confusing sidelong looks.

Zach's temple social experiment was a success, but he still felt like he had a lot to say about the political climate of the times, and no outlet. He needed a Plan B to meet his need to talk politics in a socially appropriate way. He looked online and found that his political party needed workers to help get out the vote. He volunteered and found other like-minded people who also enjoyed talking about politics. As long as he remembered to take turns and not lecture, the discussions were lively and left him feeling invigorated and positive. He was glad to meet people who agreed with him and shared his passion for politics.

For Zach, a Plan A for curtailing his impulse to hijack social conversations, combined with a Plan B to find people who shared his interests, improved his social interactions.

MARIA, 45

Maria rarely went out, and she was beginning to feel more and more lonely and isolated. She used to attend church when her children were young, but it was difficult to make herself go when she didn't have the twins to motivate her. Not only that, she felt embarrassed by her divorce and didn't want pity. Eventually, though, she listened to her mother and sister's advice and decided to give church another try.

First, she thought about what she liked and missed about going to mass. She enjoyed the familiar liturgy, the sacred music, and Father Gonzales' hopeful and uplifting homilies. She felt more relaxed after prayer and quiet reflection. Maria wanted these things back in her life, but she needed to feel comfortable getting back into the church routine.

Maria's church was a hugging and handshaking church. She hated hugging strangers, and she didn't shake hands because of germs. She didn't want to look rude by refusing. They might think she was uppity or a snob, which certainly wasn't true. She needed a Plan A to avoid contact.

Hugging and handshaking usually happened before and after service, while people were milling around and finding their pews, and then again as they lingered on their way out. Maria decided to avoid much of this contact by arriving early and sitting in the center of a pew near the front. She knew most people preferred to sit at the back, so there would be fewer people near her. Also, if she wasn't near the aisle, it would be difficult for anyone to reach her. She could smile and wave from a distance, and avoid all but the most tenacious huggers and hand-graspers.

Still, some were persistent and could try to hug her or shake her hand on the way out of church. Maria needed a Plan B to avoid those she couldn't escape from. She thought about how some people did a high five or fist bump instead of shaking hands or hugging, but that wasn't her style. She decided that whenever a handshake or hug seemed imminent, she would place her

CHAPTER 3

palms together under her chin, in an almost prayer-like attitude, and bow her head slightly toward them with a polite smile. It might look quirky, but it would make her unavailable for a hand-shake or hug, without insulting the other person.

After making her Plan A and Plan B, she went to mass the following Sunday. She found the service uplifting and was glad she came. She avoided most contact by leaving quickly through a side door as soon as the service was finished. Overall, she called it a success. Maybe someday she might even stay for the coffee hour after service. One step at a time, though.

Maria's Plan A, to arrive early, sit front and center, and leave quickly after the service, successfully helped her avoid most physical social greetings. Her Plan B, pressing her palms together with a slight bow of the head, worked to stave off the more insistent church huggers and hand-shakers. These two plans helped her to reduce her social anxiety about going to church.

ROBERT, 62

The OGC, Old Geezers Club, is a group of retired men who hang out in a diner where everybody knows their names. Robert relished being in the OGC and bonding with other guys, but sometimes they snorted or looked away at something he said or asked. It seemed he was putting them off, but he didn't know what he was doing wrong or what to do about it.

Just yesterday, after ten minutes of conversation, Cliff stood up with a look of disgust and said, "Robert, just can it! Look over your shoulder, there's the line you crossed!" Then he threw some bills on the table for his coffee, stalked out, and drove away.

Something Robert had said must have really bothered him, but he had no idea what it was. No one else would talk to him, they just told him he'd gone too far and he should mind his own darned business. Robert left.

He thought about what Cliff had said about looking over his shoulder to see the line he crossed. He had looked back at the time, but there was no line there. What did Cliff mean? Then he realized that, of course, "crossing the line" in conversation meant saying something offensive. There was no literal line, but Robert must have said something inappropriate. What was it?

Cliff had returned to the group after a brief hiatus for cancer surgery, and everyone had asked how he was doing. That seemed to be the friendly thing to do. But something about what Robert had said or asked made everyone mad at him. Why? The surgery was for prostate cancer. Robert knew that cancer could be fatal, so he asked Cliff how long he had to live. They all laughed as if he had told a joke, although the laughter was definitely awkward.

Robert also knew that some men become impotent following similar surgeries, so he asked Cliff about this, too. He thought he was being a good friend to ask about this important part of a man's life, and they were all friends, right? Wrong, apparently. That one overly personal question had been the last straw, making Cliff walk out and everyone else mad at him.

Robert needed to apologize. He also needed to learn to filter what he said rather than running off at the mouth. Just because he had no problem talking about personal stuff didn't mean that everyone else felt the same way. His Plan A would be the apology. It was never easy for Robert to say he was sorry, but he knew he would have to if he was to stay in the group. A good apology should include a promise not to keep doing the same thing, and this would be hard.

His Plan B would be to share about his autism. He wanted them to understand that he might put his foot in his mouth again, but that he wanted to learn to pull it back out.

The next morning, Robert arrived a bit late to make sure everyone else was already there. Before he sat down, he pulled out the apology he had written in advance and read it aloud. It said, "I want to apologize to Cliff, and to all of you. I was way out of line yesterday, and I realize that now, although I was clueless at the time. I guess you should know that I have AGS: Awkward Geezer Syndrome. That means sometimes I accidentally act like a jerk without meaning to. I don't know how what I say comes across. If you accept my apology, and you guys don't mind me blundering about sometimes, I would love to keep on as part of the OGC. If you're done with me, I understand, and I'll go quietly."

Cliff accepted his apology, and the guys all told him to sit down and quit getting maudlin on them. They also promised to give him a smack on the back of the head the next time he stepped out of line. Plan A, the apology, was a success. It was time for Plan B.

Robert talked about his grandson's autism and how it affected his ability to socialize with other kids his age. He also said that when he said he had AGS, he really meant that he had autism, too, just like Bobby. It was not easy for him to talk about it, but he wanted his closest friends to know what he was learning about himself. As it turned, most of the guys either had a relative on the autism spectrum, or they knew someone who did. That sparked a whole new discussion.

By examining what had happened right before everyone got mad at him, Robert was able to figure out his social mistake. Plan A, apologizing, was the beginning of his social solution. For Plan B, he told his buddies that he had autism, and asked for feedback if he crossed the line again. Having friends who accepted him as he was really helped Robert.

SPEAKING FOR OURSELVES

"Sometimes I want to go to a social event, but I know that I might have difficulty with remaining in a social situation, especially if things don't go to 'plan.' I have things I want out of a party or gathering, but if those things don't happen, it can greatly affect my ability to enjoy myself. Having a backup plan helps. if I can't go to a party with a friend that I know, who I'll be able to talk to if I don't see anyone else I know, then I can plan to sit quietly and listen until I feel comfortable joining in. If I'm going to be at a gathering in a house for a long time, I might plan to duck into the kitchen for a while if I start to feel overwhelmed. And if all else fails and I'm too overwhelmed for that, or not having the good time I thought I might, I can apologize for having to leave early and go. Knowing that I have a plan for when things don't go the way I want makes it easier for me to enjoy myself. There's less fear and mental pressure when I know what my escape plan is."

— *Cat, autistic adult*

CHAPTER 4
INTRO TO SENSORY CHALLENGES

———————

(When You Just. Can't. Even.)

Most people with autism experience some sensory challenges, or unusual responses to typical sensory experiences, that affect the way they process sensory experiences. This includes the basic five senses of auditory (hearing), visual (sight), tactile (touch), gustatory (taste), and olfactory (smell). In addition to these five, we can add vestibular (movement and balance) and proprioception (deep pressure, muscle and joint information).

Some people are sensory seeking. If you under-react to sensory input and need things to be exaggerated in order to really experience them, you might be a sensory seeker.

For example, do you like to turn your music volume way up to eleven and beyond? Do you often tap your feet, rap a pencil against the desk, or hum? You might be an auditory seeker.

Do you love to closely examine or inspect tiny things, holding them close to your eyes? You could be a visual seeker.

Do you love to touch certain textures? Maybe you still have your childhood blanket because touching it calms you down.

Perhaps you can center yourself by petting your cat or dog, or holding a furry toy. If so, you might be a tactile seeker.

Maybe as a child you were constantly licking things or putting them in your mouth. You might still chew your pens or your fingernails, or be curious about how various objects taste. If so, you might be a gustatory seeker.

Do you look for things that have pleasing or strong aromas? Do you find yourself smelling each bite of food? Did you love scented markers and stickers as a child? It's possible you're an olfactory seeker.

What about movement? Do you tend to be in constant motion, seldom still? As a child did you often run, climb, and balance on high places? You might be a vestibular seeker.

Perhaps you crave firm, prolonged hugs, or the feeling of wearing tight clothes, or being wrapped up in a blanket like a burrito. You could be a proprioceptive seeker.

It's good to be aware of what kinds of sensory experiences might help you calm yourself when you're under stress. If you have an idea of what experiences make you feel better, you can keep possible sensory solutions with you on your daily travels. For example, if you know that the smell of lavender calms you, you can carry lavender-scented hand sanitizer or lotion. If you are soothed by soft textures, put your keys on a furry key chain you can hold when you feel stressed. On the other hand, many autistic people find certain sensory experiences to be distressing, overwhelming, or even painful. This is sensory avoiding.

Do you find it nearly impossible to pay attention when there is more than one sound source, such as background music and conversations? Do certain sounds or pitches tend to hurt your ears or make you cringe, such as a baby crying or tennis shoes squeaking on the gym floor? If so, you might be an auditory avoider.

Do you find that some colors, stripes, or patterns bother you or hurt your eyes? Does it take you longer than most to adjust to the light after walking out of a darkened theater? It could be that you're a visual avoider.

Do you hate certain clothing textures, tags in clothes, seams in socks, having to shake hands with people, or being touched lightly or unexpectedly? You could be a tactile avoider.

Were you called a picky eater as a child, and do you still have a self-restricted diet? Maybe you don't eat mushy or crunchy or squishy foods. You might still cringe when different foods on your plate touch each other, and having two different foods in your mouth at the same time might make you lose your appetite. If so, you might be a gustatory avoider.

Do some common smells give you a headache, turn your stomach, or cause a gag reflex—even odors that other people seem to take in stride? Do you have to avoid detergent aisles in grocery stores and perfume stores in the mall? You could be an olfactory avoider.

Would you rather sit quietly than go for a walk or do some other physical activity? Were you the child who would read books in the library instead of playing on the playground? Do you worry about losing your balance if you have to move quickly from one position or place to another? You might be a vestibular avoider.

Do you dislike firm hugs and tight clothing? Have you been told that you have a weak handshake? Do you hold your pen so gently that your handwriting is faint or shaky? If so, you could be a proprioceptive avoider.

It's possible to be both a sensory-seeker and a sensory-avoider. Many autistic people are strong visual learners who also overreact to loud or unexpected noises: seeking visual and avoiding auditory.

Sometimes a person can be both a seeker and an avoider of the same sense. For example, someone might love to crank up the volume of their music, speak in a loud voice, and make noise by tapping things. They are an auditory seeker of sounds that they control. The same person may become overly startled if there is an unexpected noise, such as a car backfiring or someone dropping a dish. This means they are also an auditory avoider, avoiding sounds that are unexpected and outside their control.

Someone else might love to look closely at tiny things, a visual seeker. The same person might find that stripes that are too close together hurt their eyes, so they are also a visual avoider related to some patterns.

Whatever your relationship is with the sensory world, you can find solutions that smooth the road along your journey. Let's see how each of our five fictional characters handled their sensory challenges.

JACOB, 18
(Proprioceptive and Tactile Seeking, Olfactory Avoiding)

Jacob knew that he sometimes annoyed his parents, but he was tired of hearing them complain about things that seemed perfectly normal to him. For example, they were always telling him to quit stomping around the house, even though he didn't think he was stomping. He wasn't angry or anything, he was just walking.

They also told him to quit hanging all over them when he hugged them. That seemed cruel; what parent doesn't want a hug from their child?

Finally, he was nearly always in the doghouse for not cleaning the dog poop out of the back yard, which was his job—his horrible, horrible job.

Jacob wanted them to get off his back about these three things, and he also wanted to learn more about himself and why he seemed to bother them so much.

First, he thought about the stomping. Jacob considered stomping to be what a child did with one foot for emphasis during an argument. How could walking be classified as stomping? He asked his mother and she told him that he walked more loudly than anyone else. They could hear him walk anywhere in the house, even when they were asleep upstairs and he was in the kitchen. Jacob said that he was heavier than his mother so it was only natural that his footsteps would be louder. Then his father stood up and walked across the room. "I weigh more than you do. Did you hear that?" Jacob didn't. "Now you walk, and listen." As Jacob walked across the room, he could hear his steps, and noticed the firm feeling of his feet hitting the floor, the pressure vibrating up his legs. It was a good feeling. But now that he listened closely, he also heard the glasses clink on the shelf with every footfall. Did he do that? He was frustrated. "Why does it make noise when I walk normally, but not you?"

His mother told him that when he had been evaluated in school, one of the things they told her was that he was a proprioceptive seeker. That meant that feelings of deep joint and muscle pressure helped him self-regulate. It made sense when he thought about it. But he realized that if his stomping annoyed his parents, it could seriously annoy other people someday when he got a job, or was in a relationship, or hanging out with friends. He wanted to control how he walked.

Even if he learned to control his stomping, he would still need to find a way to get his proprioceptive need met. What were some other things that might give him the same kind of deep-body feedback? He brainstormed with his parents. When he was a kid, his occupational therapist (OT) used to have him jump on a little trampoline, but they didn't have one at home. Jumping rope would give him the same feedback through his feet and legs, but it would be even louder than stomping. Jogging outdoors would definitely give him the kind of firm foot-fall effect that seemed to feel right to him. He also tried doing wall push-ups, leaning against a wall with his feet set back and bending and straightening his arms. That felt good, too. Jacob decided to make an exercise plan for himself that included proprioceptive feedback activities.

Jacob also needed a plan to learn how to walk more softly, since the way he walked seemed normal to him. He practiced ninja-walking, not making a sound. He knew he would forget sometimes, though, so he asked his parents to remind him if they heard him stomping. His mother said she didn't want to irk him and then have him react in irritation. How could his parents let him know without annoying or embarrassing him? They decided on a secret signal. His parents would catch his eye and quietly say or mouth the word "propes," which was what his OT used to call proprioceptive activities. That would remind him to be mindful of how loudly he was walking. If they had gone to bed and heard him walking, they would text him the word. He agreed to accept their feedback graciously, since he had asked for their help. If he felt annoyed about it, doing a few push-ups against the wall would help him self-regulate.

The second thing his parents nagged him about was what he called a hug and they called "hanging all over them." Jacob thought this complaint was mean. He loved his parents, why wouldn't he want to hug them? His mother pointed out that there's a difference between giving a person a hug, and what he usually does: lunging at them and flinging his full weight onto them. When he was little it wasn't so bad, but now he was taller than his mother. She told him that a hug means standing close to another person and putting your arms around them, giving them a brief but gentle squeeze, and then releasing and stepping back. It also requires consent, either verbal or nonverbal, so that it's clear both people want the hug. Just because someone loves you does not mean that they welcome a hug any time of day, especially when they're busy with something else. She said that it sometimes hurts her when he ambushes her, running or jumping at her like he did when he was a small child, and then taking some or all of his weight off himself and putting it on her. Also, she said sometimes it doesn't feel like he's giving her a hug to say he loves her, but for his own need to let off excess energy or a need for physical contact. Jacob didn't understand this, and was hurt. He went to play video games and try to forget about it.

About fifteen minutes later his mother rushed into his room, flung her arms around him from behind his chair, covering his face, and leaned all of her weight onto his back. "I love you, Jacob!" she said into his ear while leaning forcefully against him. He tried to push her away.

"Let go, you're messing up my game!"

"I want to hug you because I love you so much!" she said, squeezing him even more tightly.

He tried to pry her arms off from around his neck, but she clung to him.

"You're too heavy, get off my back! I'm trying to play my game!"

She finally let go. "Now do you see what I mean?"

"I don't do that!" Jacob thought about their discussion. "Do I really do that?"

"Yes, you do, actually. You don't notice that I'm trying to read a book or cook dinner, you just attack me with a hug any time without warning, and then you let your full weight hang on me. You're not a little boy any more, I can't hold you up." Jacob was quiet for a moment.

"Does that mean I can't hug you any more now, because I'm an adult?"

"You can always hug me, no matter how old you are. But grownups make sure someone wants a hug first, and they don't lean on them or keep squeezing after they are ready to stop. You have to think about the other person."

"But what if I want a big bear hug, like when I was little? Hugs make me feel good."

"You can always ask your dad or me for a bear hug, and sometimes we'll say yes, as long as you don't try to pick up your feet and put your whole weight on us. But if we're too busy right then, ask yourself if you really need affection, or proprioceptive feedback. Maybe instead of a hug you could do your wall push-ups. You can lean your whole body on the wall instead of on us." Jacob thought that was a good idea.

CHAPTER 4

"It might be a need for touch instead of propes," his father said from the doorway where he had been watching. "When you were a baby you used to fall asleep touching your mother's hair, and sometimes when you hug her now you pat her hair. What if you found something else you like to touch, like your blanket? You could see if you need touch instead of pressure."

The next time Jacob felt like a big hug, he would first ask himself if what he needed was affection or sensory feedback. If he wanted affection, he would ask for a hug, and if they said yes, he would give a gentle hug and stop before it went on too long. If they said no, thank you, to a hug, he could tell them he loves them verbally rather than hugging. If he needs deep pressure or touch more than he needs affection, he'll find other ways to meet his sensory needs.

There was one other thing his parents always nagged him about. The family's dog, Mulligan, was Jacob's responsibility. Jacob loved walking and playing fetch with Mulligan, and he didn't mind feeding him, either. What he really hated was cleaning up his poop. He couldn't stand it! The smell made him gag and wretch, and he was afraid he might vomit. He would put it off for as long as possible until his parents complained that they couldn't enjoy sitting out in the back yard because of all the poop. They nagged, he put it off, they nagged some more, on and on.

Jacob begged them to take over that job. He even offered to trade any job they asked, but it was no good. Mulligan's business was permanently Jacob's business.

Because they had been talking about sensory issues, Jacob realized this might fall in that category. Maybe he avoided smells because they were more overpowering for him than they were for other people. So, how could he solve this problem? Mulligan wasn't going to stop pooping just to make Jacob's life easier. He needed to mask the smell long enough to get through the hated task. After trying a few things that didn't work, he settled on swimmer's nose plugs and a hospital face mask from the drug store. Sometimes he put on the nose plugs so he couldn't breathe through his nose at all, but they pinched, so sometimes he wore the mask. He put some pure vanilla extract, a scent he enjoyed, on the mask before putting it on. As an odor avoider, he was able to manage a stinky task by either blocking the bad odor or adding a good odor to mask it. Being aware of his own sensory needs really helped Jacob.

EMILY, 22
(Auditory Avoiding, Visual and Olfactory Seeking)

Emily hated loud noises. She always had. Any unexpected sound—from a dropped pen, to the refrigerator ice machine clunking, to a plane flying overhead—could stop her in her tracks. She would freeze until she figured out what made the noise and determined there was no danger. Emily was an auditory avoider. As a child, she remembered many times she had been in a restaurant with her parents when the sounds of people eating, silverware tapping on plates, ice clinking in glasses, conversations everywhere, and even the sounds from the kitchen completely overwhelmed her. She would put her fingers in her ears, but it wasn't enough. Eventually, she found that if she hummed a high pitch it would block out the worst of it. The more uncomfortable she felt, the louder she hummed, trying to keep it together. At that point her

CHAPTER 4

parents packed up the rest of their meal to finish at home, which was a huge relief to Emily.

Her mother told her it was rude to put her fingers in her ears when someone was talking, and that humming in public was weird and made people wonder if something was wrong with her. Emily thought that something was, indeed, wrong with her, which was why she needed to plug her ears and hum. The only mystery was why everyone else wasn't doing the same.

Emily knew that in her quest for independence she might need to curb some of her behaviors in public. When she did things that were out of step with what everyone else was doing, people looked at her differently. They might think she was strange and not want to be near her. She didn't want to put everyone else off, but she also knew she had rights, too. She shouldn't have to be uncomfortable to make everyone else comfortable. There must be a way to take care of her own needs without bothering others too much.

So, how could she meet her need to protect herself from auditory overload without plugging her ears or humming? Emily decided to wear her wireless ear buds when she went to public places that might be noisy. This was a good first step. But what if the noises kept getting louder? Since she already had her ear buds in, she could turn on music to mask it. She made a playlist on her phone of soothing instrumentals. Wearing ear buds whenever she went out and playing her own familiar, calming music when the noise got to be too much helped her cope.

Emily is a visual learner. She finds it easier to process and remember things she sees than things she hears. She also loves looking at tiny things. As a child, she found it calming to find the tiniest toy in her doll house and hold it right up to her eyes to examine from every side. She loved to pound the arm of the sofa and watch the tiny dust motes shine in the sun as they drifted. She also liked to pick up sand on the playground and watch it sift through her fingers, marveling at the patterns that formed as they dropped and the way the sunlight changed as the sand passed between the light and her eyes. Emily had always found these visual sensory activities to be calming, almost hypnotizing. Could she use her love of visual experiences to cope with stress?

Like most people, Emily had times of feeling anxious. She knew it wasn't constructive to keep worrying about things she couldn't change, but she didn't know how to break that loop. Then she thought of using something visual to distract her from the worry cycle. She felt she was too old to sift sand or pound the sofa to watch the dust settle, but she still liked looking at tiny things. She found a virtual paint-by-numbers app on her phone. Filling colors into the tiny spaces helped block worried thoughts. By the end, she felt much calmer, plus she had a beautiful picture to look at. It worked to use her visual sensory-seeking inclination as a self-soothing strategy.

As she was learning about herself and her sensory peeves and preferences, she thought of one more. Emily's mother was always saying, "Stop sniffing things! You're not a dog!" Emily knew she was not a dog, this was obvious, but she didn't understand why she shouldn't sniff things if she felt like it. Her mother said it looked weird to other people. Emily didn't think smelling things was weird. If she saw a bouquet of flowers, or she was served a delicious-looking meal, it seemed natural to her to take a big, satisfying sniff. And why not?

Emily's mother agreed that most people like to sniff flowers and food. She was concerned about Emily's sniffing because

CHAPTER 4

when Emily started kindergarten, she used to sniff everything—the crayons, paper, pencils, desks, books, carpet, and even the other students and her teacher. It had been a big problem at the time, but she learned not to do that long ago. What bothered her mother now about her sniffing things?

Her mother admitted that she worried because she didn't want her daughter to revert to socially inappropriate sniffing. Also, when she sniffed books, it seemed odd to her mother because most people don't smell the books they read. Emily loved the aroma of a new paperback book even more than the smell of a new car or a new doll, although she loved all those smells, too. She told her mother that she planned to go on smelling flowers every time she passed a bouquet if she wanted to, and that she would keep on inhaling the aroma of food. She agreed to try not to excessively sniff every single bite, as that might seem like she thought something was wrong with the food. She also agreed not to sniff books in public, but she knew she would always cherish the moment of being alone in her room with a new book and holding it to her nose to breathe it in. She wouldn't change who she was as a person who loves aromas, but if certain kinds of sniffing bothered other people, she could try to keep their sensibilities in mind.

ZACH, 33
(Auditory and Vestibular Seeking, Gustatory Avoiding)

Zach did some things that bothered his parents. They complained about noise, safety concerns, and his eating habits. Could he get them to stop worrying about these things?

First, he thought about the noise problem. They were always telling him that he talked too loudly, which annoyed him because it interrupted his train of thought. They also complained about how loud he played his music, which he also ignored; all parents said that kind of thing to their children, and it was just a case of different tastes in music.

But one day his parents sat him down and said they really had to discuss this with him. They told him that when he talked in his "normal" conversational voice, it was much louder than most people. Even their next-door neighbors could hear him clearly, and had mentioned it to them. At first he disagreed, and said that was normal.

He always heard every conversation in a restaurant, which he found distracting, but he assumed everyone else had the same experience. His parents let him know that most people don't hear as well as he does. When the neighbors can hear him talking from their house, that means he is using an unusually loud voice.

Zach wasn't sure how to change this, but he figured he'd better give it a try. He practiced with his parents. They gave him a signal, holding a hand out palm down and lowering it slowly, to let him know when his voice was getting too loud. He found he was able to control his volume purposefully. It sounded too quiet to him, but they assured him that it was fine.

Once he started talking about something that interested him, though, his voice naturally got louder and louder with his excitement. He'd have to keep working on this so as not to annoy people, and he asked his parents to keep reminding him with the hand signal whenever he got too loud. They agreed, as long as he would agree not to react to their cue with impatience, exasperation, or rolling his eyes. That seemed fair; since he had asked for their help, he'd try not to overreact.

The safety concerns his parents worried about involved Zach climbing on the tree in their backyard and walking along the high wall behind it. He loved to be up high among the branches, and the feeling of looking down at his feet and the ground far below while he walked on the wall. Being up high had always been a rush for him; his parents had pictures of him on top of the refrigerator when he was two years old.

For his birthday his parents had given him a membership to a local gym, which he had yet to use, and now they reminded him that the gym had a climbing wall. His dad had considered installing rock climbing holds on his bedroom wall so he could climb any time, but they didn't really have room to make it safe and functional. With the gym membership, they hoped that Zach would get his need for climbing met, and it would also get him out of the house to socialize. Climbing would be a healthy change, since much of his day revolved around the computer.

Zach wasn't sure at first, but he looked up the gym's website and checked out the pictures. Familiarity with what he would see gave him confidence and he decided to give it a try. He loved the rock-climbing wall. The gym had high ceilings so he could really get up there, and there were safety harnesses and a cushioned floor so his parents wouldn't worry about him getting hurt. Going to the gym broke up his days and gave him something to look forward to. He also stopped climbing the tree and wall at home, which made his parents happy.

The last thing Zach's parents nagged him about was his eating habits. His mother said he'd always been a picky eater and it was her job to change that. As a child, she insisted that he had to tolerate a new food on his plate, then touch the food, then sniff it, then kiss it, and eventually try a tiny bite. They had been going through this for years, but he was an adult now. It was time for her to let go of this. She said that no matter how old he was, she still worried about his health if he didn't eat a balanced diet; she wanted him to be a member of the clean-plate club.

Zach needed her to stop treating him like a child. How could he get through to her?

"Mom, you know how you feel about liver?" he asked one day.

"Yes, I hate liver. That's why I never cook it," she said. "But I don't need to eat liver, there are plenty of other healthy proteins to choose from."

"Just try a tiny bite. Wouldn't you learn to like it if you keep trying?"

"Of course not. I already know I hate it."

"Exactly!" said Zach. "You know what you hate. And I know what I hate, too. Please stop nagging me to try foods that you already know I don't want."

"But when I make you try new foods, sometimes you like them."

"That may have worked when I was a kid, but I'm an adult now," he said. "It's disrespectful for you to treat me like a child at the dinner table. I want you to please stop."

"But I worry about you. You can't live on chicken nuggets and french fries, you know."

Zach agreed to research healthy diets for picky eaters online. He added the word "adults" to his search to avoid all the sites for parents trying to get their picky toddlers to eat. He told his mother that he would be responsible for his own nutrition. If he didn't like something she was serving, he would politely decline to eat it and fix himself something else if necessary. He would be sure to eat plenty of the fruits and vegetables that he did like, such as peas, apples, carrots, and broccoli, to make up for the fact that he would not eat green beans, bananas, or salad.

His mother agreed to trust him, and to stop nagging him about being a picky eater. All adults have foods they like and foods they don't like and shouldn't be labeled "picky" just because they may have fewer or different foods they enjoy. She knew it wouldn't be easy to break her own thirty-year nagging habit, but she said she would try if he would remind her and forgive her when she fell into old routines. Zach and his mother finally agreed that it's okay to avoid unpleasant gustatory (taste) experiences, as long as you maintain a healthy diet.

MARIA, 45
(Tactile and Vestibular Avoiding)

Maria wanted to make some changes in her life. She knew she shouldn't sit around at home all day in her nightgown and robe, that she should exercise more, and she should try to improve her relationship with her family. She decided to take things one step at a time and analyze the problems to see if she could come up with solutions for herself.

First, she thought about how comfy and cozy she felt when she stayed in her nightgown all day instead of getting dressed. But she also thought about how embarrassed she was if she had to answer the door in her robe. She always coughed before opening the door a crack, so they might think she was sick. She asked herself, what was so great about her PJs compared to regular clothes? She noticed that her nightgown was 100% cotton and tag-less. She picked up her other pieces of clothing one at a time and asked herself how she felt about wearing them. The polyester ones she put right down because they didn't feel good to her. She put each of those garments in a bag to donate. The fabrics that felt good to her were usually made of cotton. She still rarely wore most of them and saw that these had scratchy tags. It was like getting stabbed in the back of the neck every time she wore them. Maria assumed everyone felt that way every day, but that most people were stronger than she was and better able to ignore the pain. She got out her sewing scissors and cut the tags out of every cotton shirt and dress she owned. Then she went back with a seam ripper and picked away at the remaining shreds of tag so that they would feel smooth to the touch. She decided that from now on, she would look for 100% cotton, tag-less garments when she shopped. Once she got rid of uncomfortable fabrics and tags, she felt like she could get dressed in the morning, and that would probably improve her outlook on life.

Maria's sister in another city got them matching step-counters for Christmas and showed her how to download the app and connect online. They made a date to walk together three mornings a week, even though they'd be walking in different cities. Their pedometers would be connected and show their steps. She also taught Maria how to text, something she thought she'd never learn, so they could chat at the end of their walk.

It seemed like a good idea, but every time she went for a walk, Maria felt nervous and old. She viewed every crack in the sidewalk as a potential falling hazard, so her progress was slow and not fun for her. Her sister kept trying to encourage her, but it felt like criticism. She started dreading their walking dates.

CHAPTER 4

Maria wondered what it was about the experience that was so uncomfortable. First, being outside on the street alone with no real purpose, other than walking, made her feel vulnerable. She could make herself go out when she had someplace to go, but not just for the sake of walking. Also, her fear of falling made for slow going. Finally, the stress of knowing her sister was walking at the same time and possibly judging her progress elevated her anxiety. She was grateful for the gift and the concern, but knew she would have to do this her own way.

Maria decided she would rather walk inside her own house. She didn't have a treadmill, and no place to put one even if she could afford it. She tried walking around and around her house in circles, but it was a small house and she bumped into things a lot. Finally, she decided to march in place. It might not be the workout her sister was getting walking around her city, but it was a level Maria was comfortable with and it was certainly better than sitting and watching TV. In fact, she decided to record one of her favorite thirty-minute television shows to watch while she marched in place. She would only watch that show while walking, so it would be her reward. She even started walking four or five times a week rather than the three times she walked with her sister, so she could watch more often. Also, she felt better and stronger when she exercised. After they had walked for a half hour, her sister stopped at an outdoor coffee shop, Maria fixed herself a cup of tea, and they had a text conversation. It turned out that texting was less stressful for Maria than talking on the phone, as she could visually check what she wanted to say before sending it. The two sisters compared notes on how many steps they had walked and caught up on each other's news. Maria appreciated having this time with her sister, as she had feared they were growing apart. Doing it her way made it possible for her to increase her exercise in a way that worked for her, while also improving her relationship with her sister.

ROBERT, 62
(Gustatory Seeking, Visual and Proprioceptive Avoiding)

There were three sensory issues that Robert wanted to tackle once he learned about his autism and sensory stuff: he was always putting things in his mouth, he had a problem with light, and he hated tight clothes and firm hugs. Now that he was learning more about autism and sensory needs, he decided to see if he could change things for the better.

First, he couldn't seem to stop chewing on pens. He'd quit smoking many times, but always went back to it. His wife assumed his chewing was related to withdrawal from cigarettes, but Robert knew he'd been a pencil-chewer long before he was a smoker. His mother used to tell stories about the times he ate a rock, or a bug, or how he'd chewed the collars and cuffs of his shirts to shreds. His wife was tired of picking up a pen and finding his tooth marks all over it, and she let him know, in no uncertain terms, to stop. So, what could he do instead?

Robert's grandson, Bobby, seemed to have the same need to chew that he did, and the school gave him a "chewy" toy of food-grade hard plastic that was safe for him to bite on. He wore it on a string around his neck so it would always be handy. They even made necklaces for adults to wear, but there was no way Robert would be caught dead wearing or chewing on something like

CHAPTER 4

that. He needed something that a guy his age might use without looking weird.

His daughter had been reading a lot about the environment and sharing articles about what they could do to help. It seems disposable straws were a big no-no, and she said they should all start using permanent, reusable drinking straws from now on. The aluminum straws she bought hurt his teeth, but Robert found one that was made of firm plastic instead of metal, and he found it felt good to chew on. He bought several and started carrying them around. When he got a soda at the diner, he would bring out his own straw. The guys gave him a hard time at first, but when he said his daughter wanted him to do it to save the planet for his grandson, they backed off. Robert discovered that he enjoyed chewing his straws even more than pencils, which tended to get yellow paint on his lips, or ballpoint pens, which sometimes broke and gave him blue teeth. He'd solved his need to chew while helping protect the environment at the same time.

Second, Robert hated going from dark to bright light, especially coming out of the movie theater after a matinee. He suggested only going to movies at night, but his wife said they could fall asleep in front of the TV for free. Robert found a long-billed fisher cap that looked like the baseball caps he and the other geezers usually wore, but the bill was extra-long to shield his face from the sun. He bought a blue one and tried it out the next time they went to a matinee. When he came out, he pulled the bill down low over his eyes and kept his head down until he got used to the sunlight. It worked. He stopped complaining that he couldn't see, or making his wife wait in the lobby until he felt comfortable venturing outside. The other geezers didn't even seem to notice the new cap, so he was satisfied he'd fixed that problem.

Finally, Robert hated things that felt tight, like wearing ties, buttoning the top button of shirts, or big hugs. His wife had learned early in their marriage that gentle hugs were best for him, so she didn't try to squeeze him when she hugged him. He usually wore T-shirts or sweatshirts, maybe a polo shirt for church. He rarely had to go anywhere that required a tie, so that was okay. The only problem was that his grandson was the kind of kid who loved firm pressure, the opposite of Robert. He would run up and fling himself at Robert and latch his arms around his neck, squeezing with all his might. As much as he loved Bobby, Robert found himself getting short of breath and had to push him away. He hated to disappoint the boy, and he wasn't sure how to handle it.

One day when he dropped Bobby off at school, he noticed something interesting. The teacher met each student at the door with a routine of hand claps, fist bumps, and jazz hands, plus other arm movements Robert wasn't familiar with but the kids seemed to know. It was a slightly different routine for each child, and they had clearly been practicing every day. Bobby seemed to love it. It gave Robert an idea. That afternoon when he got home, Robert told him he wanted to create a special "grandpa greeting" for the two of them, kind of like what his teacher did at school. The boy was delighted. Together they came up with a routine that started with a salute and ended with Robert holding both of Bobby's hands and counting together while he jumped five times. It was fun for both of them, and the jumping at the end provided deep pressure feedback. Problem solved, and a fun new ritual created.

CHAPTER 4

SPEAKING FOR OURSELVES

"I have a lot of sensory issues, mostly avoiding and some seeking. Certain things are really unbearable. I used to get physically ill every time I went to the movies, for instance, until I started wearing noise-canceling earbuds. Without a separate source of sound running through them, they dampen sound the way earplugs would, but feel more physically comfortable to wear. I also wear them, and play music, to try to counteract the worst parts of getting dental work done. The vibration and the noise created can be uncomfortable, and music can't completely block that out, but for me, it's better than only having the sound of a drill or cleaning tool. Similarly, using music in noise-canceling earbuds while doing dishes helps cover the kinds of sounds that set me off most, like the clatter of china or glass.

"A lot of things are very much trial-and-error. I was well into adulthood before I learned that earbuds could work for me, even though I couldn't handle earplugs. It's been helpful to look for the things that can help, like eliminating certain fabrics from my life where I can or finding perfume oils that don't contain any of the chemical or synthetic scents that make me ill. I can use them to cope with unexpected odors in public, or just as something to dab on before handling more odor-heavy household chores, like cleaning my cat's litter box."

— *Cat, autistic adult*

CHAPTER 5

INTRO TO INTERESTS AND BEHAVIOR PATTERNS

⟵━━━⟩⊃●⊂⟨━━━

(Honoring Geek Culture)

In the past, the word "geek" was used as an insult directed at someone who was technologically skilled but socially inept. Today, many people use "geek" to describe someone who is an enthusiast, or who has a lot of knowledge and strong interest in their hobby, work, or passion. It is not unusual for a put-down to be turned around and embraced by the people it was intended to harm, and now you will meet a lot of proud, self-proclaimed geeks. And why not? Being passionate about something should be honored and celebrated, rather than apologized for or hidden away.

Many autistic people have strong interests that capture their attention and passion. Some people are fascinated by unusual things, such as appliances or light switches or numbers. Their family and friends may not understand what is so beautiful about pi or a specific brand of vacuum cleaner, but that doesn't matter. People love what they love, even if they don't know anyone else who shares that interest. In today's world, of course, it is much easier to find others who understand your personal passions. Just do an online search for a fan club for Deforest Kelley, or a collector of smoke detectors, or a devotee of dragon lore, and you will find your people. They are out there, and whatever your interest, there is someone else who shares it.

Some Aspies have interests that are shared by many, but their passion is much more intense. Plenty of people enjoy fantasy or science fiction or comic books, but to a lesser degree than their autistic friends. The fierceness of an autistic passion is pure and beautiful, and often misunderstood. But isn't it better to be passionate than apathetic?

You have every right to be you. If that means that you're fluent in both Elvish and Klingon, or you collect vintage flashlights, or you dress up for renaissance faires, so be it. Let the rest of the world get to know your amazing self rather than trying to be just one of the crowd.

On the other hand, don't shut out the rest of the world, never noticing that other people have interests, too. Keep your balance; don't let your passions dominate all of your time. The English novelist George Eliot said, "Hobbies are apt to run away with us, you know; it doesn't do to be run away with. We must keep the reins."

Now, let's see how our five characters honored and balanced their personal passions.

JACOB, 18

Jacob loved his mining-crafting video game with a passion. He felt like he could play all day without noticing the passage of time, even though he knew he shouldn't give in to that

CHAPTER 5

temptation. He worked on time management to make sure he didn't get swept away by his obsession with this game, but he still spent several hours on it every day.

His dad didn't understand why he liked a game where all the images were so basic, like blocks. He wondered why Jacob ignored the game his grandparents gave him for his birthday, the one with beautiful scenery and images that look so lifelike. Every time he brought it up again, Jacob said, "You don't understand!"

One day his father said, "You're right, I don't. Why don't you explain it to me?"

Jacob had never been asked to talk about why he loved his game before. He thought about it for a while to try to put his feelings into words. Finally, after he had gathered his thoughts, he said, "There are three benefits to my game as compared to those pretty games with all the artistic scenery. One is that I can go as far as I want through the game universe and keep on creating more and more things. There are no limits, really, to how far I can go and how much I can craft in this game. The pretty games have boundaries. They put so much into making it pretty that you can only go so far, and no farther."

"I never realized that," said his father.

"Also, I guess I like the predictability of my game. Every item, every animal, every plant and building are all built from uniform cubes. You know what to expect, and there's no real surprises and no messiness about it." Jacob went on to demonstrate his game to his father, showing him the things he had crafted and the places he'd gone. "Not only that," he added, "but in my game, I am in complete control. In real life, that never happens, but here I am in charge."

"Thanks for sharing this with me," his father said. "I had no idea. This is much cooler than I thought it was by glancing at your screen. There's a lot more than meets the eye."

Jacob was glad that his father seemed to understand. It felt good. This was a passion he knew he had to control in order to have a balanced life, but one that he would never give up.

Jacob had another strong interest he would never give up, and that was the environment. When he read about the melting polar caps and disappearing ozone layer, he got angry at humans for messing up a perfectly good planet, the only one we have. He would rant and rave about the stupidity of the people who continued to harm the environment until he got himself all wound up. When he felt overwhelmed he would go play his game, where he controlled his world.

After another long rant to his parents about the environment, his mother asked him, "Why don't you do something about it, instead of complaining?"

"I can't fix the environment by myself! Everybody has to change how we do things to reduce our impact. One person can't make it happen!"

"Maybe you can't do everything, but you can do one thing. What can you do?"

Jacob thought about that long and hard. He started researching online to find out what one person could do to help save the environment, and there were actually a lot of suggestions. He knew switching to reusable straws wasn't enough. He wanted to reach out to more people. Jacob decided to start a blog about helping the planet. He would share about the tips he had found online, link back to them, and encourage readers to follow the suggestions in their own lives. Writing about his feelings about the planet was a great outlet for Jacob, rather than ranting to his parents. He learned early on to delete comments that were hurtful or were probably bots trying to sell get-rich-quick schemes, but he replied to the positive comments. A few of them even became online friends. Their shared love for the planet was a strong connection.

EMILY, 22

Emily had two things that she loved above everything else: Alpeggy, her stuffed alpacorn (a winged alpaca with a unicorn horn), and Alexander Hamilton. She never went anywhere overnight without Alpeggy, which had resulted in being teased at slumber parties, but her loyalty to her faithful alpacorn was greater than her desire to be accepted. Alpeggy was not only a friend, but practical, too. Emily hugged her when she felt stressed, with her topknot fluff right under her nose, and breathed slowly until she calmed down. When she was using her cellphone to go online for long periods, she fitted Alpeggy under her elbow for support. She loved Alpeggy so much, she sang to her when she was happy.

Her mother was embarrassed when Emily sang in public, so she tried hard not to sing, covering her mouth when the music started to slip out. She thought there must be something wrong about singing if her mother was embarrassed by it. Now, as an adult, she realized that being embarrassed by singing was her mother's problem, not Emily's. Singing was her favorite. She decided that if singing helped her express her joy, she would sing, as long as it wasn't disturbing people. She liked what Buddy said in the movie *Elf*, "Sing out loud for all to hear." And Alpeggy made her so happy, she couldn't say her name without singing it.

Speaking of which, Alexander Hamilton is another of Emily's passionate favorite subjects. She knows everything about this founding father, she's read all the biographies in the library, and she sings along on every song from the musical. The music reminds her that she is original, inimitable, and that she is the one thing she can control. As an autistic, she has felt out of control for so much of her life that she clings to this like a lifeline. Singing songs with a positive message about making a difference in the world gives her the confidence to go forward with her own pursuit of independence.

ZACH, 33

One of Zach's passions was politics. He knew a lot about what was going on in government and had strong opinions about it. He found that by volunteering at his political party's office, he could find others who shared his interest and were always up for a lively discussion. Not only that, but his volunteer work made a difference. It was a good feeling.

Zach had another interest that he didn't like to talk about. After he graduated from college and was home all day, he watched a lot of TV. One show that unexpectedly captured his attention was a cartoon about six ponies. There was something about the characters' clearly delineated personalities and their strong friendship that struck a chord in him. In each episode, he found himself learning about social relationships along with the ponies. He came to feel as if these characters were his friends, to a far greater extent than the people he knew. The pony friends faced challenges every week, but at the end of the episode their friendship was closer than ever. From them, Zach learned a lot about what it means to be a friend.

Zach never told anyone about the ponies. He searched online and found other fans who weren't little girls. Once he even drove through a fast food window and ordered a kid's meal because the toy was a small plastic figure of his favorite pony. He pretended he had a child at home, but he threw away the box and kept the toy hidden in his pocket. Remembering the courage of the pony character made him feel brave and calm when he found himself in awkward situations. He used it like a talisman, but an embarrassing one he would forever keep secret. What would people think if they knew? Would they assume he was too immature to be a real adult?

Zach didn't want to stop watching his show or carrying his pony toy. He loved and learned from the show, and his pony reminded him to be brave. Someday he might tell his parents how this show was a friend to him, but for now, he'd keep his interest private.

MARIA, 45

Maria's favorite thing to do in all the world was to watch Sloth Live Cam TV. Sloths were her favorite animals. She thought they had adorable faces, and their fur looked so soft. But the best part was when they moved. Watching a sloth move so slowly along a branch, one hesitant foot at a time, always calmed Maria. Sometimes she noticed that an hour or more had passed with her sitting absolutely still, gazing at the sloths on her computer monitor. Her children often gave her stuffed sloths for her birthday, Christmas, or Mother's Day when they couldn't think of anything she needed, and she displayed them all on her bed in a particular arrangement that was pleasing to her eye. Although she never wanted to stop watching sloths, she knew it wasn't good for her to spend the majority of a morning doing nothing else. She decided to use the timer on her phone to regulate how long she watched sloths. First she had to try out all the different alarm sounds, because a lot of them were startling and would ruin the calming effect of the sloths. She chose one that sounded like gentle wind chimes, set the volume low, and turned off the vibrate function, which she found stressful. When she turned on her sloth TV show, she decided how long she wanted to watch and set the alarm. After an anxious night she'd give herself more time, and when she had to go out she'd set a shorter time.

This plan worked well at first. Then she noticed that when she didn't have anything planned, she ignored the alarm and wasted half her day watching sloths. She felt groggy after these long sessions, rather than the pleasant calm she felt after a shorter sloth session.

Maria decided to create appointments for herself on her phone calendar, daily. It might be to go to the grocery store, or do laundry, or write to her children, or make banana bread. Deciding what to do after watching the sloths was difficult, so watching more sloths always won out. When she planned in advance what she wanted to do next, it was easier to turn off the sloths and she felt more productive. She knew that she'd have sloth time every day, which was a comfort, and she could always come back to the sloths later in the day if she felt anxious.

CHAPTER 5

Maria's other passion was robots. She loved giant robots with pilots in their heads controlling their movements. She loved robots that transformed into vehicles or animals. She really loved transforming robots that joined together to form giant robots with pilots. She collected models and comic books as well as the DVDs of all of the giant robot movies, as well as the toys. She kept her collection out of sight in her closet out of embarrassment. Her family thought her sloth fascination was quirky and cute, but she was afraid they would think her transforming robot collection was too weird. Sometimes, when she had to go somewhere stressful, like to a doctor's appointment, she imagined her body as a giant transforming robot, and herself as the pilot in her head. Nothing could hurt her, and she was in complete control of where her robot body went and what it did. If she was overwhelmed and started to freeze, she could be the pilot and tell the robot to leave the area and proceed to a safe place. No one but her knew she was thinking this, but it gave her strength and courage to face what must be faced.

ROBERT, 62

When Robert was ten years old, he found a discarded television set in an alley. He was fascinated by all the tubes inside, and he kept them in an old shoe box under his bed. He didn't know what was so cool about them, he just knew he loved them and wanted more. Perhaps this passion led him to a career in television repair.

By the time he retired, Robert had an extensive collection of cathode ray tubes from television sets of all kinds and ages. He put up wire shelves in his garage, each shelf filled with large plastic bins full of tubes. As his collection grew, the space in his garage shrank, so that all three of the family cars were permanently relegated to driveway or street parking. This annoyed his wife and daughter, but what else could be done? They didn't want his collection in the house. He offered to put a shed in the back yard, but they pointed out that Bobby needed that space for his trike and swing set. A shed was out of the question.

Finally, one day the women of the house put their feet down and said he would have to get rid of some or all of his collection. This was so distressing Robert couldn't even talk about it. When his wife saw how difficult this was for him, she offered to help him take pictures of everything in his collection so he could see exactly how many of each type of tube he had. Cataloging it might be fun for him, too, since he rarely looked at his collection any more.

Robert agreed, and they began to go through each box and photograph everything. After they finished, he decided to keep the best single tube of each category. Later he could choose to sell or give away the duplicates, the ones he could bear to part with.

It took a long time, but at the end he had one wire shelving unit full of individual cathode ray tubes spanning the decades, the best example of each. Everything in the "sell or give away" boxes had been photographed. After spending another day looking through those boxes, Robert decided to let them go. He didn't want to have to do it himself, as it felt almost like a parent giving away a child, so he asked his wife to find good homes for them all.

CHAPTER 5

After going online and finding websites populated by other collectors of cathode ray tubes, his wife sold his excess collection. She took some of the money and made a hard-back book of photographs of his entire collection. She then took out the six oldest antique tubes from his boxes and had them professionally mounted in a beautiful shadowbox frame. Robert had never been happier with a gift in his life.

Robert had a second passion: he was a huge fan of a short-lived science fiction TV show from the 1960s. He owned the DVDs of all three seasons and watched them again and again. One year his wife and daughter gave him a small, portable DVD player with ear buds so he could watch his show as much as he wanted while they watched something else on the main TV.

Robert's favorite character was the half-alien, half-human first officer, because he was so logical most of the time, but he also had human emotions that he tried to cover up. Before being diagnosed on the autism spectrum, Robert sometimes felt as if he were an alien, not quite as human as everyone else, struggling to cope on a strange planet.

One year his wife and daughter planned a vacation for the family to coincide with a convention of his favorite show. Since he usually barely tolerated vacations, preferring to stay home where everything was familiar, they thought this would keep him busy while they enjoyed themselves. He was hesitant at first, but once he got there and found himself surrounded by others who shared his passion for the show, Robert had the time of his life.

Having his passions respected and honored by his family meant the world to Robert.

SPEAKING FOR OURSELVES

"Sometimes it's hard, with a really intense interest, to feel at ease in conversation. I often feel like I'm talking about what interests me 'too much' when I'm with neurotypicals who don't share that interest, but at the same time, it feels so uncomfortable to hold all of my excitement in when I've learned something new about a subject I'm passionate about. Even with people I feel comfortable with, I can get physical symptoms of an anxiety attack when I feel like I'm over sharing, not only because I worry that my areas of interest might seem weird or boring to others, but because it can feel like sharing something personal about myself. I can't separate the things I'm passionate about from my identity.

"Even though it can feel difficult or socially awkward, though, I like having things that are this important to me, because they also have the power to make me feel better and safer. A picture of a favorite character or actor on my phone becomes something I can look at when I need to calm down in an anxiety-inducing situation, like a blood draw or a waiting room. A song that reminds me of a favorite book or TV show can elevate my mood when I've been down or stressed. Wearing a T-shirt with dinosaurs on it can make me feel more capable of doing whatever 'adulting' I need to get through. Despite the challenges in loving something so intensely that it's part of yourself, it's also a source of strength and emotional well-being to be able to turn to these things for comfort or inspiration, and I wouldn't change the way I feel about my interests for anything."

— *Cat, autistic adult*

CHAPTER 6
INTRO TO MANNERISMS

(Celebrating Quintessential Quirks)

Along with unique interests, many autistic people also engage in repetitive behaviors, quirks, or mannerisms. Some of the most common are shaking or flapping their hands ("jazz hands"), fiddling with their fingers, rocking, spinning around, spinning objects, and tapping their body or objects. Movement can express pure joy often related to a strong interest. Often, movements are used to self-regulate stress or self-soothe. Whether movement expresses happy excitement or signals distress that could escalate to a meltdown, it serves a purpose.

If the people in your life try to stifle your natural inclination to move your body, especially if they tell you to have "nice hands" or "quiet hands," it can seem condescending or insulting. You might politely ask them to stop using those phrases. Then, take a moment to consider why they might feel the need to tell you to stop using your mannerisms in the first place. If you don't know why, ask them. Are they embarrassed by your behavior? If so, that's their problem. Now that you're an adult, it's about time for them to accept you, quirks and all.

Are they afraid that others will realize that you're "different" somehow? Most of the time other people already know, and anyway, there is no shame in having autism.

Are they worried that you won't be able to find friends or get a job if you rock or shake your hands when you're nervous? Finding work and making friends are issues everyone faces. While it's true that autistic people often have more challenges in these areas, just stopping a mannerism will not suddenly open doors. Friendship and employability are complex issues which should be addressed, but not by simply trying to keep yourself from moving.

Do you, yourself, want to change some of your own mannerisms? Have you been embarrassed by people staring at you or giving you a funny look when you're engaging in self-stimulatory behavior such as flicking your fingers or rocking, also called stimming? Do you think it would be a good idea to stop, like breaking a habit? You can change your own behavior, but before you try to quit, you should ask yourself why you move your body in these ways. Is it usually when you're uncomfortable or anxious? If so, you may be using movement as a pressure-relieving escape valve to help you regulate stress. Think about what else you could do to relieve your stress instead of the movement you want to quit doing. If you just stop doing one thing without giving your body something else to take its place, you're doing yourself a disservice. Always have a way to meet your own needs for stress management.

On the other hand, do you usually do the behavior when you're happy or excited, as a way for your body to express the joy you may not have words for in that moment? If so, and you really want to quit that particular movement, replace it with another way for you to physically express yourself. Watch how other people your age move their bodies when they're excited. Do they use jazz hands? A fist pump? A dance move? If you really want to stop doing your thing, you could practice imitating what other people do in similar situations and see if it feels as good to you. If not, maybe you shouldn't try to change yourself. People are diverse, with many unique forms of self-expression. Let other people get used to and accept your personal style of self-expression, rather than trying to change something that works for you. In fact, some people who try to quit a behavior that serves a purpose for them end up with a different behavior that takes its place, and it could be more extreme than the original behavior. Maybe you don't need to stop doing what feels natural, but try to educate others to accept you being you.

Our five characters have their own ways of moving their bodies that could be called stimming. Let's read about them and their stims.

JACOB, 18

There were a couple of mannerisms or quirks that Jacob's parents often asked him to stop. One of them was hitting his head, and the other was rubbing his fingers.

Jacob realized that he often pounded on his head, but he didn't know why that should be any of their concern. He didn't do it hard enough to hurt. He took a closer look at why he might be doing it. What did it feel like to pound on his own head? He could hear a dull thump when he did it, and a pleasant feeling of pressure that sort of bounced off. The way it felt best was to use the heel of his hand against the corner of his forehead above his temple. Was there a pattern to when he did it? To find out, he kept track of what was going on each time he hit his head.

Over the next few days, whenever his parents asked him to stop hitting his head, he made a note about what was going on. Usually it was when he was thinking hard about a homework problem, or when his game was taking a long time to load, or when he was just plain bored.

At school, Jacob wrote a note asking his special education case manager if any of his teachers had ever complained about him hitting his head. She replied that at the beginning of the year a new teacher had commented that she thought Jacob was engaging in self-injurious behaviors (SIB). His case manager told the teacher that this was not considered injurious, since he only used the soft part of his palm against a firm part of his head, not near his temples or his eyes, and never with force. At school it was not considered to be a problem.

Jacob told his parents that gently pounding his head made him feel better, like his "propes," jumping or doing wall push-ups. Since it wasn't hurting anyone, he politely asked them to try to get used to it or look the other way if they didn't like to see it. He assured them that he would never actually harm himself but now that he was an adult, he would appreciate it if they accepted him as he was, quirks and all. They agreed to try.

The other habit or mannerism they noticed was that he sometimes rubbed his thumb pads against his fingertips in a circular motion, usually getting faster and more agitated over time. At first it was always mild and not really noticeable, so

CHAPTER 6

most people would ignore it, but sometimes he kept rubbing his fingers faster and harder, eventually ending up with his hands in front of his face and his eyes squeezed shut while his fingers kept on rolling. Again, Jacob took notes about the behavior. He realized that this usually happened when he was under stress, and the stress was increasing. The speed of rubbing his fingers was directly related to how anxious he was at the time. It felt like his emotions were rolling and bouncing around inside of him and he didn't know what to do with them. When it was at its peak, he realized this must look weird to other people, and he didn't like the idea of everyone seeing how stressed he was by his mannerism. At the same time, if he tried to stop doing it, he wasn't sure what would happen to all the stress.

Jacob did an online search for "how to relieve stress" and found a lot of suggestions. The ones that felt most useful to him were to notice which body parts were tensed up and do relaxation stretches, to get more exercise, and to laugh more. The next time he noticed himself rubbing his fingers rapidly, he stopped and checked out how his body was feeling. He realized his shoulders were extremely tense and pulled up almost to his ears. Jacob consciously relaxed them, bringing them down to their normal position, then he slowly rolled his head and rotated his shoulders while slowing his breathing. It really helped him calm down. He also did jumping-jacks or wall push-ups. If he was still upset about something he couldn't change, he found something funny to watch online, such as memes about his mining-crafting game or funny dog and cat videos. That usually got him laughing, and he felt much more relaxed afterwards.

For Jacob, asking his parents to be more tolerant of one of his mild head-pounding mannerism, and finding better ways to meet his own need to reduce stress instead of the rapid finger rubbing, were two good solutions.

EMILY, 22

Emily knew she had little habits that her mother was always nagging her to quit. She was tired of her mother telling her, "Stop squinting, you'll get wrinkles!" or "Take your hands off your ears!" or "Stop waving, use quiet hands!" She decided to look at each of the three habits separately and try to figure out what bugged her mother about each one. Then she could decide if she wanted to change the behavior, or if she'd rather try to get her mother to accept it.

First of all, Emily knew that she squinted every time she went outside, or when her mother opened all the blinds on a sunny day. The light hurt her eyes, and she wasn't about to let her eyes be in pain because her mother thought she would get wrinkles. She figured wrinkles were a normal part of the aging process. However, since her eyes hurt even when she squinted, she tried to think of ways to help with that—for her own sake, not because her mother was uncomfortable. She had considered buying sunglasses, but she already wore glasses. If she had to keep switching from her regular glasses to sunglasses, she was afraid she'd lose them. She didn't need one more thing to have to keep track of. Then she realized that she could get prescription glasses that would turn dark in the sunlight and then lighten up again when she went indoors. Emily chose a pair with larger lenses than her old glasses to give her more coverage in the sun, with floral print frames for fun. She was surprised at how quickly they

CHAPTER 6

got dark and then returned to normal inside. In addition to the darkening glasses, she got a broad-brimmed sunhat. Between the hat and the glasses, her eyes felt much better when she went out. No more squinting! Although her mother was happy, Emily made this change for herself, not for her mother.

The second thing her mother told her to stop was tapping her ears. Emily frequently found herself cupping her hands around her ears and moving them in and out, covering and slightly uncovering her ears. When she did this, she heard a sort of rushing sound like the ocean, getting louder and softer as she moved her hands. When she moved her hands slowly, it sounded like waves hitting the shore. When she moved them faster, it created a different, interesting sound effect. She also liked how it felt on her ears. Sometimes, when she was really bored or really stressing, she ran her hands down the sides of her head and over her ears, folding them over as her hands passed, and then letting them spring back. For some reason, this felt really good. She never really thought about what it might look like to someone else when she was doing it. Emily watched herself in the mirror while tapping and rubbing her ears, and realized that it did look kind of strange. She never saw anyone else do that. People might look at her funny or have weird thoughts about her if she acted really different from everyone else. Emily thought about this. She didn't want to stop her stim of tapping and rubbing her ears because she found it enjoyable, but she also felt awkward doing it in public now that she had seen how she looked in the mirror. She decided to keep on rubbing or tapping her ears at home whenever she felt like it, but to try not to do it when they had company or when she was out in public. She asked her mother to leave her alone if she was playing with her ears at home, and to quietly remind her if she started to do it around other people. Her mother agreed.

The last thing that her mother nagged her about was the one that bugged Emily the most. Her mother would tell her, "Quiet hands!" That was ridiculous! Hands couldn't talk, and the way she moved her hands didn't make any noise. It's not like she was clapping or hitting things. She asked her mother why she kept telling her to have quiet hands. Her mother said that when she was little, a teacher told her that she should stop Emily from flapping her hands because it made her look autistic, and that "quiet hands" was the proper way to correct her.

"But I am autistic," Emily said. "Why shouldn't I look autistic? Is there something wrong or bad about who I am?"

"Of course not," her mother replied. "We didn't want you to look different from the other children. We didn't want them to know about your special needs."

"Newsflash, Mom, everyone already knew I was different. Having 'quiet hands' isn't going to make me not autistic. And I wouldn't want to be not autistic, it's who I am! Do you wish you had a different daughter, one that doesn't have autism, instead of having me?"

"No, no, not at all! We love you, we wouldn't change you for the world!"

"Then stop telling me to have quiet hands," said Emily. "I move my hands when I'm excited, when happiness bubbles up inside of me and there aren't enough words in the universe to express it. My hands speak joy for me."

"I never thought about it that way," said her mother.

"Well, I'm glad you're thinking about it now. And another thing, sometimes I move my hands in front of my eyes because

CHAPTER 6

I need to filter out the bright sunlight, and it makes it cooler and more comfortable, plus, it's interesting to see how it looks through my fingers."

"Can't you stop, now that you have dark glasses and a sun-hat?" asked her mother.

"The thing is, I don't have to stop. It makes me feel good. Please stop thinking 'autistic stims' and start thinking 'jazz hands' or 'sunlight filters.' That's what it is, and I like it." Emily's mother agreed to stop trying to make her change things that she didn't want to change.

ZACH, 33

Zach had a few repetitive mannerisms he did a lot. He liked to spin around in swivel-chairs, he hummed, and he tapped things around him.

His parents asked him to stop spinning around in the rocker. It was distracting when they were trying to watch television or have a conversation, and they worried he would break it. Zach doubted he could break the chair, but he did an internet search: "Can I break my chair if I spin it too much?" While it was unlikely to break, it could come loose from the base if it was turned too much in the same direction. Also, Zach wanted to respect his parents' need for a less-distracting environment. He decided he should stop spinning around in the living room, and when he felt the need to spin he would use the desk chair in his room. He figured if he alternated direction, he wouldn't have a problem. He also decided not to spin in the chairs where he volunteered; he didn't want to bother people or have them think he wasn't serious.

The second quirk his parents complained about was his incessant humming. Apparently, he hummed nearly all the time, although he wasn't aware of it. He asked them for feedback about when he seemed to be humming. They told him that when he was under stress, he tended to hum tunelessly, a prolonged vocalization, like moaning with his lips shut tightly. They said that at other times, when he seemed to be happy, he hummed melodies that they did not recognize but were clearly songs rather than random notes. He decided to study his own humming behavior, with their help. He asked them to tell them each time they noticed he was humming, and to tell him if they heard a song or a one-note hum. After he got some feedback, he realized they were right about his feelings being connected to his humming. When they said he was humming one note, it had been when he was worrying about something. When that happened, he would try relaxation techniques like deep breathing, rolling his shoulders, or going for a brief walk. When they told him he'd been humming a melody, he recognized it as the theme music of his pony cartoon show. It always made him happy to hear the opening music, so that must be why he hummed it when he was happy. He didn't tell his parents what song it was, but he did tell them that they were right, he was happy when he hummed that one. They were glad to know he was happy, and they wouldn't bother him about it unless it got too loud.

Finally, Zach's parents (and his teachers, when he'd been in school) often asked him to stop tapping or drumming on everything. It was as if his pencil or fingers were drumsticks. This was a problem when it got too loud, or if he got out of control and started tapping on people or on their things. Zach realized he could control this habit, now that he understood what bothered people the most about it. He still liked to move his fingers, but when he was around other people he tried to minimize the noise, such as tapping on his leg rather than on a hard surface. Because it relaxed him, he wouldn't try to stop, but carry on in ways that were less annoying to others.

MARIA, 45

Maria always felt some stress when her girls came home during college breaks. She loved them dearly and missed them when they were away, but she always felt vaguely uncomfortable by the way they acted around her. Sometimes they rolled their eyes, or sighed loudly, or got up and walked out of the house, and she could never figure out why. Finally, she decided to ask them. They told her that they were embarrassed to bring their friends home to hang out because she acted so weird. Maria was shocked and hurt. She always tried to behave properly and had no idea what they meant by "weird," so she asked them to explain. They told her that it looked weird when she fluttered her hands in the air meaninglessly, or twisted her hands together, wringing them like an old-time damsel in distress, or pressed her hands against her face so hard it looked like she was going to push her fingers right into her skull. This took Maria aback. She hadn't realized that she was doing these things, or even that things she did might look weird to others.

After taking a day to process what they told her and to get over her hurt feelings, Maria brought up the subject again. She told her children that these things that embarrassed them might be related to the autism she believed she had. They told her that at first they didn't believe she had autism and thought she was making up excuses, but after being away at school and then coming home and looking at her in a new light, they believed her. Still, they said, they wished she wouldn't be so "weird." Maria said she could try to change some or all of the behaviors that bothered them, but she would need to know when she was doing them, because these were unconscious actions. She asked them to help her: if they saw her moving her hands in the air, they could say, "Fluttering." If they saw her rubbing and twisting her hands together, they could say, "Wringing," and if they saw her pressing her hands hard against her cheeks they should say, "Cheeks." Maria kept a small notebook with her, and each time they pointed out her mannerisms, she wrote an "F" for fluttering or a "W" for wringing or a "C" for "Cheeks." Then she jotted down a brief description of what was going on and how she was feeling at the moment.

After a week of this, Maria had a much better idea of when and why she was doing the things that bothered her children so much. Usually when she fluttered her hands it was when she was excited about something, such as watching sloth videos or scrolling through images of giant robots. Fluttering her hands like butterflies expressed the joy she felt about sloths and robots, in a way that words never could. She decided that there was no reason to change this behavior, and if her girls wanted to invite friends over, she would go upstairs if she wanted to watch sloths or robots. When it was just family at home, she expected them to accept her fluttering hands as her way of showing how happy she was.

Maria noticed that most of the time when she twisted or wrung her hands, she was feeling uncertain or slightly nervous.

CHAPTER 6

When she asked her phone, "Why do I wring my hands?" she learned that hand-wringing told the world that you were feeling anxious. When she asked, "How can I stop wringing my hands?" there were several suggestions, like doing something different with her hands. Maria didn't want her mannerism to give the impression that she was extremely anxious when she was only slightly nervous, so she wanted to do something else with her hands. She pulled out a prayer shawl she'd started knitting for the church years ago, and she decided to finish it. She put it in a basket near her favorite chair, close to hand. She asked her girls to let her know if they saw her wringing her hands, and then she'd decide if she wanted to knit instead.

Finally, Maria realized that when she pressed the pads of her fingers hard against her cheeks, it was usually when she was the most anxious or upset. Her hands shook and she started to feel as if she couldn't control her facial expression, that she might grimace or cry. She was afraid she might have a panic attack, so she pressed her face to hold it, and her shaky hands, still. She really pressed hard, too, and left red marks on her cheeks. This was not good, but she would need to do something when she felt that uncomfortable. After asking her phone for advice again, she found many articles about how to cope with feelings of panic or anxiety. Maria chose a combination of tips. First, she would tell herself that this feeling may seem strong, but it would go away. Second, she would take ten deep, slow breaths and consciously relax her body, especially her neck, shoulders, and hands. Then she would ask herself if her anxiety was about something she could fix, or if it was outside her control. If she could fix it, she would. If she couldn't fix it, she would tell herself to let it go or shake it off, while actually shaking her hands. Finally, if she was still anxious about something she couldn't change, she would temporarily distract herself by watching a sloth video. After laughing at their funny ways, she felt better.

Maria found that some of the behaviors that embarrassed her children were things she didn't want to change, and others she could work on. Most teens were embarrassed by their parents, so it wasn't the end of the world if her girls felt that way. They would all survive, and might even grow closer as they encouraged her to change those things she wanted to change.

ROBERT, 62

Robert had a couple of quirks that bothered his wife and daughter. One was that he always seemed to be clearing his throat. He was unaware he was even doing it until one of them offered him a cough drop. He did a bit of online research and learned that repetitive throat clearing could be a habit, a tic, or an autistic self-stimulatory behavior. Since excessive clearing could be bad for his throat, he decided he should break this habit. He started carrying a bottle of water around with him, and whenever his wife or daughter told him he was clearing his throat, he would take a sip of water. This would also keep his wife from nagging him about staying hydrated. After a couple of months, he rarely cleared his throat unless he had a cold or allergies.

The other habit that got on their nerves was when Robert patted his thighs in a specific pattern, again and again and again. They were sick of it. He always repeated the same routine of two pats of his open palms against his thighs, followed by closing his hands and thumping his fists, then waiting a beat and

CHAPTER 6

starting over. Pat, pat, thump. Pat, pat, thump. It drove them crazy. Robert hadn't even noticed when he was doing it, but once they pointed it out he recognized the beat immediately. In his head he heard his favorite song from the 1970s. The performers and audience all stomped their feet twice and clapped once, paused, and then repeated the rhythm. It was a powerful beat, but he realized maybe he didn't need to share it with the world. When he tried to stop tapping along to the tune in his head, he found it difficult to focus on anything else except trying not to pat his thighs. He sat with his hands clasped together and didn't hear a word his wife or daughter said, he was trying so hard to keep his hands still. Finally it got to be too much, and he took off and headed for the diner. His friends were there, and he ordered coffee and sat down with a sigh of relief to be away from the women and the need to control his mannerism. As the guys sat around and shot the breeze, he noticed that each of them had a habit, too. One drummed his fingers on the table, another jingled his keys, and another rubbed his moustache. He asked if it bothered them when he patted his thighs, and he demonstrated what he was talking about. Immediately they all joined in, stomping their feet and clapping and singing the chorus of the song together, until the other diners turned to stare. They stopped singing and laughed, then told Robert that they had noticed his habit, but it never bothered them. Everybody has their quirks, and his was no big deal.

Robert decided to tell his wife and daughter that they were stuck with a guy with rhythm. He would try to keep the volume down, but he wouldn't stop tapping along with the music in his head. It made him happy. They agreed to tolerate it, but said they would let him know if he got too loud or if he started doing it in church. Robert felt this was fair. He put on his favorite album, and the whole family stomped and clapped along, especially his grandson.

SPEAKING FOR OURSELVES

"When it comes to 'looking normal' versus being able to live and function and be a happy, healthy autistic adult who stims, I would definitely take the latter. Because 'looking normal' drains your energy, it's terrible, you have to put up with all of the negative sensory input with no way to self-regulate ... A better option is to encourage society to learn and embrace different neurotypes."

— Amythest Schaber, autistic blogger, vlogger, and advocate
Neurowonderful.tumblr.com and
Ask an Autistic on YouTube

PART II
HOUSING

————◆————

A Place of
Your Own

"'Home' is the nicest word there is."
— *Laura Ingalls Wilder*

"Earth is the nest, the cradle, and we'll move out of it."
— *Gene Roddenberry, creator of* Star Trek

CHAPTER 7
LEAVING THE NEST

(You Can Fly!)

For most of us, the word "home" conjures up visions of comfort, safety, familiarity. It's the place we return after a hard day at work or school, where we can let our hair down and kick off our shoes and troubles. You may live in the same home you grew up in, or you may have lived in many places throughout your life. If you're one of many adults on the autism spectrum, you may still live at home with your parents. You know it's not an ideal permanent living situation, but you're okay with the status quo. You're with the family you love, in a place you know well, your comfort zone. Your home is your world, so why would you ever want to move out?

There are a number of reasons. Sometimes it's a desire for independence, to stretch your wings, to control your environment. Sometimes it's a necessity. Maybe you got a job offer in a different city. Maybe your parents are moving to a condo or retiring to a seniors-only community. Perhaps a parent is getting re-married and establishing a new home elsewhere. Parents have their own lives, too, and their long-term plan might not include parenting in retirement. Worst case, parents don't live forever; no one does. You don't want to cope with learning to live on your own for the first time while simultaneously mourning the loss of your parent. It's in everyone's best interest for you to move out on your own while your parents are still around to offer support.

Whatever your reasons for moving out, go for it. Sure, there are financial and social considerations. How will you know you're ready to live independently? It may seem overwhelming, but we can break it down and make it more "whelming." Here's how.

Financial Considerations

You can't move out if you don't have funding. It might be income from your job, or a trust, or disability income. Whatever it is, if you want to move out, you need an income. Dr. Jed Baker wrote in *Preparing for Life: The Complete Guide for Transitioning to Adulthood for those with Autism and Asperger's Syndrome*, "Although there is more to life than money, having a comfortable amount of money can improve the quality of your life by allowing you to make more choices ... The more money you have, the more freedom you have to choose what you do and where you live." (Baker 2005, 344). Learn more about money matters in Chapter Twelve of this book: Money Management (Be Your Own Banker).

Social Considerations

There are also social considerations to keep in mind when making decisions about moving out on your own. Will you miss your family, and how will you stay in touch with them? Will you live

CHAPTER 7

alone, or with roommates? What should you do (or not do) to be a good housemate if you don't live alone? The following chapters offer solutions for these issues.

Readiness Considerations

Are you emotionally prepared to move out on your own? How much responsibility can you realistically handle? If you're not quite ready for independent living straight out of school, don't worry or put yourself down. Everyone moves at their own pace. It's not unusual for autistic adults to move out at a later age. The important thing is, you're on the path toward independence, so keep going. One step at a time will get you pretty far down the road to your own place.

Our five fictional characters have each faced challenges with their living arrangements, and they found their own path. You can, too.

JACOB, 18

Every Wednesday, Jacob had to attend a Social Skills for Adulthood group with his school psychologist. There were several other guys in the group, a lot of them autistic. It was sometimes interesting, sometimes boring, but it was not optional, so he went.

One week, the topic was to dream about your future. Each group member shared about what they wanted to do in their future, what kind of job they wanted, and where they wanted to live. The leader asked a few follow-up questions after each person shared. When it was Jacob's turn to share, he said his goal was to live in Sweden. The man who created his favorite video game is Swedish, and it sounded like a cool place to live. Whenever he did an online search for Sweden, the images all looked awesome. It would be so cool to live there! His group leader asked follow-up questions, like if he wanted to live in a city or in the country. Jacob preferred the city because he thought the country might smell like a dairy farm, which he hated. The leader asked if he preferred a house or apartment, with housemates, or alone.

"I'll live in a house in Stockholm, with my parents," Jacob said.

"With your parents? I thought they lived here."

"They do," said Jacob, "but they'd have to move to Sweden, obviously."

As soon as he said it, a couple of the guys laughed, and then stifled it. He couldn't tell who was laughing or why. He passed on the other questions and kept quiet.

When he got home, Jacob replayed that scene in his head, worried about why they laughed at him. What had happened right before the laughter? He said his parents would have to move to Sweden. Now that he thought about it, he realized that was an unexpected answer. They were talking about where they wanted to live when they grew up, and he assumed wherever he wanted to move, his parents would have to come, too. He'd always lived with them and had never thought about moving out before. Now he thought about it. He realized most adults move out as soon as possible, but the idea scared him. He'd never lived alone and didn't know if he'd like it. By the time his parents got home, he'd decided that he was not ready to move out when he graduated. But at least now he was thinking about it, instead of assuming he'd always live with his parents. At the age of eighteen, he wasn't ready to take that step yet, and that was okay.

EMILY, 22

Emily was tired of her parents' rules and their helicopter-hovering ways. Sometimes she felt smothered by their love. If only she could get away and have her own apartment! She would love to live in one of the condominiums in town. They had lovely grass lawns and smooth paths, bridges across brooks meandering between buildings. What a perfect place to live!

She made an appointment to talk with her case worker about moving out. They'd already discussed this at a previous meeting and agreed to move forward with support toward independent living. Emily told her case worker about the beautiful building she wanted to live in, and that she would like two bedrooms so she could get a cat. Her case worker looked up the information and learned that the monthly rent for the place she wanted was more than double her disability income. There was no way she could afford such a place. She needed to be realistic.

Emily was disappointed, but she still wanted to find a place within her means. Unfortunately, since she wanted to stay in the same city as her parents, there was nothing she could afford. Then her case worker told her about some local group homes that served young adults like herself, people with disabilities who are able to do most things for themselves.

They toured a few places and found one that Emily loved. She would have her own bedroom and bathroom, and share the kitchen and living room. They even had a cat. There were house rules posted, which kind of reminded Emily of living with her parents, but it was different when the rules were for the group and not dictated by anyone's mom or dad. She was especially drawn to one staff member, Sarah. Emily thought she was cool. It would be fun to live here.

After joining them all for dinner several times, Emily was more than ready to commit. This was the place she wanted to live, and the people she wanted to live with. It was only a few blocks from her parents so she could see them often, but now it would be as an adult child coming home to visit, not as a little girl living under their roof. She loved the feeling of freedom her new living arrangements gave her. She was finally living her own life as an adult.

ZACH, 33

Zach knew he was too old to live with his parents. He felt like a failure. The guys he went to school with were all married with jobs and kids. His parents didn't pressure him to move out, but all their friends had empty nests. Zach didn't blame them for wanting the same.

He knew he couldn't afford it, but he kept checking online for cheap apartments near his parents and the temple. Unfortunately, the perfect apartment never magically appeared.

One day after the social group, Zach got to talking with the rabbi about his dilemma. The rabbi said that they were looking for a live-in caretaker to stay in a basement apartment at the temple, rent-free. The responsibilities would include locking everything up after the last function each night, making several rounds to be sure the property was secure and as a deterrent to vandalism, and unlocking the buildings in the morning. The rabbi said that if Zach would fill out the application, he would put in a good word for him. They wanted to hire someone who participated in synagogue life rather than a stranger, so he had an edge.

Zach was excited by this idea. He immediately filled out the application and was thrilled to be offered the position. It didn't pay much, but it provided him with a roof over his head and utilities, as well as a small income for food and other necessities. His parents seemed relieved that he had found a place and were glad that he'd be living nearby in the temple. It was a win-win! Participating in social activities and reaching out to his rabbi as a mentor worked together to help Zach take that first giant step out of his parents' home.

MARIA, 45

Maria had lived with her parents until her wedding day, and then with her husband until he left her. Now that her daughters had gone off to college, she found herself living completely alone for the first time. It was a struggle learning how to pay the bills herself, but after a few times of getting her power shut off and asking her sister to help her figure out what to do, she now had her bills on auto-pay. She'd settled into a routine, and she quite enjoyed having the entire house to herself. When her sister told her it was a waste to have such a big place for one person and suggested she sell the house and get a condo, Maria nodded, but she never followed through. Even though money was tight sometimes, she couldn't bear the thought of leaving the home where she'd raised her girls. For her, moving out was not an option.

ROBERT, 62

When Robert met and fell in love with his wife, they were twenty-eight years old. She had an apartment and he was living with his mother. Although she was surprised that he'd never moved out, she assumed he stayed because his mother was still mourning the loss of her husband. When they started talking about marriage, she suggested he should move out and live alone before he committed to living with her for the rest of their lives. Robert happily agreed to anything she said. He was in love, and believed that all of her ideas were brilliant. However, he never actually took any steps forward to look for a place of his own. He had enough money from his job repairing television sets, but he didn't do anything about his living situation. Eventually, she gave up on that idea. She was confident that he wasn't going to get wanderlust and leave her just to have the experience of living alone. If he hadn't left his mother's home in twenty-eight years, it was unlikely that he'd leave hers. They happily moved forward with their wedding plans.

In all the years they'd been married, he hadn't once yearned to live alone. If he wanted privacy, he would sit in the back yard or tinker with his collection in the garage. For Robert, the perfect living situation was the one he had been fortunate enough to find. He felt no need to ever live alone and hoped his wife would outlive him so he never would.

CHAPTER 7

SPEAKING FOR OURSELVES

"The best thing you can do while you still live at home is to make the most of every opportunity to become more responsible, educated, and employable ... The sad truth is, sooner or later, you will have to leave the nest. If you can't see the day when you can fly out on your own, then you need to let your family know that you eventually want to have the best living situation possible and prepare for it ..."

— *Jerry Newport, autistic author,*
Your Life is Not a Label

CHAPTER 8
LIVING ALONE

───➤●◄───

(The Ruler of All You Survey)

Sometimes the greatest comfort of all comes from living on your own. No parents, no roommates, no one to move your things, play music when you want quiet, or compete for the remote. If this sounds like your idea of paradise, you may want to find a way to live without housemates. As with anything in life, there are pros and cons to following this road.

The positive side of living alone is that no one else shares control of your environment. You don't have to share wall space with other people's ideas of art, or have their knick-knacks gathering dust on your shelves. No one will eat your food or borrow your jacket. No one will make a mess and leave you to clean it up, or complain that you have made a mess and left them to deal with it. No one but you will control the thermostat. There is no hassle about who pays for which utilities, what portion of rent each person is responsible for, or who gets the larger bedroom or closet. You are blissfully unencumbered by others' expectations or intrusions.

There are downsides to living alone, as well, and not everyone has the luxury of this option. First off, it usually costs more. When you plan your budget, take into account not only the rent but all the other living expenses that you will be solely responsible for if you live alone.

Home Owners Association Fees — If you are able to buy or rent in an area with a Home Owners Association (HOA), you can expect to pay fees. If you rent, your landlord might pay the HOA fee, but check your renter's agreement to be sure.

Utilities — Before you move, find out approximately what you should expect to pay for electricity, gas, water, sewer, and trash pickup. You can ask your prospective landlord or do an online search. These will not be exact figures you can count on, but should be in the ballpark of what you can expect to pay. If your landlord offers to pay for some or all of these utilities, that is awesome, but make sure it is stipulated in writing before you sign the lease or rental agreement.

Internet — Wireless or dial-up internet monthly prices can vary depending on location, services included, and servers. Research ahead of time. For most of us today, internet is not a luxury, but a necessity. Budget for it accordingly.

Telephone — In the past, you may have been included on your parent's family phone service, and if that continues, count yourself fortunate. If you will need to pay your own phone bill, check out several plans, what they offer, what they cost, and what you can afford. If your plan does not include unlimited minutes or data, learn to budget your phone time so you don't get surprised by a huge bill at the end of the month.

Television — Check out the available cable or dish services if you like to watch television, like most of us do. If you want a particular movie channel or service, factor it into your budget.

If you plan to forego having roommates, all of those bills will be yours alone to pay, which is one of the big downsides to living alone.

Another con of the roommate-free life is loneliness. If this is your first time living on your own, you may find yourself feeling lonely at times, and that's natural. No matter how much you may value your privacy, there may be times when you feel safer or more comfortable if there is someone else nearby. Before you decide to live alone, you might try spending time alone beforehand. Do you know someone who is going on vacation and needs a house sitter? Volunteer. If it drives you crazy, reconsider living alone. You might be happier with housemates.

If you do decide to live alone, plan what to do if you feel lonely. Is there someone you might call, like a parent, sibling, or close friend? (Don't use a school-friend or work-friend for this if you never socialize with them outside of school or work.) Ask them if it's okay to call them sometimes if you need to talk. For the ones who say yes, put their names and phone numbers on a card that says "who to call if I'm lonely." Put it where you'll see it easily.

Another thing you can do about loneliness is to be active. Many Americans today spend much of their days sitting, often looking at one screen or another. It's good for your mental and emotional health as well as your physical health to get up and move. Try putting on your favorite music and dancing like there's no one watching (because there literally is no one watching). Try going for a walk. Try yoga or Tae Kwon Do or stretching or jumping rope. Anything to increase your activity level. You'll be surprised at how movement improves mood when you're lonely.

If you are allowed to have pets where you live, and if you know you have the time, energy, and responsibility to take on another little life, you might consider having an animal roommate. A small dog, cat, or even house rabbit or bird can provide unconditional acceptance and unlimited company. You're not alone in a house that has a pet. However, don't choose this option without carefully considering your ability to maintain the level of work required to care for a pet. If you had a pet at home and your mom or dad stepped in to help take care of it when you were stressed, then you may not be ready. When you live alone, there is no backup when you don't have the fortitude to deal with a pet emergency. If you love animals but know you aren't ready for the responsibility of full-time pet-parenting, consider volunteering at a no-kill animal shelter or pet adoption agency. Offer to cat-sit, or to walk your friend's dog. Animals can be a great stress-reducer, but being a single pet-parent has the potential to be stressful. Don't take on pet ownership unless you know you can handle it.

Let's see how each of our five fictional characters feels about living alone.

JACOB, 18

Jacob didn't like to think about moving out on his own. He didn't like to be alone. Often he went to find his parents and make some kind of connection with them, although he now tried to hold off on hanging on them like he used to. He wanted to be reminded that they were there and that he wasn't alone. When they went out in the evening without him, he found himself getting spooked if he walked by a dark window, so he tended to stick to his room, pull down the blinds, and play video games until they got home. He knew that he would probably always want someone else living with him. Living alone was not in his comfort zone.

EMILY, 22

Emily loved living at the group home. She had her own room and bathroom, which was great, and the house was never empty. She appreciated knowing that if she got lonely there would always be a housemate around, or she could find Sarah, her favorite staff member, to talk to. When socializing got to be too much for her, she could go to her room and close the door. She finally felt like a grown up, even though she'd technically been an adult for four years. Not living under her parents' roof was truly liberating. Group home life, with lots of people around, was the perfect solution for her and she had no desire to live alone. She was just too socially oriented.

ZACH, 33

Zach felt like he had won the jackpot with his new living situation. He was out of his parents' house at last. He didn't have to worry about rent or utilities because they were included in his new job as night security guard. His evenings were usually spent in his room, reading or watching shows on his laptop or playing video games. If he had to adjust to having a roommate or house-mate around, it would be difficult for him. He had certain ways he liked to do things. Living alone was the best solution for Zach.

MARIA, 45

Although she loved and missed her twin daughters when they were at college, Maria found living alone to be restful and calm-ing. There was no one leaving things in the kitchen or bath-room, no one playing their own music or watching shows that she found stressful. Most of the time she didn't even play music, she simply cherished the quiet in the house with no other feet walking and no other lungs breathing. When her daughters first went off to school, they told her she should get a little dog to keep her company since she loved animals so much. She thought about what it would take to care for another little life, like a baby that would never grow up. Even thinking about it made her tired. She didn't want a pet, she preferred her online sloths that could never make a mess in her house. For Maria, the peace of living alone was just right.

ROBERT, 62

If you asked Robert whether he would ever want to live alone, there was no hesitation or consideration. No, he would not. He loved his wife and daughter and grandson and the life they had together. Although he wanted his daughter to feel like she was getting her life together, he knew he would be sad when the time came that she could move out on her own. Any time the ladies were out and about and Bobby was in school, he'd head on over to the cafe to hang out with the geezers. It gave him the creeps to be alone in the house, although he didn't like to admit it. He knew himself well enough to know that he would never want to live alone.

SPEAKING FOR OURSELVES

"I have lived the past decade of my life as a single person and have concluded that it is not only okay for me but in fact better to be alone ... I am never lonely. I have many friends and many options for social activities. But these things still don't really interest me as much as my other interests. Even at my age, I am a raft and I am strong, and while I have found my island, I still explore and push my comfort zone. I am surrounded by people who love and support me, and yet, I am still alone, and that is okay."

— Karla Fisher, autistic senior technical
program manager for Intel
Different ... Not Less

CHAPTER 9
LIVING WITH OTHERS

(A New Family of Housemates)

You may have decided that living alone is not for you. You might be living with family until the time is right for you to move out. Perhaps you're ready to move out, but you need someone to share expenses. Or maybe you're happily living alone, but some day you'll want to get married or live with a significant other. How can you prepare yourself to live with someone? Even if you just want to have friends over to visit, this chapter has something for you. It's all about getting along with others who inhabit your living space.

We'll cover four areas: communication, social, sensory, and responsibility. These are issues that affect many aspects of adult life. Having a map will help you navigate so that potential road blocks become manageable detours on an enjoyable road trip.

Communication

Whether you're living with family, friends, your spouse, or a college dorm roommate, communication is key to maintaining a harmonious living arrangement. What's your most comfortable communication style? You may prefer texting or instant-messaging even if you're both in the same room. You might prefer emails because of reduced pressure to respond in real time. If you hate talking on the phone, you might not even set up your voicemail or listen to messages if they come in; if this is you, let people know not to try to call you. Leaving sticky notes around the house might be your go-to approach for communication.

Know your preferred communication style, and share it with those you live with. Before deciding if a potential housemate is right for you, it may be a good idea to disclose your autism to them. (See Chapter Fifteen for more about this.) They need to know if something is a mild preference that you can be flexible about, or if you have specific needs that can't easily be changed. There's an important distinction between "won't" and "can't." If your roommate assumes that when you don't communicate the way they do that you're choosing to ignore them, that could be a problem. If you really can't talk on the phone, let them know up front. You're not ghosting them when they don't get a call back, you may be literally unable to make that call.

Time and place is also important. Talking before coffee is impossible for many, but might be the peak time for others. If only one of you is a morning person, first thing in the day would not be the best time to discuss the utility bill. If you always come home exhausted, let your housemate know they shouldn't take it personally when you head straight to your room without saying hello. If one roommate thinks talking to someone through a closed bathroom door is acceptable, they should just stop that. Most people prefer privacy in the bathroom, and unless the apartment is on fire, conversation can wait. You can make an appointment to talk about anything serious or emotionally charged, so you both can be ready.

CHAPTER 9

Remember, communication is a two-way street. Ask them how they prefer to communicate. If they hate sticky notes, or don't even notice them, then don't leave them all over the fridge, mirror, or computer screen. Work to find the communication style that suits you all.

If there is a communication breakdown, treat it like any other solvable problem. Look at both sides and don't try to always have it your way. There's no shame in asking for help from a conflict negotiator, like a professional counselor or an impartial friend. The risk of losing a roommate over a misunderstanding is worth working to solve your differences. Remember not to make this into a fight. The purpose is to understand the other person's point of view. It may not be your default setting to try to imagine what someone else is thinking, but you are smart and capable. If you're not sure, ask them how it looks to them, and then really listen. You can usually find a middle ground where each person feels heard and that their needs are respected.

Social

We all have our social needs and limitations. Some people measure their social tolerance in teaspoons, and others in buckets. Knowing your own capacity for socialization is important, and letting your roommates know where you stand will help avoid hurt feelings. Just because you live together doesn't mean that you have to do everything together. If your roommate is going out and you're not invited, don't take it personally. You each have your own lives. If you'd like to do more things with your housemates, invite them to events that you all might like.

Think about everyone's situation when planning social events. If some of your housemates have well-paying jobs and others are under- or unemployed, don't suggest an expensive restaurant or concert. Check online for free or low-cost events in your area and invite your roommate to join you. If you get turned down but they seem open to the idea of getting together socially, try again later. If you get rejected three times, then stop inviting. You might have a house-sharing relationship but not a social relationship outside the home, and that's okay, too. It's important to know whether you are friends, or you just have a financial living arrangement, and act accordingly. (More about friendship in Chapter Eighteen.)

It's crucial to share your social styles and preferences up front. If you want quiet and privacy in the apartment after 9:00 PM and he has a standing invitation to his friends to drop by any time into the wee, small hours of the morning, you may not be well-matched roomies. If you need music every waking moment and she craves quiet, come to an agreement before moving in. If your musical tastes don't mesh, invest in some good earbuds or noise-canceling headphones so you can keep enjoying your beats even if your housemates don't share that enjoyment.

Discuss in advance how everyone feels about overnight guests. Is it expected that partners can sleep over occasionally, or regularly, like every weekend? If a housemate's significant other moves in, will they pay their share? Talk about it up front.

Of course, when you're living with a spouse or significant other (SO), there are some differences. There is clearly a stronger tie than with a housemate; you're sharing a life and a future with this person, and they deserve to have you take their social needs seriously and accommodate them. (More about relationships in Chapter Nineteen.)

Sensory

Many autistic people have strong sensory needs and aversions. (Remember Chapter Four?) It's good to know yourself and your own sensory responses, especially if they're intense, and share this knowledge with potential roommates. If you need a scent-free household, you won't want a housemate who loves cologne. Comfort with sound level differs between individuals (see Social, above), so don't forget to keep your headphones handy. Decide together about wall decor in common areas, and don't use extreme colors if it gives one housemate a headache. If you have food allergies or severe aversions, find a roommate who can live with your restrictions. Any food which, when you breathe it in, makes your throat constrict and hinders breathing, is a sign of a serious allergy which should never be ignored. If breathing pea-nut dust could kill you, any potential housemate must under-stand that they will never be able to eat peanut products at home. If the smell of certain foods turns your stomach, it may be a sen-sitivity, not a true allergy. Check with your doctor before taking any risks. If there are a lot of typical foods that make you feel ill but aren't dangerous for you, consider making accommodations yourself. If your list of banned foods is extensive, you signifi-cantly limit the pool of people who might be willing to live with you. Restrict that list to medical allergies which endanger your health, not aversions. Block or cover up unpleasant odors. Some people keep a hospital face mask to cover up smells. A drop of vanilla, lavender, or other extract can be added. For extreme odor challenges, some people purchase more expensive but effective respirators used by painters to block out toxic fumes.

Responsibility

With great independence comes great responsibility, to paraphrase Stan Lee. It may seem easy to split expenses equally, but there's a lot more that needs to be responsibly shared. You've probably spent your life so far in a world where light bulbs, toilet paper, and salt were always available. Now, there is no one else to replenish things when you run out. Each person living under the same roof needs to take equal responsibility for shared items. Go to a big box store together and split the cost of household staples. Put a sticky note on the next-to-the-last item on the shelf to remind you to buy more before you run out.

As far as personal items, such as deodorant, toothpaste, soap, shampoo, razors, and feminine hygiene products, each housemate should stock and replenish their own. If you all share a bathroom, consider assigning each person a shelf of the medicine cabinet or a drawer to keep their toiletries in. Or, each person could buy a shower caddy to hold those things, which can be kept in your own room and carried to the bathroom when needed. This way no one can accuse someone else of using up their conditioner. Be sure to stock up on these personal items, too. Don't keep adding water to an empty shampoo bottle to eke out one more shampoo, or rolling an empty deodorant over your pits hoping the last molecule of deodorant will do the job. It won't.

Another thing to take responsibility for is proper nutrition. Plan your meals in advance and stock up on the items you need.

CHAPTER 9

You may be happy to have the same breakfast and lunch foods daily and repeat dinner menus weekly, such as Meatless Monday, Taco Tuesday, or Fish Friday. Search online to learn what you should eat to maintain good health. But don't lecture your housemates if they don't make the same healthy choices you do. They're adults, too.

Let's see how our five fictional adults managed sharing living space with someone else.

JACOB, 18

One afternoon, Jacob was reading a manual with tips and hacks for his mining-crafting video game when the light bulb on the lamp beside him burned out.

"Mom! The light bulb burned out!" he yelled.

His mother was on the couch with a cup of tea and a book. "Yes, I see," she commented.

After a few minutes Jacob called out, "Mom! Didn't you hear me?"

"Yes, I heard you," she said. "You said the lightbulb burned out." She kept reading.

Another few minutes passed, and Jacob looked up from his book, surprised that it was still dark. "Mom, what the hey! I can hardly see over here!"

"That's because the light bulb burned out, dear."

"I know that! When are you going to put in a new one? I've been waiting!"

His mother put down her teacup. "Do you know where we keep light bulbs?"

"Sure, hall closet, top shelf."

"Then, if you need a light bulb, I suggest you go get one and change it yourself. You're an adult now." She picked up her book and began reading again.

Jacob was astonished. He'd never even thought about changing a light bulb, but he figured he'd better learn. How hard could it be, right? He went to the shelf and got a new one, then asked his mom if he should turn off the lamp first. She said yes. He carefully unscrewed the old bulb, screwed in the new one, and turned the lamp back on. It worked, and it was easier than he thought. Then he realized he was still holding the burned-out bulb. He asked his mom what to do with the it and she told him to put it in the specialty recycling bin, so he did. As simple as that.

"That's the way a good housemate handles a problem," his mother told him. "When something needs doing, they don't wait for someone else to take care of it, they just get it done. And if you're not sure how, ask. Even adults have to ask how to do things, but they don't let that stop them, and neither did you." Jacob was surprised at how proud he felt after doing what was, essentially, a small thing. But for him, it was a big step toward being an adult instead of a kid.

EMILY, 22

Emily loved her new life living in the group home. She had people around when she wanted company, and she could go to her room when she needed to be alone. The only problem was the house was not as sound-proof as she'd like. She loved listening to her music, but if someone else's music was playing anywhere in the house, she could hear that, too. Hearing two different songs playing at the same time drove her crazy. She didn't like confrontation, so she decided to leave sticky note messages instead of directly talking to her housemates about it.

After about a week, she was called into the living room where she found all of her housemates and staff members. "Sit down, Emily," Sarah said. "We need to talk."

Emily sat down slowly in the only available chair, facing everyone. She was confused and a bit frightened. "Is this an intervention?" she asked. She had seen this sort of thing on TV. "I don't drink or take drugs, so I don't need an intervention."

One of her housemates spoke up. "We're tired of you always yelling at us about our music. It hurts our feelings. We have a right to listen to music just as much as you do, and we never complain about how often you play *Hamilton*."

Emily was shocked. "I never yelled at anyone!"

"Look at these notes," one of the staff members said. "Did you write these?"

Now Emily noticed that the entire coffee table was plastered with pink sticky notes written in purple ink. "Yes, those are mine. I didn't want to yell, that's why I left notes instead."

"Look at this," said one of the women. "All caps and five exclamation points. That's yelling, and it really hurt my feelings."

"And look at this one, where you said my music made you want to vomit. Why would you say such a hurtful thing?"

Emily realized she had written those notes when she was upset. Not having the person in front of her, it had been easy to let out all of her frustration without thinking about how the person reading it might feel. She froze, unable to speak, as the realization of how her notes affected her housemates rushed over her. She felt her face grow warm as she was flooded with emotion and shame. Finally she found her voice. "Can I still live here?" she whispered.

"Of course you can still live here," said a staff member. "This is not about wanting you to leave, it's about wanting you to be sensitive to the people you live with and their feelings."

"But it hurts my ears when they play their music and I can hear it over my music."

"Is your right to listen to your music more important than their right to listen to theirs?"

"No, I just never thought about it. At home, when I put on *Hamilton*, my parents never turned on any other music or TV, because they know it bothers me."

"So your parents let your preferences take priority over their own."

"Um, I guess so. I never thought about them having preferences, they're my parents."

"Things are different for adults living together," said the staff member. "One person can't dictate when or what music other people can play. I think we have two issues here we can resolve as a group: being respectful of others' choices, and communicating respectfully."

The group decided together that those who could afford it would purchase noise-canceling headphones or would ask their family to consider them as birthday or holiday gifts. Those who could not afford the headphones, or who had sensory problems with the feeling of headphones over their ears, could still play their music, but never above an agreed-upon volume.

CHAPTER 9

As far as respectful communication, no one had a problem with sticky notes, as long as the notes were not mean or used in excess. They came up with these sticky note rules:

1. Avoid using all caps and multiple exclamation points. (It looks like yelling.)

2. Be kind and respectful. (No name calling or put-downs.)

3. Only one sticky note per issue. (Don't spam someone's door with multiple notes.)

4. Keep it positive. (A happy face can let the person know you're not mad at them.)

Emily smiled. At first, she had felt like everyone was against her. Then she felt bad about hurting her housemates' feelings. Now, she felt like part of a team again. Everyone in the house would be working on respectful communication, not just her, and no one was mad. A good day!

ZACH, 33

Even though Zach loved living alone and could easily drop by his parents' home to visit (and do his laundry and get a home cooked meal), he occasionally felt lonely. It would be nice to have friends over sometimes. Of course, wishing for visitors wouldn't make it happen; he needed a plan. He made a list to help him prepare:

1. WHO? He had to decide who to invite over for a visit. A couple of the guys from the social group at the temple

played the same video game he did, so he would invite them over to play.

2. WHERE? His apartment, naturally. It was a one-room studio, but his mother had given him cushions to make the bed into a daybed-sofa during the day. That would work.

3. WHEN? After the social group, because they'd already be at the temple.

4. WHAT? What would they do? Obviously, they would play the video game.

5. REFRESHMENTS? Zach would buy soda, chips, and cookies, and make popcorn.

Zach was stoked when both guys said they'd come. When they got to his place, he put out the grub and sodas, which the guys dug right into. He moved his laundry off the daybed so they could sit, then sat down at his desk and turned on his PC to show them his newest games. After a while Noah asked where the bathroom was, and as he pointed it out Zach wondered how clean it was. Too late to worry about that now. A while later the guys got up, thanked him for the snacks, and left. He said bye over his shoulder without looking up. When he came to a good saving place, he realized they'd only stayed, like, twenty minutes. He thought parties usually lasted longer.

The next day while doing laundry at his parents' house he told his mom about having the guys over, but that he was disappointed they left so early. She asked him what they had been doing, and he told her about the snacks and how he'd been showing them his new video game.

CHAPTER 9

"Did anyone else get a chance to play the game, or just you?" she asked.

"I was showing them, so I was playing and they were watching. It's a new game, they'd have to watch me play it for a while to understand all the tips and tricks I've picked up."

"When you bought the game, who showed you how to play it?"

"Nobody, I just started playing it."

"So, what makes you think they couldn't do the same? Are your friends too dumb to figure out how to play a video game on their own?"

"I didn't say that! They're smart, but I've been playing it longer, so I know more about it than they do. Anyway, they didn't say anything, so I assumed they were fine with it."

"Sounds like they let their feet do the talking."

"Sometimes I don't understand you at all. Feet don't talk. What do you even mean?"

"They walked out. They used their feet to let you know that watching you play your video game was boring, so they left."

Zach hadn't thought about that. He'd been so into his game he hadn't considered whether they were having fun. His first try at sharing his living space with friends had failed miserably. He felt discouraged, like he would never invite friends over again, until he realized he needed to plan differently and put himself in their shoes.

Several weeks later, he invited the guys over to his place to watch a ballgame after the social group. They could all watch together and he wouldn't be tempted to hijack the evening. He was excited when they agreed, and determined not to make the same mistakes.

The day before the big game, Zach looked around his apartment with fresh eyes. He saw dirty dishes, so he washed them. He saw piles of laundry on the furniture, so he folded and put away the clean ones and dumped the dirty ones in the hamper. He checked out his bathroom and did a thorough cleaning, realizing he hadn't actually cleaned it since he had moved in.

When the guys arrived he put sodas, chips, popcorn, and cookies out again, and turned his computer screen toward his guests. He started streaming the game and then sat back to enjoy it. Occasionally he glanced at them to see if they were bored, but he didn't stare at them; that would be creepy. The guys seemed to enjoy cheering for their team and groaning when they lost. On their way out, the guys thanked him and gave him fist bumps. They all said they should do it again and offered to take turns hosting. At the end of the night, Zach felt like he had won, even though his team lost. Sharing his living space socially had been a big success.

MARIA, 45

Maria shuffled her way to the bathroom sink. She looked down to see that she was almost ankle deep in empty toilet paper tubes. They were all over the floor, gathering dust. What would her daughters think when they came home from college next week for their break? They would think she was crazy. They would be right, this was crazy. Who lets toilet paper tubes take over the entire bathroom floor like this? Sloths would never live this way. But then, sloths only went to the bathroom once a week,

CHAPTER 9

and they didn't use toilet paper. Trying to be like a sloth would be no help at all in this situation. She felt deeply ashamed and wondered what was wrong with her. Why couldn't she handle simple life tasks the way everyone else did? She bent down to pick up a tube, then recoiled in disgust as her hand touched the dusty cardboard. She washed her hands and then made herself a cup of tea to de-stress.

She hated the feeling of the cardboard on her fingers, and the sound it made. She looked over at a mountain of delivery boxes she'd opened but left in the hallway without flattening and recycling them. Another mess to be cleaned up before the girls got home, but the same problem. When she thought about her hands brushing against cardboard, she imagined the painful sound and it made her skin crawl. Did everyone feel this way when they touched cardboard? Were they all strong enough to overcome it? Maybe not. Her senses were different; neurotypicals might be unaware of the intense sound of a hand brushing against cardboard. So what could she do?

She sipped her tea and pondered possible solutions. Then she went to the store and bought kitchen gloves, ear plugs, and an extendable grabber stick. When she got home, she put on the gloves and ear plugs, gingerly picked up a cardboard box between two gloved fingers, and carried it to the bathroom. She used the grabber to pick up the tubes and drop them in the box. When the floor was empty and the box was full, she carried it out and put the whole thing in the recycling bin. It was a distasteful task, but it hadn't taken as long as she feared. She made another cup of tea, set the timer for a half-hour of Sloth TV, and settled in to relax. Later she could wear gloves and ear plugs again to fold up the remaining boxes from the hall. Having a plan to avoid embarrassment when sharing her space with her daughters was a great relief.

ROBERT, 62

Robert sighed. Once more, Bobby was pitching a fit, and he had no idea why. He turned back to the game on TV to try to cover up the sound of the screaming and the women folk trying to help him calm down. Some things in life were a mystery, and he figured his autistic grandson was one of them. He adored the boy, but every once in a while he just screamed, out of the blue, for no discernible reason. Best thing was to turn the game up and tune the boy out.

Now he couldn't help but notice that his wife was standing between his chair and the TV, arms crossed, staring at him and tapping her foot.

"You make a better door than you do a window," Robert said. He'd never quite understood the phrase, but he knew people used it when someone blocked their view. She took the remote out of his hand, and turned off the set. "Hey, what gives?" Robert was astonished.

"You can't keep doing that and leaving us to clean up your mess!" She was steamed.

He looked around the room, but didn't see any mess. "I don't know what you're talking about," he said. "Give me the remote, I'm missing my game!"

"You'll miss more than the game, mister!" Why was she mad at him? Robert had no clue.

"Why, for heaven's sake? I cannot figure you out."

CHAPTER 9

"You can't just waltz into the room, turn off Bobby's favorite show with no warning, and then watch your sports while he has a meltdown. We have to deal with it, and it's not fair!"

Robert blinked. Had he done that? When it was time for the game he had just turned to the game, like always.

"Why don't you watch the DVD that we gave you instead of interrupting your grandson's after-school unwinding time?"

"I can't watch a game on DVD, it's live. Anyway, I need the big screen to see the plays. What's this about after-school unwinding time?"

His wife sighed, as if he ought to know this, but it was news to him. "School is difficult for Bobby. He works hard to hold it together all day, and comes home exhausted. He really needs to have some down time to watch his favorite show. Then, when it's time to do homework and eat dinner, he has the emotional and social strength to go on. But when you turn it off in the middle of a scene, without asking, preparing him, or apologizing afterward, you ruin his day. He's crushed, he can't cope, and now he's in a full meltdown that your daughter has to deal with. And here you sit, watching your game as if nothing happened."

Robert tried to process what she said. He'd been so focused on his game he hadn't even noticed Bobby. When the screaming started, he had no idea that he'd caused the problem.

"Wow," he said. "I am such a jerk."

His wife sighed, and seemed a bit less angry. "You're not a jerk, you're a good man who sometimes acts like a jerk. There's a difference."

"But I was so clueless!"

"Everyone's clueless until someone gives us a clue. Life is about learning how to not be a jerk. So, what are you going to do now that you have a clue?"

Robert thought. "What do you think I should do?" he asked.

"Well, you can start by turning his show back on, that will help with the immediate problem. Then you can apologize."

"I've been getting a bit of experience apologizing lately," said Robert, remembering his falling out with the Old Geezers' Club.

"But after fixing it and apologizing, you need to stop doing this again and again. Do you have any idea how often you put him through this?"

"Uh, every time there's a game?"

"Exactly. I kept expecting you to pick up on it and do the right thing, but you clearly were never going to on your own."

"I just thought the kid had a lot of tantrums and needed to be disciplined. I thought I'd leave that to his mother."

"There is a big difference between a meltdown, which he can't help, and a tantrum. His behavior is communicating when he doesn't have words. All that screaming is Bobby communicating his pain at having his favorite show ripped away from him with no warning."

Robert felt terrible, and quickly turned the set back to the cartoon and got out of the way as his daughter led her son back to the set. Before long, the meltdown subsided and the boy was able to focus on his show again.

"So now the question is, what are you going to do differently next time?"

"I don't know," Robert said truthfully. "I want to watch the game on the big screen, but I want him to have his down time, too. What should I do?"

CHAPTER 9

They brainstormed some ideas. He could record the game and watch it later that night. That would work for Robert and Bobby, but it wouldn't be great for his wife and daughter, who wanted to watch other things in the evenings.

A better idea was to let the boy play DVDs of his favorite show on his grandpa's special DVD player, which was usually off-limits for everyone except Robert. They called it "Grandpa-Bobby Switcheroo Time." Bobby would wear his grandfather's cap, sit in his grandfather's chair, and drink his milk out of the "World's Best Grandpa" coffee mug while watching his show on Robert's DVD player. He loved the idea, and asked everyone to call him Grandpa while he was watching his show. Once he was settled into it, Robert could turn on the big TV and watch the game. He really got a kick out of watching his grandson pretend to be him.

After this incident, Robert decided he needed to turn up his personal radar to notice when his preferences might conflict with others in the family. He didn't live alone, after all, and everyone in the household deserved respect.

SPEAKING FOR OURSELVES

"Unwritten rules like, 'Don't parade around naked ...' 'Don't swear like a sailor ...' 'Close the door when in the bathroom ...' and 'Pick up your mess ...' exist so that masses of people can function with each other. They provide guidelines, they define appropriate versus inappropriate behaviors so we can all live and work together as a society. Now, a person can do any of those things in private if he wants to."

— *Dr. Temple Grandin, autistic author and professor*
Unwritten Rules of Social Relationships

PART III
INDEPENDENCE

———⊰⊷●⊶⊱———

The Holy Grail of Adulting

"I am no bird, and no net ensnares me;
I am a free human being with an independent will."
— *Charlotte Bronte, author*

"One of the most jolting days of adulthood comes
the first time you run out of toilet paper. Toilet paper, up
until this point, always just existed. And now it's a finite
resource, constantly in danger of extinction, that must be
carefully tracked and monitored, like pandas?"
— *Kelly Williams Brown, author,* Adulting

CHAPTER 10
TIME MANAGEMENT

(Conquer the Clock)

A ctivist Susan B. Anthony said, "Independence is happiness." If this is true, then the road to happiness goes through management: managing our time, transportation, money, and ourselves.

Time is one of those things that we all have, but we can't see or touch, and it can be difficult to know what to do with it. Many autistic adults struggle with time management in three areas: time comprehension, time planning, and time transitions.

Time Comprehension

People with time comprehension challenges don't understand lengths of time, such as the difference between fifteen minutes and an hour. That's why they're often late or early. Their friends and family members might think they're flaky, but that's not it. Their brains function differently than neurotypical brains (different, not less, as Temple Grandin says). It's smart to learn time comprehension so you can be in control of your own time, rather than feeling like time is an unfathomable mystery. You can learn this. It will take some effort initially, but most worthwhile pursuits take work and practice to master. Here's what to do.

For every task in your routine of getting ready for the day, time how long it takes you to do it, and write down the activity and time. For a week, log how long it takes you to shower, to dry your hair, to dress, to brush your teeth, and other things you do daily. Pay attention to how long things take, and which things seem to take the same amount of time. For instance, does showering and drying your hair take about as much time as watching a sitcom? As you compare the length of time different things in your life take, you'll be learning to grasp relative time.

Time Planning

Now that you know how much time things take, you can begin the time planning process. Average out a week of times for each task to determine about how long it should take you to do each thing. Then, add up the times for showering, brushing your teeth, fixing your hair, getting dressed, eating breakfast, and so on. How long does all that take you? Work backward from the time you need to be ready to go out. With this knowledge, you can plan to get up and start getting ready in plenty of time to do everything. Keep track of how often you hit the snooze alarm, factor that in, and add extra time for the unexpected.

On the other hand, if you are one of those people who starts early, gets ready quickly, and then has an hour before your ride arrives, plan something to do while you wait. Consider having a book at hand that's easy to put down, so that you won't get caught up in a story you can't pull yourself away from. Self-help books are good for this, and you can learn something new while you wait. Or fold clean laundry, put away clean dishes, or have a sketch pad handy so you can draw. Anything to keep you actively engaged in something that will be easy to leave, so you don't become anxious standing around waiting to go.

Time Transitions

Many autistic people have difficulty transitioning from one activity to another. Is it hard for you to get started on a new project? Do you have trouble stopping your video game or putting down your book in order to do the next thing in your day? If so, you may need to plan ways to help you transition instead of getting stuck, never getting around to other things that need to be done. When you were a kid, you may have played a game until your parents made you stop. If they hadn't been there, would you have played all night? If so, you need time transition help.

You are the adult in the room now. If you don't want to spend all your time on video games, it's up to you to figure out how to transition from one thing to another. The best way is to find an interim activity to put between the thing you don't want to stop and the thing you have trouble starting. If you tell yourself you must stop doing the thing you love most and then immediately go to a chore you highly dislike, you might ignore your own advice and keep doing the fun thing. However, if you place a medium task in between, it'll be easier to stop doing the really fun thing to do the kind of fun thing, and then stop doing the kind of fun thing to do the least fun thing. Then plan something else that you enjoy as a reward after you do the thing you hate to do. For instance, instead of going straight from binge-watching your favorite show to taking out the garbage, you might go from watching your favorite show to watching a brief "how-to" video, to preparing a snack to put in the fridge for later, to taking out the garbage. After you take out the garbage, you can reward yourself with the snack you made. Write down each step and check it off as you complete it. You'll feel more productive than if you let time slip away until you realize it's after midnight and you've done nothing but watch television all day.

Jerry Newport, autistic author of *Your Life is Not a Label*, wrote "For those of us with autism, especially, scheduled time adds a lot of needed security. It becomes something dependable ... schedules appeared in my ocean like little ice floes. I jumped on them whenever possible. Today, there are enough of those in life's ocean that I don't have to tread water too long before I find something to grab onto ... It's up to you ... The more you use your brain to make wise choices about your time, the more control you will have over your life."

Let's see how our five fictional characters managed time in their lives.

JACOB, 18

When Jacob was a child, it seemed as if his life was ruled by visual schedules. His teachers and his parents had charts everywhere with hook and loop stickers for picture icons. As he finished each task, such as brushing his teeth, he would move the picture of a toothbrush over to the "all done" column and go on to the next thing. Jacob hated those charts. He was relieved when they quit pushing them on him in middle school. School was so structured he always knew where to go, and when he got

CHAPTER 10

there the teachers would tell him what to do. At home, his mom would tell him when it was time to do something, which was fine with him.

Then one day, he missed the bus to school. His new alarm clock didn't wake him, and when he finally got up, he went through his morning routine at his usual pace. He figured his mother would tell him to hurry if he really had to, but she hadn't said anything. He was shocked to find he'd missed his bus. He threw down his backpack and yelled at his mom that she'd made him late and now she'd have to drive him to school. She said, "I don't deserve to be yelled at. If you missed your bus, you can walk to school." Then she got in her car and drove herself to work.

Jacob was shocked. He couldn't believe what had just happened. He angrily walked the mile and a half to school and had to get a tardy slip from the office before he could be admitted to class. Being late put off his routine and he was in a grumpy mood all day because of it.

When his mother got home, Jacob shouted at her about the rotten day he'd had and how it was all her fault, but she wouldn't listen. She picked up her laptop and went to her room, telling him to let her know when he'd calmed down enough to talk without yelling at her.

Jacob played his video game for a while to cool off, but he couldn't stop thinking about how different his mom was acting. Eventually, he turned off the game and knocked on her door quietly to say he was ready to talk. She told him her point of view, which he hadn't considered.

His mother had been waking him up and rushing him through his morning to get to the bus on time since he had been in kindergarten, and now that he was a legal adult, she was done.

"But why didn't you tell me?" Jacob asked.

"I did, don't you remember?" He didn't. "When we bought you the alarm clock, I said that I wouldn't be waking you up and getting you ready for school any more. You can do that for yourself now. That's why we bought the clock, remember?" Jacob vaguely remembered that she had been talking about something while they were shopping for the clock, but he was focused on finding one from his video game. He didn't remember what she had said and realized now he should have paid attention. His mother went on, "I told you that from now on, it was up to you to get yourself up and ready, and if you were late, you would have to walk to school."

"Do you mean you're not going to be, like, my mom anymore?" he asked her.

"Of course not, I'll always be your mom," she said. "But now I'm a mom of an adult, not a little kid. As an adult, you need to get yourself up in the morning and get yourself ready in time to catch your bus. Going upstairs to shake you awake three times, and then reminding you to hurry and brush your teeth and hair and get out the door is not my idea of a good time."

When she said it like that, Jacob realized it really didn't sound like fun for her. He had never thought of his mother as a person who might not enjoy all the things she did for him. "Is it terrible being my mom?" he asked. "Has it been awful for you?"

"Not at all! I've always loved being your mom, and raising you has been a joy. But you're eighteen years old now. It's time for me to step back."

CHAPTER 10

"What if I can't do it?" Jacob asked. "I was late this morning. What if I'm always late? I might get kicked out of school."

"First off, you won't get kicked out of school for being late, although they might want to talk to you about it if it happens too often. Just get up when your alarm clock goes off and get yourself ready and out the door. You know what to do." Jacob realized she was right.

"Secondly," she went on, "if you really need help, you can always ask me. I'll always be here for you to help solve problems that come up when you need me, but I'm not going to insert myself into your problems if you don't need me. You get to decide when you need help."

"When you say you'll help me, do you mean you'll tell me to hurry if I need to?"

"No, we're not going to go backwards to me treating you like a child again. But if you need help making sure your new alarm clock is set correctly, or if you need me to help you make a list of what needs to be done by certain times in the morning to be on time, I can help you get those things set up. Then it's up to you, as an adult, to take it from there."

That sounded reasonable to Jacob, and he decided he could manage his own mornings now that he understood that it was his job.

The next morning, Jacob over-slept again, but then he rushed through his morning routine double-speed and caught the bus just in time. That was twice his alarm clock didn't wake him up; it turned out he had set it for 6:00 PM instead of 6:00 AM. After that, Jacob rarely had problems, but when he did, he investigated to see what went wrong. Did he stay up too late the night before? Had his alarm clock come unplugged? Did he get distracted during his morning routine? Whatever it was, he could figure out a solution, or ask for help if he got stuck. Taking charge of his own morning time management made Jacob feel like an adult. He liked the feeling.

EMILY, 22

They were doing it again. Her housemates were bugging her about the dishes. She might as well be living at home the way these Nagatha Christies were on her case all the time. She knew it was her turn, but it would only take her a minute to do them. She just had to finish responding to friend on the *Hamilton* website. But they wouldn't stop interrupting her.

"Do you have to keep reminding me every second? I said I would do it!"

"You said you would do it last night, and then again this morning, and now it's 4:00 in the afternoon." This time it was a staff member rather than her housemates. "Today's dinner team needs to get to work and they need a clean kitchen. You need to do your job."

"But I know if you let me finish this one email, I can do the dishes really fast!"

"You said that thirty minutes ago. Are you still answering the same email?"

"Well, I answer, and then they answer me back, and then I have to reply to their answer. We're trying to have a conversation here!" Emily felt frustrated when people interrupted her.

"Your responsibility to the house comes first; you know that. Do the dishes now."

CHAPTER 10

Reluctantly, Emily shut down her laptop and went to the kitchen. "I don't see what the big deal is, I can get this done in, like, five minutes." She rinsed the dishes and had to scrub the casserole dish that had been hardening all night and day. When she got the dishes in and the dishwasher running, the staff member stopped her before she could get back on her computer.

"Emily, you said you could do the dishes in five minutes, right?"

"Sure, it hardly takes any time at all."

"It actually took you thirty-five minutes to get the dishes into the dishwasher, and now it will be another hour before the dishes are clean. Today's dinner team wants clean dishes. By not doing your job when you were supposed to, you created a problem for them."

Emily was shocked. "I didn't think it took that long!" She hadn't thought about making the other team late with their dinner prep. She'd volunteered to do the dishes yesterday when her team was ready to cook, but she didn't want to stop listening to *Hamilton*. They were happy to do all the cooking without her if she'd do all the clean-up, so she agreed. But that was yesterday, and she had kept putting it off. She couldn't blame today's team for being upset with her.

"I'm sorry," she said. "I guess I'm clueless at estimating times. Five minutes seemed like how long it should take. I didn't even think about how long the dishwasher would take."

The other team told her it was okay this time. They didn't need the casserole dish and there were enough plates, but no one liked looking at dirty dishes in the sink all day.

The staff member told Emily that she could learn how to understand and manage her time better. He suggested timing how long certain jobs took, since she admitted that she didn't have a clue. She agreed to try it for a week and then they could look at the times together. Emily used a timer on her phone for every house chore she did and wrote it down in the notes section of her phone. She was surprised. Some jobs she thought would take practically no time, such as dishes and taking a shower, took longer than she realized. Other tasks, like cleaning the toilet, seemed like they'd take an hour, but really only took a few minutes.

The most important thing Emily learned was to do a job right away and get it over with. It felt great to relax with no chores hanging over her head. Learning how long jobs take, and tackling them right away, were good solutions for her time management problem.

ZACH, 33

Part of Zach's job was to make the rounds at the synagogue three times each night. He wasn't told exact times, but they said he should make the first rounds at least an hour after closing up, the second one later at night such as right before he goes to bed, and the last one early in the morning at least a half-hour before unlocking. He was not expected to get up and make rounds once he went to bed for the night, which was a relief to him.

When he first started the job, he often forgot to make some of his rounds. He would be about to go to bed and suddenly realize that he hadn't made either of the two rounds that should have been done before bed. Other times, he overslept after getting involved in a game long into the night before and missed his morning rounds and unlocking the building. A couple of times someone had to call him or knock on his door to get into the offices. A member of the trustees spoke to him about it and he said it wouldn't happen again.

Zach set alarms on his phone to go off at 7:00 AM to make his first rounds, at 8:00 AM to unlock the buildings, at 5:00 PM to lock up again, at 6:00 PM to make his first evening rounds before dinner, and at 10:00 PM to make his final rounds. Once he had his alarms set, he was methodical in getting the job done. He did not want to disappoint the rabbi who had recommended him, and he certainly did not want to lose this job and have to move back home. Setting the alarms solved his problem of losing track of time and forgetting to do his job.

One night, as he made his usual 6:00 PM rounds, he thought he saw someone between the buildings, but when he shone his flashlight that way they ran off. He assumed it was kids looking for a place to hang out. He walked around one more time. When he made his 10:00 PM rounds later he was shocked to find offensive graffiti painted on a wall. This was disturbing. At first, he felt frozen in place. Then he pulled out his phone, took a picture of it, and cleaned it up.

The next morning, he showed the rabbi the photo of the graffiti. He told him he had cleaned it up, but that he was worried about it happening again. The rabbi thanked him, asked him to forward the photo with an email describing what he had seen, and said he would share it with the trustees and the police. Then he asked about the usual routine for making the rounds, and Zach explained his new system that made sure he never forgot his rounds again. The rabbi suggested that he vary his rounds so that it was not always at exactly the same time. The taggers could have been able to predict that after the 6:00 PM rounds they would have a window of four hours during which they could vandalize the building. Zach thought about this. He had really liked the routine of his system, and he was uncomfortable with something less structured. It made sense, but he worried if he didn't have alarms, he might forget. He decided to find a way to use alarms with unpredictable times.

Zach got out some index cards and wrote different schedules for rounds. They were not equally distant from each other, but were irregular to make it difficult to predict when he might come back. In most cases he left himself a full eight hours to sleep with no rounds scheduled, since the temple did not expect him to interrupt his sleep; however, he decided that once every couple of weeks he would have one round scheduled for the middle of the night. He ended up with eight different schedules. None were at the exact hour or half-hour, but times like 6:04 AM or 10:49 PM. Then he programmed alarms into his clock for each time. He labeled each card by a letter of the alphabet and named those alarms to match, such as "A, Morning," or "C, Evening," or "G, Night." Each night he would pick the top card, set the alarms for the next day to correspond with the letter on the card, and then put it at the bottom. He shuffled the deck weekly to mix it up.

Zach felt better knowing that no one could anticipate when he might be making his rounds, and the card system worked. At first, he thought he would hate having a different schedule each day because a predicable routine was comforting to him, but soon the routine of choosing a card and selecting the corresponding alarms became his new normal. For Zach, setting up a system solved his time management problem.

CHAPTER 10

MARIA, 45

Maria blinked her eyes. When had it gotten so dark? A glance at her phone told her it was after 8:00 PM. How had that happened? She stood up and sat back down again quite suddenly, dizzy and shaky. She saw an empty water bottle nearby, but no plates or food wrappers. Had she remembered to eat today? Another try at standing up let her know that she had probably forgotten. She made her way to the kitchen unsteadily and quickly drank some juice. Then she had a piece of cheese and an apple and started to feel more like herself.

Where had the day gone? How could she forget to eat all day? She had been excited about the twenty-four-hour robot movie marathon and settled in first thing in the morning with her tablet beside her tuned to Sloth TV. If a movie got boring, she could go back and forth between her favorite things. That was twelve hours ago.

As she fixed herself a cup of soup to follow the juice, cheese, and fruit, she started to worry about herself. Was she so incapable of taking care of her own needs that she went all day without any nourishment? What if the girls found out? They might want to put her in a home, or make her wear one of those electronic emergency buttons that old people wear. She wasn't that old. So why was she acting so helpless and out of it?

The next morning, after sleeping on the problem, Maria decided to set some alarms on her cell phone. She'd never needed reminders for things like eating, doing laundry, or washing dishes; she assumed she could manage the basics on her own. But looking around her house, she could see that she'd been wrong. Dishes, laundry, trash, and recycling were piling up. When the twins were home Maria was always on alert, trying so hard to be a good parent. Her self-image as a mother was her focus, but now that she wasn't actively parenting, she needed help.

Maria opened the calendar section of her phone. She made calendar appointments with alarms for getting up, for showering and brushing her teeth and hair, and for eating breakfast. As she went forward through her day, she included everything she wanted to do, like putting her breakfast dishes into the dishwasher. Most of the appointments were things she should do every day, so she programmed her phone to repeat those daily. Others, like taking out the trash, grocery shopping, and doing laundry, she set for weekly. She made a monthly reminder to balance her checkbook. Then Maria went to her phone settings and listened to the alarm options, choosing gentle chimes that made her feel calm.

The first day she put her plan into action, she resisted opening her phone when it chimed. She didn't want to see what the reminder was for. How could she get herself to follow her own plan? What might make it more interesting to look at her phone instead of ignoring it? She decided to devote an afternoon to searching for images online of sloths and of giant transforming robots. She copied links for the images she liked and put one in the Notes section of each of her reminders. She would have to open the appointment and click on the link to view the image. Her reward for completing each task would be to look at the image that she had hidden there for herself. She also put an emoji of a robot head at the beginning of each task that she had completed, saving for that date only, not for future appointments. At the end of the day, if she looked back and saw robot heads on most of her appointments, she'd know that she had gotten a lot of done that day. After a month, she could look back at all the days and see if there were certain tasks that she consistently skipped and make a plan to get those jobs done. Even though they were simple, daily things that others might not need reminders for, she didn't trust herself to do everything unless she had a structure for her days. For Maria, creating daily reminders with pleasant alarms, rewarding herself for each job done by looking at a picture she enjoyed, and then checking off her finished tasks with robot head emojis made her feel confident about managing her own time.

ROBERT, 62

"Hurry up!" Robert called up the stairs. "What's taking everyone so long? Let's hit the road!" His wife, daughter, and grandson were still getting ready for their outing to the farmers market, and he was the only one downstairs. He impatiently jangled his keys in his pocket. "Let's go, get a move on!" he called again.

Finally, his wife came downstairs. "Will you stop all this racket? We're not leaving with your grandson half dressed."

"Well, maybe his mother should light a fire under him. I've been waiting for twenty-five minutes."

"Robert." His wife gave him The Look. "The plan was to leave at 9:30, and it's only 9:05. Keep your shirt on and quit yelling. You're only making everything more stressful."

"But I'm ready now. I don't see why it should take everyone so long to get out the door."

"You're almost a half-hour early. That's not our fault.

Yelling at your family about your poor planning won't win you any brownie points, you know."

"But I started getting ready right after breakfast, and now I'm ready to go. Why not get on the road early if we can? We'll have that much more time when we get there."

"It takes the rest of us longer to get ready than it does you. Your daughter is upstairs helping Bobby go through his morning routine, but every time you yell, he freezes. She has to wait for him to calm down before they can get back on track."

"I didn't know that," Robert admitted. "But how am I supposed to get everybody out in the car without calling up the stairs? Do you want me to go up and help her?"

"No, please don't. She's got it handled, she just needs you to cool your jets."

"We'll never get there, there won't be any parking places when we do, and all the best vegetables will be gone before we even get out the door," Robert complained.

"We decided last night that 9:30 would be the best time to leave. It's not our fault if you're ready to go early. Find something to do with yourself, and I don't want to hear a peep out of you until 9:30. Not one peep!" His wife went back upstairs, leaving Robert feeling up-in-the-air. What should he do? Just standing there was driving him crazy. He poured another half cup of coffee and sat down, pulled a tablet and pen over, and started making notes.

"Things to do when I'm ready too early," he wrote at the top. Then he tapped the pen on the paper a few times, thinking. Finally he wrote this list:

1. Have another cup of coffee

2. Read the newspaper

3. Do a crossword puzzle

He looked around the kitchen, remembering how upset his wife was with his yelling. What could he do that might make her happy? He added to the list:

4. Put away clean dishes from the dishwasher

5. Wipe down the island and counters

6. Clean the inside of the microwave

Robert decided to start with number six. He got out a clean sponge and wiped down the inside of the microwave and the door, inside and out. It really wasn't a difficult job once he had the sponge in his hand. He looked around for something else to clean, and started wiping off the counters, island, and then the front of the dishwasher. He was contemplating whether or not he should take his grandson's artwork off of the refrigerator to give that a good cleaning, too, when his family came downstairs and headed to the car. He quickly rinsed the sponge and put it back, glancing at the clock. 9:29. They were a minute early.

"Sorry about all the yelling before," he said sheepishly to his daughter.

She sighed. "Don't worry about it, Dad. It went a lot faster once you stopped shouting."

"Yeah, I heard." He glanced at his wife. "I won't let it happen again."

"I notice you've been cleaning." She smiled. "That's very helpful."

"I aim to please," he said as they all piled into the car and headed off to the farmers market, right on time. For Robert, making a list of things to do while waiting solved his time management problem. Including helpful tasks as well as things that would be fun for him made his wife happy. It was a good reminder to make a useful contribution to the household.

SPEAKING FOR OURSELVES

About Time Scheduling (Making a Plan for What You Will Do)

"Scheduling has helped me in more ways than I could ever imagine. By personally creating a list of things I would like to get done that day, I am controlling my day. When I write out my schedule, I'm making room for balance in my life. I can attest that scheduling has worked for loads of different folks on the spectrum and it can work for you, especially if you're a visual learner. It will feel way more inspiring and encouraging if you create it yourself than it will if someone in authority makes your schedule for you."

About the Time Log (Writing Down What You Actually Did)

"My strategy is to try and be conscious of the log, softly reminding myself to keep it updated with what I am doing every half hour. Should I feel ashamed, nervous, or guilty about putting down that I didn't have a very productive day, I don't let it get to me. I am completely turning my life around from depression to optimism and passion. It takes time to develop a new routine that reflects the Morgan who wants to be a well-rounded

CHAPTER 10

person. I am consciously using my schedule and log to *change myself for the better.*"

> — *Morgan Marie, autistic writer and blogger*
> *https://confessionsofanautisticfreak.wordpress.com*

CHAPTER 11
TRANSPORTATION MANAGEMENT

———⟫●⟪———

(Go Where You Want to Go)

There are lots of ways to get from one place to another. You can walk, bike, carpool, use a ride-hailing app, take public transportation, or drive yourself. They all have advantages, and also aspects that might be more challenging for some autistic people.

Walk

Walking has great advantages. You are in complete control of where you want to go. It's great exercise, good for the heart, and can even reduce anxiety and depression.

On the downside, walking is limited by weather, distance, daylight, and how much you can carry. For instance, you might be able to walk to a grocery store, but you won't be able to take a cart-load of groceries home. Many people bring a small rolling cart and shop more often.

There are other things about walking that can bother some autistic adults, like unpredictable social stressors. Will you see

155

someone, and if so, what do you say? As a general safety rule, especially for female-presenting people, it's better not to greet unknown men you pass on the street to avoid giving the impression that you're open to a relationship. If you're male-presenting and you pass a woman you don't know, don't sustain eye contact or try to start a conversation. Regardless of gender, a simple, courteous nod and a brief, "hello" is plenty. This is non-threatening, without coming on too strong. Don't make full eye contact or slow down, but veer slightly to the side away from the other person so as not to crowd them, allowing plenty of passing room. Then, keep walking at the same pace without looking back.

The reason for this has to do with how the other person, usually a neurotypical, might interpret your actions. An NT man walking past a woman who looks at him, smiles, and says hello, may think, "She must be interested in dating me. I should try to get to know her and see where this goes." A woman walking alone past a strange man who makes prolonged eye contact or speaks to her may feel uncomfortable, or even threatened. Also, if you are a man walking behind a woman going the same way, you may not know how fast to walk. If you keep the same pace trailing her, she may feel she's being followed or stalked. If you speed up to pass her, you should keep up that speed or she might think you've passed her in order to then slow down and perhaps force an encounter. Some people go so far as to cross the street to avoid any kind of confrontation at all. It sounds complicated, but the bottom line when sharing a public sidewalk is to maintain a comfortable speed, allow plenty of passing room, and avoid interacting with strangers. It's safer not to phone-and-walk, not only because you could walk into a lamp post, but also because people focused on their phones look distracted and vulnerable.

Another aspect of autism that can affect walking is increased fatigue. For some, social interactions are exhausting. If this sounds like you, be sure to save enough energy to walk all the way home after a social event. Even going to a library, museum, or store may include social interactions with staff and other patrons.

If you plan ahead, walking can be an excellent mode of transport in the right situations. It provides healthy exercise and works to help decrease anxiety and depression.

Bike

If you can ride a bike, your horizons are expanded. Biking shares the advantages of walking while increasing speed and distance. Many bikes have baskets for a few groceries.

Some autistic people have great motor control, and others have trouble with balance. If you find it takes a lot of concentration to stay in the bike lane without wobbling, then you may not be ready for street biking. Keep practicing; this is a skill that you can improve.

If you do have the balance and control needed to safely ride a bike, remember to wear a helmet, know the biking laws for your state, use bike lanes, and ride with traffic. In America, that means staying to the right and going the same way as the cars. Get yourself a bike lock, mirrors, and lights as well as reflectors for night biking. Even if you don't intend to bike at night, there may be times when the sun sets before you get home. Dress for comfort, flexibility, and visibility, and keep your bike in good repair.

Carpool or Get a Ride

If there is a regular activity like school, work, or a club meeting, there may be others you can carpool with. Carpools are great for the environment and traffic, with fewer cars on the road. Plus, you can take advantage of carpool lanes on some freeways.

If you are in a carpool, there are ways you can make it fair. The first and simplest is to be grateful. Thank your driver each time they give you a ride. Of course, gratitude alone won't put gas in the tank. If you can't take turns driving, offer to help pay for gasoline, buy coffee for the others in the car, and refrain from smoking, "backseat driving," or talking in a loud voice.

Carpools are great, but sometimes you need to go to a one-time appointment. If you have family or close friends who give you rides, here are some things to keep in mind.

If your parents have always driven you everywhere, be aware that this is not a permanent solution. You may appreciate their help, but as an adult you will need to manage your own transportation needs. Brainstorm other options. This doesn't mean your parents should never give you rides, but you can reduce your dependence on them. When they do give you a ride, thank them. Even parents have other things they could be doing, and gratitude is appreciated.

If you have a sibling or friend who gives you rides, that's great, especially if you're both going to the same place. However, if it's one-sided, you should offer to help pay for gas. Don't back off too easily when they politely decline. Tell them you wouldn't feel right not helping with gas money, and they will be grateful. This is especially true when they're driving you somewhere as a favor to you, not just because you're both going to the same event.

CHAPTER 11

Ride-Hailing App or Taxi

There are a number of ride-hailing apps. Some are familiar, and others you may not have heard of. Check out the reviews, noting how many reviews there are as well as how positive they are. If a service has a five-star rating based on four reviewers, those may have been written by their friends. A four-star rating based on thousands of reviews is more telling. Some provide a photo of your driver and their car or license plate number, so you know who's picking you up. Always be safe, and never get into a car unless you're sure this is the car you hailed. One safety rule is not to ask, "Are you here for ___?" telling them your name. Instead, ask them, "Who are you here to pick up?" If they're your driver, they'll know your name.

You are not obliged to make small talk with your driver. If they try to chat and you don't want to, put in earbuds and/or take out your phone, tablet, or a book. This sends the signal that you're not up for conversation. If they still try to chat with you, respond briefly, then turn your attention away.

Most of these apps let you pay and tip online. It's a good adult practice to always tip when you have been the recipient of a service. If you felt you received excellent service, such as a clean car with items like bottled water, tissues, and mints available, you might want to tip 20 percent; for good service that was not exceptional, consider tipping 15 percent. You can always do an online search to see what the going rate for tipping is in your geographical area.

Taxis and shuttles are similar to ride-hailing apps. In some cities, like New York, you only need to raise your arm to hail a cab because there are so many. You can call for a taxicab or arrange a shuttle bus online, by phone, or app. Again, use the internet to find one that suits your needs and is available in your area. Socially, the taxicab experience is similar to ride-hailing, as you are not obliged to chat with your taxi driver. Do be polite, and don't forget to tip.

Bus, Subway, or Train

Most cities have some kind of a bus system available, and some also have subways or commuter trains. Check online for what is available in your area. There are pluses and minuses for each, and it's up to you to decide what's best for you.

On the plus side, public transportation can be more affordable than other options. Having a pass can open doors to your community that may otherwise have been closed to you. There may even be specialized transportation or rates available for people with disabilities which you may be eligible for. Check online for disability services in your area.

On the minus side, there are things to take into account that may mean the bus, subway, or train may not be right for you, including sensory, social, and safety considerations.

Sensory problems can include smells; either the smell of the vehicle itself, exhaust fumes, or the body odor or perfume of others riding with you. If you are sensitive to odors, plan ahead to make your ride more pleasant. One way is using a cloth handkerchief soaked in water with a few drops of a scent you enjoy such as vanilla extract. Once it dries, you have a vanilla-scented handkerchief you can hold to your nose against the stench of a bus. You can also buy scented key chains and other small scented items you can carry in your pocket or purse.

CHAPTER 11

Unwanted social interactions can be handled just like in a taxi or ride-share: carry a book, phone, or earbuds and ignore strangers who try to talk to you. Public transportation is not a safe place to make new friends, so keep to yourself until you get to your destination.

Don't take up more than your fair share of space. Aim your knees straight ahead at hip width rather than spreading out to the sides. Don't cross your legs if it would put your foot in the aisle or your neighbor's personal space. Keep your bag, back-pack, or purse on your lap. If you must stand and hold a strap while riding because there are no seats, keep your possessions in front of you. Try not to touch others if possible (it's not always possible), and avoid eye contact.

The safest place to sit on a bus is as close to the driver as possible. Don't talk to the driver, but if you're close, people are less likely to try to bother you. The back of the bus is the least safe place; avoid it when you can. If you must sit next to another person, try to choose someone of your own gender presentation to sit by. On a subway or commuter train, find a car that is not empty if you can. It may seem like a good idea to get in an empty car to avoid people, but at any stop another person could get on. If that person has bad intentions, you don't want to be alone in a car with them. Choosing a car with other people decreases the likelihood that you will be alone in an unsafe situation.

As long as you plan ahead for sensory, social, and safety concerns, public transportation is an excellent way to expand your horizons.

Drive

Autistic adults can be excellent drivers. Some learn to drive as soon as they are old enough to get a license, and others prefer to get their license when they are older. Some choose not to drive, perhaps because being responsible for a large steel object traveling rapidly amongst other large steel objects is too stressful. Some people are uncomfortable with non-symmetry; they like things to be the same on both sides of their body, and the idea of pressing the brake and gas pedals with only the right foot is uncomfortable. Other people would be excellent drivers in highly controlled situations, but they don't react well to surprises. If a car honked, or an animal ran in front of their car, they might freeze. Knowing yourself and how you react under stress is important. To drive or not to drive is a personal question, and no one should pressure you to make a choice that's not right for you.

Factors to consider include the cost of purchasing a vehicle: licensing, insurance, gasoline if it is gas-powered, and regular upkeep. Upkeep is vital; if you don't take care of regular maintenance, the consequences are expensive and dangerous. If you have an electric vehicle, never go so far that you lack power to get home, and know where to find charging stations.

As you can see, there are many options and considerations for transportation. Be responsible about your choice. Don't be pressured into something you're not comfortable with. Now, let's see how our five fictional characters managed their transportation needs.

CHAPTER 11

JACOB, 18

Most of the seniors at Jacob's school had their driver's licenses, many of them drove their parents' cars to school, and a few even had their own cars.

Not Jacob. His father offered to help him get his learner's permit, but Jacob kept putting it off. He had taken driver's ed in school because he had to, but he had no desire to drive. Just the thought of getting behind the wheel made him anxious; he pictured himself crashing the car and possibly killing himself or other people. It made his stomach hurt.

There weren't a lot of places Jacob needed to go, actually. He rode the bus to school, and he enjoyed the exercise of walking to the bus stop. After school, he walked Mulligan. He loved being alone outside after being cooped up in classrooms and navigating crowded hallways. Walking alone was a great stress-reliever for him, and he welcomed it, even in rain or cold.

His parents had offered to buy him a used car for his eighteenth birthday, but Jacob talked them out of it. They got him a top-of-the-line bicycle instead, with mirrors, lights, a sturdy locking chain, and a helmet. He'd learned to ride as a kid but hadn't ridden in years. He found that he really did remember how to balance and steer, and that he was good at it—I guess you could say it was just like riding a bike.

It seemed to access a different part of his brain than he usually used, and relieved stress. The invigorating feel of the wind in his face made him happy. Since then, he'd been exploring his town on weekends, riding to the library, the local game and comic book stores, and even the mall. He found he could tolerate the crowds in the mall for longer periods after a bike ride to get there, and with the bike ride home to look forward to.

For Jacob, walking and riding a bike were satisfying transportation solutions. His parents still drove him to appointments and places that were too far to bike. He knew that someday he'd have to come up with other options, but for now, while he was still living at home and going to high school, he wasn't going to worry about it too much.

EMILY, 22

Emily never wants to drive. Not ever. This wasn't always the case, though. When she was a teen, she begged, but her parents refused to let her get a learner's permit. They didn't believe she was mature enough to drive safely. She used to complain that they were mean to not let her try, but they wouldn't budge. Finally, she gave up and let them drive her everywhere.

One day her case manager asked if she wanted to learn to drive, since as an adult she wouldn't need her parents' permission. Emily thought about it long and hard. She knew she wanted to go out and do things, but when she thought about driving now, she realized it might not be for her. She recognized a pattern in her responses to sensory things in her environment. Once during dinner, she was in the middle of telling a story when someone dropped a pan in the kitchen. The loud, unexpected clatter shocked her and she froze with her mouth half open, unable to continue talking. When her housemates asked her to finish the story, she still couldn't talk. She couldn't even finish her meal because her stomach was in knots. What if she

CHAPTER 11

were driving a car, and there was a sudden, loud noise, like a car honking or backfiring? How would she react? She didn't want to find out while driving. Emily decided that driving was not for her.

She asked her case manager about other ways to get around town. The group home had a shuttle bus that took groups on scheduled outings, but if Emily wanted to go somewhere else on her own, the shuttle wasn't available. There was a pretty reliable bus service in their city, but Emily had never ridden a public bus and she was hesitant to try it alone. Her case manager told her that there might be several people who felt as she did. She scheduled a group outing to the movies, but instead of taking the shuttle, they would all ride the bus together.

Before the trip, they had a group meeting to go over what to expect. One of the staff members made a slide show, and they also watched a video about riding the bus. Most of her housemates scoffed a bit and said they already knew this stuff, but they all watched it anyway. Emily felt confident after the meeting. There was nothing surprising about riding a bus, but seeing it on a video helped her feel more secure about doing it herself.

The next day, they were ready to go. They reviewed the bus schedule and knew which bus would take them to the theater and about what time it would be at their stop. Everybody had enough money for the bus to the theater, movie tickets, snacks, and for the bus home again. Everyone had their phones in case they got separated. They walked the few blocks to the bus stop together.

Soon, the bus arrived. Emily was in the middle so she could watch someone else pay before it was her turn. Some people had prepaid cards to scan to pay for their ride. Emily had cash. There was a place to slide in a paper dollar, and a receptacle for change, and she paid her $1.50 with a one-dollar bill and two quarters. She was a little nervous, but she didn't mess it up. She sat by someone she knew. The ride to the movie theater wasn't long and she enjoyed chatting and looking out the window. Later, a woman wearing heavy perfume got on the bus and Emily's seatmate pulled her sweater over her nose, clearly bothered by the smell, but Emily didn't mind. For her, the hardest part was the squealing brakes, traffic sounds, and occasional shock of a honk or siren. She had planned for this, though, and she put in her noise-canceling earbuds to make the sound level tolerable.

When they got to their stop, they walked to the theater. Emily bought herself a movie ticket, soda, and popcorn, and settled down between friends from her group home to enjoy the movie. She kept her earbuds in because the volume in the theater was pretty high. She had a great time. Going home, she felt even more confident as she scanned in her dollar and dropped in her quarters before finding her seat. She thought one day she would feel comfortable taking the bus on her own. It felt like her world was expanding, and she liked the feeling.

For Emily, the bus was the best solution to meet her transportation needs. Knowing what to expect and going in a group gave her the confidence she needed to be independent.

ZACH, 33

Zach still had the used car he got when he graduated from college about a decade ago. He couldn't afford anything newer, so he hoped it would live forever. Unfortunately, he hadn't been able to afford the kind of maintenance an old car needs. The morning it wouldn't start, he wondered what was wrong. Did it need oil? He dimly remembered some kind of light coming on, but he thought it might have been a computer glitch. Now, sitting in a dead car, he realized it had been a mistake to ignore that light. When was the last time he changed the oil? He couldn't remember. Money was tight so he kept putting it off until payday, and then putting it off again. There had been some noises, but he just turned up the volume on his music.

Zach called his dad. His father's roadside automobile service membership would cover towing his son's car. The mechanic's verdict was that it would be too expensive to fix everything that was wrong. Buying a new car was out of the question. Zach's dad didn't offer to buy him one and Zach didn't ask. He was an adult now, and transportation was his own responsibility. He got $300.00 for the car for scrap metal, and said good-bye to it. His father said he should open a savings account with the $300.00 to save for his next car. That sounded smart, so he did. Meanwhile, how was he going to get around with no wheels?

Zach thought about the places he usually drove. He had to go to the grocery store, but there was a market within walking distance, so that was fine. He could carry his groceries home.

Since he lived and worked at the synagogue where his social group met, he didn't need a car for that. He used to drive to volunteer at his political party headquarters, but now he would have to find another way. One of the other volunteers went to his temple, so he asked him if he could get a ride the next time they had a volunteer session. He agreed to pick Zach up since it wasn't too far out of his way, so Zach figured that problem was solved.

From then on, every time there was another volunteer meeting, Zach asked his friend what time he would pick him up. This was working great for Zach, and he assumed it was just as great for his friend. It turned out he was wrong about that. The next time he asked about a ride, his friend said, "I don't know, Zach. When is your car getting fixed, anyway?"

"It's not getting fixed, it's junked," Zach said. "I thought you knew that."

"No, I thought it was in the shop and you needed a ride until you got it back."

"Um, I can't afford a new car," Zach said.

"So, what are you going to do? What's your plan?" Zach couldn't say his plan was that his friend would keep giving him free rides forever. He now realized that he'd been acting like a kid, only instead of relying on his parents, he was relying on a friend. That wasn't fair.

"I'm not sure," he said. "If I pay for gas, would you keep giving me rides?"

His friend's face relaxed into a smile. "Actually, that sounds great. I don't mind taking the time to come pick you up, but gas prices are high."

"No problem, I'm grateful for the ride, and happy to pay." Zach found a site online that gave guidelines for how much to reimburse a friend for rides. He showed up with cash in hand for every ride and offered to buy snacks or coffee sometimes. He figured that he would have been spending money on gas for his old car, anyway, and his friend needed cash. It was a win-win.

For Zach, the loss of his old car was a wake-up call. When he saves up enough for a new one, he'll put regular maintenance and oil changes on his calendar so he won't forget. In the meantime, between walking and rides for gas money, Zach's transportation needs were met.

MARIA, 45

Maria dreaded driving. She had a car, but she disliked using it, or even seeing it in the driveway. When she was married, her husband had always been in the driver's seat, and she had been happy to ride "shotgun." When he left her, he left her the family car. She imagined it was his excuse to get a flashier car for himself. The first few times she went out in the car alone after he left her, she got into the passenger side out of habit, and was embarrassed to get back out and walk around to the driver's side. The more time passed, the dirtier the car got and the more she avoided it, finding other ways to get around whenever she could.

When her girls were home from college, they drove the car to go out and see friends. They always filled it with gas and got it washed, and even got the oil changed, all of which Maria was happy to pay for. She realized that she hadn't driven it once since their last visit. Why was she holding onto it, when they could put it to much better use? She told them they could have the car as long as they didn't fight over it. The girls were thrilled, and as soon as she convinced them that it would not leave her stranded, they gladly drove it back to school at the end of break.

Looking out the window to an empty driveway made Maria feel lighter. She hummed as she puttered around the house. Then she thought about what it would really mean for her to have no car. She had been quick to assure her girls that she didn't need it, but was that true? What if there were an emergency and she had to get to the hospital? Of course, if it were a real emergency, she could call 911. But what about going to a doctor's appointment, or to church, or shopping? Maria turned, as she often did, to the internet. She searched, "How can I go places with no car?" and found lots of ideas. Walking, of course, was something she could do, although she didn't like it much. Her city had a bus system, but she got motion sickness; the thought of made her queasy and she had to lie down for a while. Later, she returned to her computer search.

Several ride-hailing apps were advertised, and she researched each and read reviews from real people. Two seemed superior, so she focused on them. She found videos showing how to use the apps, and what to expect. Some of the videos were aimed at drivers, but quite a few were for passengers like her who had never used the service before. The more videos she watched, the more confident she became. This was something she could do for herself.

Sunday morning, she decided to put it to the test. She had downloaded the app and put in her information to create a profile the day before. Now she opened the app and typed in her church's address and what time the service started. She was contacted by a driver, and the app showed a picture of the car and the driver along with the driver's name and plate number. At the appointed time, Maria waited outside her house and a car pulled up that matched the picture on the app. The window rolled down, and the driver asked, "Are you Maria?" and told her his name. She checked the app and this was her driver, so she got into the back seat. Figuring out tips was difficult for Maria when she was under pressure, but now she had time to work out an appropriate tip. After she was dropped off, she

CHAPTER 11

gave her driver the highest star rating and a 20 percent tip. Although he hadn't done anything outstanding, she appreciated that he had not pressed her to make conversation and the car was clean.

As she walked in from the church parking lot, Sofia, a woman she had spoken with several times, said hello and asked if her son had dropped her off. When Maria told her she had used a ride-sharing app, Sofia offered to drive her home so she wouldn't have to wait for another ride. Maria hesitated. She didn't want to impose, but Sofia had always been kind and friendly. She agreed, and they sat together in church.

On the ride home, Sofia shared that she was still getting used to going to church alone since her husband died, and she appreciated having someone to sit with. She mentioned they lived in the same general neighborhood, and it would be no problem to give her a ride every Sunday. Maria offered to pay for gas, but she wouldn't hear of it, as she would be driving that way anyway. They agreed and exchanged email addresses in case one of them couldn't make it.

Maria said good-bye and went into her house, feeling elated. Since her new friend wouldn't accept gas money, she tried to think of other ways to express her gratitude. Maria decided that whenever she had overripe bananas, she would make two loaves of banana bread and give one to Sofia. She also found some amusing memes online of sloths saying funny things like, "I planned on procrastinating today … but I never got around to it." She sent Sofia an email to thank her for the ride and attached the sloth meme. Since Sofia was a widow, she might need funny things to help her not feel so sad, so Maria would send her funny pictures every week.

For Maria, walking to the local grocer, using a ride-hailing app for appointments, and accepting a ride to church with a friend were all good ways to solve her transportation problems. She was happy to know her daughters would have a car at school, and to have found a new friend.

ROBERT, 62

Robert clenched his teeth and gripped the steering wheel. He could feel his face grow hot and his muscles tense. He had started to pull into the parking lot of their favorite drive-through coffee place, but now he was stuck. It was so busy they had a huge line, and he was left with his back bumper hanging out in the street. There was nothing he could do. Any moment one of those cars behind him might start honking at him to get out of the way, and he couldn't move.

The most frustrating thing was, Robert could see that there was actually plenty of room for him to get all the way into the lot. At least, there would be if each of the cars in that long line would pull up just a bit. Every car had space in front of them, but he was left blocking traffic.

"Look at them!" he complained to his wife. "If only people would pull up behind the car in front of them, we wouldn't be blocking half a lane of traffic out there! Why do they do that?"

"Mm-hmm," his wife agreed absently. Then she turned and looked at him. "When you ask why they do that, is it a rhetorical question, or do you really want to know?" She had been reading about Asperger's, and one thing she learned was not to assume her husband looked at the world the same way she did.

CHAPTER 11

"I really want to know," he said. "It's not just rude, it's down-right dangerous. We're hanging out in traffic so far, we could get hit by some crazy kid texting while driving. All they have to do is pull forward about a foot or two, and problem solved."

"Okay," she said, "I'll tell you what I think. I think no one in those other cars is thinking about you. They're thinking about getting their cup of coffee. They have no idea that you're block-ing traffic back here, or that they could solve our problem if they all worked together. They're not being mean, they just have a different perspective that doesn't include you."

"Huh." Robert was surprised. By failing to pull forward to let him in, it felt like the other drivers were conspiring to make his morning miserable. But, if they weren't even aware he was back here, then it was nothing personal. "So they're not out to get me, they're just clueless?"

"They're not clueless, they just don't have the same clues you have. Everybody looks at a situation from a different vantage point. Each of them is looking forward, and they see a car ahead of them in line. They probably don't even notice that they could pull forward a bit, and they might think it would be rude to the car in front of them if they tailgated too closely. From back here, you can easily see all of them. You visualize the sum of the spaces between each of the cars and you see a solution to your problem if they would all work together to pull up a bit and let you in. But they don't see what you see, and they can't work together. They're all separate people with their own agendas."

"So they might all pull forward if I asked each of them to help me out back here?"

"Please don't do that. Stay in the car and they'll move up when they can." Just then, the car in front got their order and everyone pulled forward. Robert got his back bumper out of the street before anyone honked. He thought about how many times he'd gotten mad when he saw careless drivers, or jaywalkers, or bicycles going the wrong way. It made him mad that they could cause accidents affecting everyone on the road. He always assumed they were doing it on purpose, but now he wondered about his own perceptions. He remembered the times he got angry about someone speeding, and his wife wondered aloud if they were on the way to the hospital. He hadn't thought of them as people with reasons to speed, only about how foolish he thought they were. Did his Asperger's make it harder for him to put himself in their shoes? He guessed he was glad his wife had shared her thoughts, not that he'd ever admit it.

Robert was a good driver, but he didn't always look at things from other drivers' point of view. Having a neurotypical wife to offer a different perspective was helpful.

SPEAKING FOR OURSELVES

"As someone who doesn't drive, transportation is an issue. It's stressful if I can't get a lift with someone I know, and I've had some bad experiences riding the bus. One weekend, my sister and I were going somewhere. We had a ride there but not back, so we used a ride-sharing app to get home. It's something I might have been nervous to do alone, but having my sister with me made it feel like something I could do. We had a fun day out, and our driver was really nice. I still avoid the bus, but using the ride-share app is a solution that works for me."

— *Cat, autistic adult*

CHAPTER 12
MONEY MANAGEMENT

———⟶➤●⊂⟵———

(Be Your Own Banker)

Money management is not easy, but it is achievable. With some attention to your income and outgo, you can master your own money. Most people would rather spend money now than plan for the future, even if the future is as close as the end of the month. No one likes having to decide whether to spend your last few dollars on gas or groceries. It's better to manage your money so you needn't worry about making ends meet.

There are UPS and DOWNS that can help you get a handle on your finances. The UPS to remember are Understand, Plan, and Save; the DOWNS to avoid are Denial, Overspending, Wishful thinking, Negativity, and Splurging.

Understand

It's important to understand how much money is coming in, and how much needs to go out. The word "budget" sounds stressful, but it doesn't have to be scary. Dave Ramsey, financial author, defines a budget as "telling your money where to go instead of wondering where it went." It's being the boss of your bucks. Whether you use a budget planning worksheet or an app, having a visual image of money flow is helpful. This can be as simple as two columns: income and outgo. You'll need to know your monthly income, your fixed bills and due dates, and other expenses like groceries and transport. Seeing your income and outgo written down is a vital first step to understanding money management.

Plan

Now that you understand your money flow, plan to control it. Your bank probably has an app to make it easy to track your money. Use the automatic bill pay to pay your bills automatically and you can stop worrying; your bank will take it from there.

Once your regular bills are taken care of, you'll see what's left. When planning your grocery budget, think about the foods you eat regularly. What are your favorite breakfast, lunch, and dinner foods? Keep non-perishable food on hand so you won't find yourself hungry and your cupboards bare right before pay-day. It's tempting to spend your food budget on cookies and chips, but don't go crazy with power. People need healthy proteins, fruits, and vegetables. Now that you're an adult you can choose, but seek nourishment rather than empty calories. Don't forget toilet paper, tissues, toothpaste, soap, shampoo, detergent, and personal hygiene products. Any time you can buy in bulk at a low price, do it. Just put a sticky note on the next-to-the-last item on your shelf reminding you to restock before you run out.

If you have money left after your basic needs are taken care of, plan what you'll spend on clothes, books, eating out, and entertainment. Rather than going out on the town, invite friends for an evening at home cooking and watching a film on TV. You can have fun without blowing your budget if you plan for it.

Save

Now that you understand your money flow and you have a plan to meet your needs, it's important to save. It may not be a lot, but adding to your savings every payday is smart. Your banking app can transfer money from checking to savings for you.

You can save for a rainy day, like your car breaking down or illness. Having a bit of money set aside can keep you from panicking when these things happen. You can also save for something fun: vacations; a new phone, computer, or car. If it helps you stay on course, try putting a picture of what you're saving for where you can see it. A photo of a new computer taped to your coffee machine can remind you that when you make coffee at home instead of getting a fancy latte, you're saving for your laptop.

Once you manage the UPS of money management, it's time to avoid the DOWNS on your road to financial mastery.

Denial

Being in denial about money is a common downfall. It's easy to close our eyes, cover our ears, and sing, "La, la, la, I can't hear you!" when the topic of money comes up. People in denial tend to write checks without making sure they have enough to cover them. They're often surprised when their card is declined, or they find overdraft charges on their statement. This leads to anxiety and financial uncertainty. Don't be in denial. Keep your eyes wide open and know exactly how much you have and what you can spend.

Overspending

Overspending is easy to do, and many young adults fall into this trap. Credit cards are especially dangerous. It's tempting to buy all the books, games, and collectibles that catch your eye and just put it on the card. But remember, everything you charge will cost more due to interest. People who pay only the minimum due find themselves over their heads in debt before long, with interest piling up. It's better to budget so you know how many books you can buy.

Wishful Thinking

Those who spend lots money on lotto tickets are indulging in wishful thinking rather than rational thinking. Very few people win the lottery, and the deck is stacked against you. Don't let wishful thinking guide your daily spending. The same goes for writers, artists, actors, and others who could have a big break at any moment. It's possible for a creative person to make it big, but don't live life as though it's already happened. If you're offered a contract, wonderful! Just don't spend money until it's in the bank.

Negativity

Few people start out making the big bucks; entry positions come with entry salaries. Many struggle to find work and live

CHAPTER 12

on a shoestring budget. Whatever your situation, try not to get bogged down in negative thinking. Sometimes the thoughts pop up on their own, intruding on your happiness. These are called Automatic Negative Thoughts, or ANTs. Recognizing you're having these ANTs is the first step to stopping them. If you find yourself having negative thoughts, like, "I'm so poor! I'll never be able to afford the things I want!" tell yourself, "Stop." Then think of a positive thought to replace it. For instance, instead of thinking you're poor, tell yourself, "I spend and save money wisely." Some people find it helpful to write their negative thought on paper, and then crumple, tear up, or (safely) burn the paper.

Splurging

Everyone gets the urge to splurge. If you've charged something you can't afford, return it. If it can't be returned, it needs to be paid off, which may mean cutting back on other expenses to cover it. Before you treat yourself, pause yourself. What seemed like a necessity at 3:00 AM may not seem quite as important at 3:00 PM. If a website is trying to pressure you to BUY NOW or you'll miss out, remember that's their way of getting your money. Don't let FOMO convince you to buy something you don't need and can't afford. You're the boss, not the internet. Those who splurge must pay the price, and the price is much higher with interest.

Read how our five characters managed their financial UPS and DOWNS.

JACOB, 18

Jacob's dad was in the doorway holding a paper, looking upset. Jacob paused his game.

"Did you spend $30.00 on in-game purchases this month?" he asked.

Jacob thought about it. "I don't know, there were some special, limited time deals. But I have $50.00 a month allowance, so NBD."

"But you also spent $40.00 at the board game store."

"I never spend more than $50.00, Dad. I pay attention to that."

"Both of these were in the same month, that's $70.00. And the online purchase didn't go to your debit card, it went to mine. I paid for your imaginary game whatever-it-was."

"I didn't know that. I thought I was paying for it."

"But you didn't have enough money left in your account. Why do you need all those board games, anyway? You never play them."

Jacob loved his board games. He loved reading the directions, sorting the cards, and the way the plastic pieces felt in his hands. He didn't need to play them to enjoy them. No way his father would understand, so he kept it to himself.

"I'll pay you back, I promise. Is there any work I can do to earn some of it?"

"I'm sure your mom will be able to think of something. The garage needs cleaning out, for a start. But how can you make sure this doesn't happen again?" That was a good question, and Jacob didn't have a good answer. He always felt that if he spent less than $50.00 at a time, he'd be okay. He guessed he really didn't understand financial stuff.

CHAPTER 12

"I'm not sure. Is there a book about it? We didn't have a money class in school."

Jacob's parents asked his case manager for recommendations. At their suggestion, he removed saved credit card numbers from sites so he'd have to type it in every time. He could keep his debit card in a lock-box in his closet, with a note asking if this purchase was necessary. They also made a "no money after midnight" rule because he was so vulnerable to special offers that popped up in the middle of the night. To wait until morning and then have to unpack his card would at least slow him down so he could think clearly. He also downloaded his bank app to check his balance easily.

Learning about financial management and using an app to monitor his account helped Jacob understand his money. Making it difficult to get to his debit card and having a rule about no late-night spending helped him curtail his splurging.

EMILY, 22

Emily was excited to go on her first grocery shopping trip since she got her food card. It was like a credit card, and she got to make up her own PIN number and everything. She felt so grown up!

She strolled up and down the aisles in the grocery store, putting everything she loved in her cart. Cookies, donuts, chips, candy, soda—all of her favorite treats. She also got the cereal she'd loved as a child, which her parents only bought her for holidays because of the sugar. Now that she was an adult, she made the rules.

A staff member from her group home met her at the checkout line. He pointed out that her cart looked heavy on snacks with little nutritional value, and that those things cost a lot of money. Would she have enough money to buy nutritious food all month long?

Emily had always relied on her parents to provide the normal, healthy foods, so she hadn't thought about buying them herself. Now she wondered. Could she afford to buy all the fun things she wanted and also buy the healthy foods she needed? She went ahead and bought what she had in her cart this time, but realized she didn't fully understand her money situation. She could easily overspend on snacks and not have money for other foods.

Later, she talked to her case manager about it. The group home decided to add two new classes: one on nutrition and one on money management. That way they could all learn to manage their money and to make wise choices at the grocery store. Understanding her finances and avoiding overspending were important lessons for Emily to learn.

ZACH, 33

Zach checked the numbers on his lottery ticket again. Close, but no joy. He gazed longingly at the new car images on his laptop. No new car this month, he thought sadly. He'd keep walking and getting rides from friends until his ship came in. He turned to his favorite quiz show. He always knew the answers, but other people walked away with millions of dollars and new cars. He could win a car if he were on that show. Unfortunately, he couldn't get to the city where they filmed it because he didn't have a car. Back to square one.

Zach was stuck in wishful thinking. He wished he could afford a new car, and he bought lotto tickets and answered all the questions on the quiz shows, but that wasn't getting him into the driver's seat. Eventually he got tired of wishing and hoping. He'd make something happen.

How much money did he spend on lottery tickets, anyway? He did the math and saw how fast it added up. He'd put that money in savings instead. Where else could he find money to save?

Sometimes the young adult group went out for coffee, and Zach was always happy to be invited. He usually got a large blended mocha, which was like a milkshake. Instead, he'd order a small black coffee, put in his own cream and sugar, and save a lot.

Another thing he probably didn't need to spend money on was in-app purchases. It took time to earn the credits to achieve higher levels, and he liked forging ahead instead of waiting. He checked his purchase history, and found those small purchases really added up.

Next payday, Zach put the money he would have spent on lottery tickets, fancy coffee, and in-app purchases into savings. It wasn't a huge amount, but it would grow. In the meantime, he stopped looking at high-end new cars and started browsing used cars online.

Zach's financial solution was to understand where his money had been going, to plan to save rather than frittering his pay away, and to sub rational thinking for wishful thinking.

MARIA, 45

Maria hummed a single, prolonged note as she shuffled envelopes at her kitchen island, tapping the bottom of the stack on the smooth tile. She used to love the color pink, but lately she was seeing more and more pink in envelope windows. Realizing pink bills meant bad news, she avoided opening those envelopes. When she'd tried to read them, her anxiety got so high it felt like she was having a heart attack, but when she watched her sloths, she felt better.

Still, Maria couldn't forget the growing pile of bills. What would happen to her if she threw them all away? She couldn't bring herself to be so willfully defiant, but she couldn't bring herself to open them, either. Now she was humming louder, shuffling envelopes faster, and tapping them on the counter harder. This had to stop before she worked herself into a tizzy.

Maria purposefully laid the envelopes down on the counter, turned her back on them, and started taking slow, deep breaths. She thought about how calm a sloth would be if sloths had to deal with bills. She thought about giant robots; they'd never be afraid of an envelope. Gradually, she felt stronger and more in control. She knew she couldn't ignore distressing things; if she didn't do something, it would only get worse. She needed to stop being in denial about her bills and make a plan to take care of them. She didn't feel strong enough yet, but she knew if she went on the internet without a plan to tackle the bills, she'd get lost and the day would slip by.

Maria put in her earbuds with her favorite music and walked around the block three times. Three was a good number; enough for a break, but not enough to exhaust her. Three times around

CHAPTER 12

the block, no more, no less, and she'd come back and open those envelopes.

Then she made a cup of tea in her favorite cup and got out the bills. She sorted them: electric company, credit card, phone. Only three companies; that felt manageable. She read the letters to see what the problem was. Now she could see a pattern. In each case, she'd missed paying a bill back when she had bronchitis. When checked her bank balance online, she had more money that she thought. The money was still there; she hadn't spent it on something else, she just forgot to pay it. She knew that if she paid online instead of mailing a check, they'd have their money sooner and quit sending her those horrible pink reminders.

While she was online, she saw a pop-up ad about her bank's automatic bill pay feature. What a perfect solution! The idea made her feel lighter. She made immediate payments on her creditor's websites and noticed that each of them had something on their drop-down menus about assistance or payment plans if she had trouble making her payments. This time she had the money, but it was a relief to know that if there were some big emergency, help was available.

Once she paid the three bills, Maria set up auto-pay. Now she could put her feet up and watch a giant robot movie before dinner. This turned out to be a good day, after all.

Realizing she'd been in denial and making a plan for the future worked for Maria.

ROBERT, 62

Robert couldn't understand. Why didn't Bobby want to go on the field trip? He'd always loved class trips. There'd never been a problem before, so why was he so dead set against it now, when they were going to a planetarium? Bobby loved stars and planets.

Finally, the boy opened up to his grandma. The real reason he didn't want to go was that this field trip would cost money, and he assumed they couldn't afford it. She told Robert.

"Can't afford it? That's crazy talk! We're not broke, why would he think such a thing?"

"Seriously, Robert? He's not deaf. He hears you complain about money."

"When do I complain about money?"

"When don't you?" she replied, exasperated. "You're always so negative about anything financial, especially since you retired, and your worries are affecting the boy."

Robert sulked, but he thought about what she'd said. Was it true? Did he talk about money too much in front of the boy, and was he too negative? Over the next couple days, he paid attention whenever money was brought up. Turns out, he complained about high prices every day. He didn't want to be that guy. They weren't rich, but they weren't poor, either.

He usually let his wife take care of household bills, but he needed to be in the know. Once he understood he wouldn't be so anxious, and he didn't want to worry his grandson.

Robert sat Bobby down and told him the field trip was affordable, and he hoped he'd reconsider because grandpa was really looking forward to it. Bobby grinned and nodded. They

CHAPTER 12

had a great time, and Robert bought a planetarium pencil for Bobby's Christmas stocking.

For Robert, understanding their finances helped him reduce anxiety and negativity.

SPEAKING FOR OURSELVES

"The lack of money was not an insurmountable problem ... I decided to create an educational website ... The success of the website meant that I was working and earning money, something that I felt very proud and excited about."

> — *Daniel Tammet, autistic savant and author,*
> Born on a Blue Day

CHAPTER 13
SELF-MANAGEMENT

---⇒≫●≪⇐---

(Stop the Nagging)

S elf-management may seem like a tall order. Your whole life, parents or teachers may have told you what to do and when to do the next thing. Now that you're an adult, it's time to do that for yourself. It's a big deal, but it's not unmanageable; self-management can be broken down into simple steps that make it less daunting.

There are seven steps in a successful self-management program: choosing self-management, defining the target behavior and replacement behaviors, setting goals, self-monitoring, choosing appropriate strategies, evaluating and re-evaluating to make sure you're on the right track, and finally, using maintenance strategies to keep you going in the direction you have chosen for yourself. Let's look at each of these steps more closely.

1. Decide to engage in self-management

Every trip starts with a map and a plan, but until you actually commit to the idea you won't get anywhere. How can you know if you really want to embark on this journey? If there's a behavior you want to change and it bothers you enough to work on it, you should plan a self-management program to make that change. If someone else wants you to change a behavior and you don't agree, ask why they want you to change. Are they embarrassed by something you do which isn't harmful? Maybe they should accept it rather than trying to change you. Mannerisms often relieve stress. If you want to quit, choose another behavior to replace it. Don't try to stop doing something helpful without substituting something else. If nothing else feels right, tell them why you'll continue doing it, and that you hope they can accept it.

On the other hand, some habits can be harmful, such as smoking or self-injury, or detrimental, such as allowing video games to interfere with your work and relationships. If you have a habit that could be self-destructive or overtake your life, a self-management program can help. If you don't feel up to taking these steps yourself, find a counselor or coach to work with you. You don't have to do it alone, but the decision should be yours alone.

2. Define the target behavior and replacement behaviors

What, exactly, is the target behavior you want to work on? Is it a thing you're doing that you want to stop or decrease? Or is it a thing you're not doing that you want to start or increase? Either way, once you choose a behavior to change, write it down and describe it clearly. Don't be vague, like "I want to be less annoying" or "I want to be more social." Choose something specific, like "I want to interrupt less often," or "I want to go to a social event twice a month."

CHAPTER 13

Now you have identified and defined your target behavior. If it's something you want to quit or decrease, think about what you'll do instead. For example, if you want to stop picking at scabs or pulling out your eyebrows while watching TV, find a hobby that keeps your hands busy, like knitting. Don't try to stop a habit without replacing it.

3. Set goals

Goals are your signposts along the road; they should be meaningful, measurable, and achievable. If you try to give up cigarettes, but after a month you're still smoking, it feels like a failure. However, if you set a goal to reduce cigarettes per day over time, and after a month you have gone from ten cigarettes a day to three cigarettes a day, you can see your progress. Don't give up on a program that's working, even if it's slow. You're on the right road, so keep going.

Goals should be meaningful to you. Not to someone else, but to you. If someone wants you to quit a habit, but you find the habit is calming and safe and you don't want to quit, it's not a meaningful goal. With self-management, the most important person is yourself. What would make you happier or healthier or more productive? That's the goal to work toward.

It's important that your goals are measurable. For example, "being healthier" is too vague to measure. Do you want to eat more nutritious foods? Reduce junk food? Exercise more? Smoke less? Choose measurable steps. Eating a sack lunch rather than fast food four days a week is measurable. Riding your bike to work rather than driving three days a week is measurable. Either you did these things, or not.

Finally, you want your goals to be achievable. It might be nice to lose 100 pounds before your high school reunion, but that goal may be unachievable. Consider asking a doctor or nutritionist to help you maintain a healthy weight over time. Remember, a goal is not a wish, it is something possible for you to achieve.

4. Self-monitor

You'll need to keep track of your progress to know how you're doing. This might mean writing down the number of cigarettes you smoke, the foods you eat, or how many steps you walk. Self-monitoring means you're in charge, and you know how you're doing.

It doesn't sound like fun, does it? How can you make self-monitoring easier on yourself? If you have set yourself a goal that requires counting things, like number of cigarettes or how often you go to the gym, you'll need someplace to log it. A record helps you monitor your progress.

The important thing is to find the one that works for you. If you love your phone, use it. If you love paper, find a notebook or calendar and pen that brings you joy. Whatever tools you use to monitor your progress should suit your personal preferences.

Once you know how you will self-monitor, decide when you will do it and stick to your plan. Will you take your data at every meal time? Each morning or evening? Every hour, or every four hours? Every time you do the thing? Your self-monitoring schedule should be appropriate to the behavior you're working on and should also fit into your days easily. Set pleasing alarms if you need to; most of us need reminders when we start something new.

5. Choose appropriate self-management strategies

It's not enough to say you're going to keep track of a behavior and change it. You'll need strategies to make it happen: antecedent manipulation, reinforcement, and social support.

Antecedent manipulation means setting up your environment to make it easier to do the thing you want to do and harder to do the thing you don't want to do. For instance, if you want to eat more fruits and vegetables and fewer sugary and salty snacks, put a bowl of grapes or baby carrots next to your chair. That makes easier to do what you want to do. Put cookies and chips in the highest cupboard to make it harder to do the thing you're trying to quit. If you really want them you can still get them, you're just not going to make it easy on yourself. Of course, you could stop buying junk food altogether, but that's your call.

Reinforcement is anything that makes it more likely that the reinforced behavior occurs again. If you want to ride your bike to work, promise yourself that every time you ride your bike you will treat yourself to a fancy coffee, but if you drive your car you will only get regular coffee at the office. If you love that fancy coffee, you'll start riding your bike more often.

Social support is another important part of a self-management program. Think about who in your life you care about and trust who also cares about you. It might be a parent, a sibling, a spouse or SO, or a longtime friend. Let that person know what you are working on and how they can help. Perhaps you want to let people know you're listening to them. Of course you know you can listen perfectly well without giving the speaker any feedback, but the speaker might wonder if you care. You may want to increase behaviors like glancing toward the speaker's face, smiling, nodding, and making vocal comments like, "Uh, huh," or "Yeah," or "That's interesting." Once you decide to do these things, let your trusted person know your plan. Then, when you're talking with them, they can let you know that they noticed and appreciate your conversational give-and-take. If you're working on something personal, like changing your eating, exercise, or smoking habits, ask a trusted person to be your coach or cheerleader. If they agree, then every evening you can text them your results. If you're on track, they'll cheer you on. If you didn't reach your goal, they'll remind you tomorrow is a fresh start. Having someone share your triumphs and challenges keeps you on the right path.

6. Evaluate change and re-evaluate self-management strategies if necessary

After a month, review your records and see how far you've come. Are you moving toward your goal? It can be hard to see progress daily, but over time you can look back and see how you're doing. If you're spinning your wheels without going anywhere, make some changes.

Why aren't you making progress? Are you fully on board with the idea of self-management? Is your goal meaningful, measurable, and achievable? Have you set up your environment to make it easier to do the things you want to do, and harder to do the things you want to quit? Do you reward yourself when you do the right thing? What about social support from family or friends? Identify your road block, make the needed changes, and try again.

7. Implement maintenance strategies

You've reached your goal! Congratulations! Now you want to maintain that success over time. Maintenance of a behavior simply means continuing the new behavior after the reinforcement has been faded or gradually removed.

After you've achieved your goal and remained at that level of success for a month or more, slowly decrease your reinforcement. If you promised yourself a fancy coffee every time you rode your bike to work, consider cutting back to a fancy coffee on Friday if you rode your bike to work all week. Pay attention, though, if you start to go backwards. You may need to return to the level of reinforcement that got you this far. If it's no problem to continue making it easy to do the right thing and difficult to do the wrong thing, then keep it up. If you want to return your environment to pre-self-management program status, give it a try, but be ready to put those snacks back up on the high shelf if you start to slip.

Continue to check in by taking data once a month, then every three months, then six months. If you're still at the same level of success, eventually you can fade it completely. Don't be discouraged if you need to return to the program every once in a while to keep on the right road. Your self-management plan is a map to help you go where you want to go, so use it.

Read how each of our five characters used self-management to achieve their goals.

JACOB, 18

Jacob couldn't believe it; he was in danger of failing a course. Why? He did well on the quizzes, tests, and classwork. The note said that failure to turn in homework was the problem. He did his homework every day after school. So, what went wrong?

This new teacher never told students to turn in their work, she just expected them to put their assignments in the "finished homework" box on her desk. Jacob hadn't even noticed the box. He was used to teachers telling him when and where to turn things in, and when she didn't specifically tell him, he never did. He kept doing the assignments because he figured the teacher wanted them to do the work even though she didn't want to grade them. He found pages of homework crammed in his backpack and more on his desk at home. It took him a while to get them all in order, but he did, and turned them in. He was lucky his teacher gave him credit, but he'd have to meet with his case manager to make a plan to manage this in the future.

His case manager's plan was for Jacob to carry a big red envelope back and forth every day to keep his homework in, so he wouldn't forget. Jacob hated the plan. It was embarrassing; no one else had a red envelope. He came up with his own plan to manage his homework situation and prove he could do it without the red envelope.

The behavior he targeted to increase was turning in homework to the teacher who never reminded him. His goal was to turn it in 100 percent of the time. It was achievable because he always turned in the homework for his other classes, and it was meaningful because he cared about his grade and he wanted to get rid of the red envelope. He'd monitor his progress in his agenda.

Now he needed strategies to make sure he got it done. He set an alarm on his phone to vibrate two minutes before class started to remind him. He slides his hand inside his backpack and into the envelope to bring out his homework without anyone else ever seeing the red envelope. He liked putting a star on his agenda daily to show his progress. The big payoff came when he earned a B+ in the class, showed his report card and agenda to his case manager, and gave back the embarrassing red envelope. Jacob didn't need to keep using the phone reminders or stars once he had the habit of turning in his homework. He was proud of himself for managing his own behavior and making his teacher and case manager proud of him gave him social support.

EMILY, 22

Emily felt slightly sick, dizzy, and "oogy." What was wrong with her? She felt so weird. When she mentioned how she felt to Sarah, she asked what she'd eaten, and if she could be dehydrated. Emily got herself a glass of water and thought about what she'd eaten that day.

For breakfast she'd had a bowl of cold cereal with milk and hot chocolate, then a frosted toaster pastry for a mid-morning snack. For lunch she had a jam and butter sandwich and a handful of cookies. Then in the afternoon, chips and a soda. She hadn't had any water, but hot chocolate and soda were both liquids, so that was okay, right? The problem couldn't be that she wasn't eating, she snacked whenever she felt hungry. Sarah told her she was filling up on empty calories. How could she expect to have energy if she didn't treat her body better than that?

Emily was invited to attend a nutrition class at the group home the following week. She learned that the way she was eating was not supporting her. She needed good fuel to feel good. It was fun to be in charge of choosing her own food, but Emily didn't like the sick feeling she had after a day of eating lots of sugar and no protein. She wanted to change her lifestyle, and her case manager helped her set up a self-management program.

Emily's goal was to eat at least five fruits or vegetables every day, to drink eight glasses of water, and to eat protein with every meal. She wouldn't try to decrease sweet snacks, because that sounded depressing. She'd rather add good things than deny herself her favorite things. This was meaningful to her, it was easy to measure, and she thought she could achieve it with help.

She'd make it easier to increase fruits and vegetables by putting an apple, a banana, and a bag of carrots in a bowl near her chair where it was easy to reach. She had a box of chocolate doughnuts in the refrigerator but she moved it to the garage fridge so it would be harder to get to. At lunch she had raisins or cherry tomatoes with her sandwich, and at dinner she helped herself to veggies.

As for water, she wasn't used to drinking throughout the day, but she knew she could do it. She'd gotten a reusable water bottle for Christmas with a picture of the Broadway *Hamilton* logo. She loved that image, so she'd feel happy using it.

Emily knew she should get more protein or she'd feel weak, but she liked her sweet cereal in the morning. She decided to have a hard-boiled egg before her cereal. At lunch, she added peanut butter to her jam sandwich or had a meat or cheese

CHAPTER 13

sandwich. There was always a protein option at dinner, so that was easy. If she didn't like it, she could get cheese or an egg or make a sandwich. That way she could be sure to have protein with every meal.

Emily made a chart decorated with pictures of her favorite things. There were boxes to check off that she had eaten at least five fruits and vegetables, protein with each meal, and finished eight glasses of water every day. When every box had been checked at the end of the day, she would put on "My Shot" from *Hamilton* and dance in her room to celebrate.

For Emily, choosing to make changes in her eating habits was meaningful, and a pretty easy choice to make after she realized how sick and weak she felt when she didn't pay attention to nutrition. Once she made the decision, she used antecedent manipulation to make it easier to make good choices by having fruit close at hand. She made it harder to make unhealthy choices by putting desserts in the garage fridge. She made drinking water fun by using a *Hamilton* water bottle. Having her house mates take the nutrition course with her and staff praise her for making good choices gave her social support.

ZACH, 33

Zach's head fell forward and he jerked awake. He was sitting in front of his game with the controller about to fall out of his hand, and his game frozen at the point where his character had died. He must have fallen asleep. What time was it? He checked his phone—after 3:00 AM! He grabbed his flashlight, rushed through his final round, then came back and fell into bed.

The next morning, he felt terrible. He hadn't been drinking; can you get a video game hangover, he wondered? He unlocked the building for the rabbi while trying not to yawn, worried that the rabbi would know that he had missed his first evening round the night before. Back in his apartment, he started to sit back down at his video game again, but then stopped. He'd been playing a lot lately. He'd missed several meetings of the young adult group, and volunteering, too, getting lost in his game for hours. Was it taking over his entire life?

Zach knew he wouldn't quit playing his game because he loved it; it both calmed and entertained him. Still, it would be useful to know exactly how much time he was spending on it. He decided to write down the time he started a game and when he paused it, all day. He put a small notebook right on top of the game controller before he went to bed with the words "Time On/Time Off" at the top of the first page. When he got up and grabbed his energy drink, he wrote down what time he turned on the game. Then he wrote what time he turned it off to go unlock the buildings. At this point he wasn't trying to change his behavior, just learn about it. All day he kept writing down his times, until he turned it off to go to bed.

The next morning, Zach did the math to see how much time he had spent on the game the day before. He was shocked. The amount of time he had spent on the game was unbelievably huge. He was embarrassed just looking at it. Was he wasting his life on a stupid game? But it wasn't a stupid game, it was a friend. He liked the feeling of accomplishment he got when he completed quests and leveled up. He felt like a success when he was in the game, but now he worried. He typed into a search engine, "Am I addicted to video games?" He didn't have most of the

CHAPTER 13

symptoms they listed, so that was a relief. Then he asked, "How much should I play video games every day?" It seemed the amount of time was less important than extent it interfered with his life. It did interfere with his job and his social life, which had dwindled to almost nothing.

Zach knew he had to balance his gaming with the rest of his life. The first thing he did was make a list of what he wanted to do more of, instead of playing video games. He started with work, because if he lost this job he'd also lose his home. Then he listed the young adult social group at the temple, volunteering for his political party, going over to his parents' for dinner, and having the guys over to watch a game. He enjoyed all these things, but it had been a while since he'd done any of them. He got out his calendar. First, he wrote in his volunteer days and the nights of the young adult group. He texted his mom and asked when would be a good time for him to visit. She said that he was always welcome, but a regular Friday dinner would be nice. Finally, he checked when the next game was, put it on his calendar, and texted to invite the guys.

Zach liked a full calendar; he vowed not to flake out on these dates. He set reminders on his phone to help him get off his game and out the door.

Zach wondered what else he could do instead of playing. He spotted a stack of books he'd gotten for Chanukah. He decided that every day after unlocking, when the weather was nice, he'd take a book out to the courtyard and read. It was always peaceful and he knew he'd enjoy it.

Reading instead of gaming in the morning was a big change. How could he keep from falling back into old habits? First, he put the game controller in a drawer, and then he put a book on the side table where the controller used to be. He could still play his game anytime he really wanted to, but he'd have to make a conscious decision to bypass the book and go get the controller. That should make it easier to choose the book over the game.

To avoid another all-nighter, Zach also decided to change his evening routine. After dinner he'd play his game if he wanted to, taking a break for his first evening round. If he had stopped the game to make his rounds on time, then he'd play again until his last round. If he hit snooze and was late with his first evening round, he would not go back to the game but would read a book instead. Either way, after his last round of the night Zach would read a book before sleeping. He slept better when he read rather than playing a video game late at night.

What else he could do to stay on track? Zach liked playing around with graphs on his computer. He'd use them to show how he was decreasing his game time and increasing social events. After a month, he pinned them to the wall next to his calendar and showed his parents; they said they were proud of him. It felt great to be in control of his own time and choices.

For Zach, his goal of reducing video game use was meaningful because he made the decision for himself. It was difficult but achievable, and it was measurable in amount of time spent on the game. Antecedent manipulations included making it easier to read by putting a book close at hand and making it harder to play the game by putting the controller in a drawer. Visual graphs showed his progress and sharing them with his parents provided social support.

CHAPTER 13

MARIA, 45

Maria had to sit down after moving her laundry from the washer to the dryer. She was breathing hard and felt quite fatigued. It seemed silly to be so tired after such a small task. What was wrong with her? She placed her hand over her heart and felt the beat return to normal. She wasn't having a heart attack, that was good. But why was she so weary? She picked up her phone and typed in, "Why do I feel so tired?" Most results didn't relate to her: she didn't use electronics before bed, and she wasn't dehydrated or diabetic. Then she saw it: "Not enough exercise." That one certainly hit home. But could not exercising make her tired? She thought it would make her more tired. The article said that exercise twenty minutes a day, three times a week decreased fatigue in sedentary adults. She guessed maybe she was one of those sedentary adults. She rarely walked since her sister was too busy to keep up with their walking dates. Maria would have to take charge of her own exercise program. What would make her want to exercise?

She searched "exercise with sloths" and found videos of sloths exercising, but they were far too slow. Then she searched "exercise with robots" and found videos with music and robots, or humans dancing like robots, or dressed as robots. If she danced or jogged along to the music, she'd get more exercise than sitting still. It was actually quite fun. The more she moved, the better she felt. To help her remember, she drew a picture of a robot on a sticky note and stuck it to her coffee maker. It made her smile and reminded her to exercise before her morning coffee.

After sticking with it for a month, she rewarded herself by purchasing one of her favorite robot dancing songs. She would buy herself a new song every month that she kept up with her plan. She really did have more energy the rest of the day when she started with exercise.

For Maria, increasing exercise was meaningful, achievable, and measurable. She enjoyed finding music to dance and move to that included robots, setting a regular time to exercise, and rewarding herself with a new song each month. These strategies helped her keep up with her plan.

ROBERT, 62

"Ew! You stink, Grandpa!" Bobby held his nose and ran to his room to play.

"How rude! Is this how you treat him to respect his elders?" Robert asked his daughter.

"The truth is, Dad, you do stink of cigarettes. I don't like it, either."

"But I never smoke in the house or the car, or around Bobby!" Robert protested. "He's just over-reacting. I can't smell anything."

"The smell stays in your clothes, and even if you're used to it, we're not. Plus, we worry about your health. I wish you'd quit."

Robert had tried to quit many times, but whenever he was under stress he went right back to it. Maybe he needed help. That night he talked it over with his wife, who was thrilled that he was serious about quitting. They looked online and found a counselor who understood both the autism spectrum and addiction. The website talked about setting up a self-management program. Robert liked that idea. He hated admitting he needed help, but having a counselor to coach him as he learned

CHAPTER 13

to manage himself was something he could get behind. They made an appointment.

From his counselor, Robert learned the seven steps for a successful self-management program. The first was deciding to do it, and Robert had already made that decision. He was finally ready to get tobacco out of his life, once and for all.

The second step was to identify a target behavior and replacement behaviors. The target behavior was obvious—smoking. For a replacement behavior, Robert thought "not smoking" was the thing, but the counselor said that rarely works. Maybe that's what went wrong all those other times. So, what replacement behavior could he use instead of smoking?

It should be something that would keep his hands busy so he couldn't smoke at the same time. He usually smoked in the back yard, listening to a mystery book on tape. He loved to solve the mysteries logically. Using earbuds, his hands were free, so he smoked. What could he do differently to break that cycle? He decided he would get a book of logic puzzles. His brain would be entertained by figuring out the solutions, but he'd need his hands to write down his answers.

The third step was to set a goal. Robert was smoking about five cigarettes a day, and he wanted to set a goal of zero. His counselor said he should sneak up on that goal rather than going cold turkey, so he'd cut one cigarette a day for a week, and then cut out another cigarette.

The fourth step was self-monitoring. Robert put a sticky note on his pack of cigarettes with the date and made a tally mark for each cigarette he smoked. He transferred the sticky note to the edge of his desk at the end of the day. He could look back over the sticky notes and see at a glance how many cigarettes he'd had each day. He wouldn't forget because it was on the pack.

The fifth step was strategies. He thought long and hard about what he would do to keep on track. One strategy was to leave, if being in the back yard made him want to smoke. It seemed whenever he walked into the yard, his hand automatically reached for his pocket for cigarettes. When the urge to smoke was strong, he'd go to the diner. Robert asked his wife how she'd feel about him taking off like that, and to his surprise she had no problem with it. In fact, she said she would go out and do some gardening each time he left, since she didn't like to be in the yard while he was smoking. Robert hadn't realized that his smoking had kept his wife in the house. That strengthened his resolve to quit for good this time.

Going to the diner was one strategy, but that wouldn't always be practical. What else could he do when the cravings got bad? He'd put his five daily cigarettes into an empty pack to keep in his pocket, but he'd never have a full pack, only his daily allotment. He locked the rest of the packages in the trunk of the car. Unfortunately, it wasn't that difficult for him to go out to the garage and pull out another pack.

One day, when he'd already smoked his daily allotment, he got such a strong urge to smoke that he was afraid he'd blow it. He had a full pack in the trunk of his car, and he got it out and stared at it for a while. Then he grabbed some plastic wrap, wound it around the pack, sealed the edges tightly, and zipped it into a plastic bag. He put it into a large plastic bow and filled it with water. The bag floated to the top. He put a can of tomato soup on top if it, holding it under water, and carefully slid the whole contraption into the freezer. Then he grabbed his keys and went to the diner. He told his buddies not to give him a cigarette, even if he begged them, and asked them to distract him until the tobacco craving passed. They took turns telling the worst jokes they could think of, and soon everyone was laughing so hard, Robert didn't even think about smoking. He noticed that, since he was smoking less, he could laugh without breaking into a coughing fit. It had been a while since that was true.

The next step was evaluating his progress and re-evaluating his strategies. What was working, and what wasn't? Robert brought his collection of dated sticky notes to his counselor and they looked for patterns. He had done pretty well at first, then went off track a bit, but got back on board after he froze his cigarettes and asked his friends to support him in quitting.

Once he got down to zero cigarettes, the final step was maintenance. First, his counselor told him he should celebrate. He deserved to treat himself because quitting smoking is never easy. Robert decided he wanted to go to a basketball game with his wife, daughter, and grandson. Inside the court there would be no smoking allowed, so he wouldn't be bombarded with second-hand smoke like at an outdoor event. Plus, Bobby loved basketball as much as he did, and their local university's team was pretty good. After the game, they all went out for ice cream and congratulated him. Robert knew he wasn't home free, because he'd quit before, but this time felt different. He had a plan. He'd continue to check in with his counselor to keep on track.

A year later, Robert was still a non-smoker. He enjoyed working puzzles in the yard while his wife puttered with the flowers. Sometimes the whole family would sit out there with tea or lemonade and watch Bobby swing or ride his bike. It felt great to share the yard with his family instead of with a cloud of smoke.

For Robert, getting counseling, following the steps of self-management, and getting buy-in and social support from his family and friends helped him finally quit smoking for good.

SPEAKING FOR OURSELVES

"If you want to change your situation, change yourself."
— *Dr. Temple Grandin, professor and author*
Unwritten Rules of Social Relationships

CHAPTER 14
SELF-ADVOCACY

(Speak Your Truth)

I n his introduction to *Ask and Tell: Self-Advocacy and Disclosure for People on the Autism Spectrum*, Dr. Stephen Shore wrote, "Self-advocacy involves knowing when and how to approach others in order to negotiate desired goals, and to build better mutual understanding, fulfillment, and productivity." As a child, others may have advocated for you: your parents by setting up play dates, or your special ed. case manager by telling your teachers about your needs.

As an adult, you are your own advocate. If someone misunderstands your intentions, you need to set them straight. If someone tries to take advantage of you, you need to stand up for yourself. You may find it hard to say no or ask for help. Whatever the situation, if no one's advocating for you, step up and self-advocate.

Liane Holliday Willey, in her chapter in *Ask and Tell*, says that self-advocacy requires both self-analysis and educating others. You need to know yourself, your strengths, and how you interact with the world so you can help people understand and appreciate your unique you-ness.

So, how do you do it? You can ACT for advocacy in three steps: Awareness, Communication, and Thankfulness.

Awareness

First, be aware of the need for self-advocacy. The first sign could be increased stress; you may notice you're breathing faster, pacing, or stimming more than usual. When you notice these things, pause and take stock of the situation. What's going on? If someone asked you a lot of questions and you can't keep up, tell them you need time to think. Otherwise, you may say "yes" just to get them to stop badgering you. You don't deserve to be railroaded into doing things you don't want to do. Sometimes work or school can be overwhelming: too many tasks, too little guidance, too many questions. It's worse if you're disrespected, bullied, or expected to do far more than your fair share. If any of these are true for you, you may need to self-advocate.

Communication

The next step is communication. Once you're aware you need to advocate, focus on communication: understanding others and sharing your thoughts.

First, check out the other person's verbal and nonverbal communication. Do their words match their expression and body language? When someone smiles while saying mean things, it's confusing. Is it a put down, or friendly banter? It's not easy to tell, so look for patterns. Do they do this often, or is it unusual? Is this how they kid around with everybody? If so, don't take it personally. However, if you're being singled out and insulted, you may need to self-advocate.

Remember to communicate calmly and rationally. Email if face-to-face conversation is too stressful. Write the issue clearly and unemotionally. You don't want to come across as a whiner, but you do want to advocate for yourself. After you write the email, save it and wait before sending it. If it doesn't breach confidentiality, run it past someone you trust, someone with a level head on their shoulders who'll tell you if your tone is angry, accusatory, or childish. Think and rethink before sending. You may decide the problem wasn't such a big deal after all. If writing it out helped you feel better, and sending it will make things worse, delete. If needed, use your best communication skills to share your side of the situation.

When you advocate for yourself, expect to be listened to and respected. If you go in projecting superiority, criticism, or hostility, it can shut down the whole conversation. On the other hand, going in feeling unworthy can also defeat your purpose. Show confidence in your demeanor and body language. Stand straight, shoulders down, not slumping or looking at the floor. A calm, positive expression and presentation are best. Know that it won't always go your way. Being gracious when disappointed is an important hallmark of successful adulting.

Thankfulness

When you advocate for yourself and someone listens and supports you, thank them. People like to be thanked, and it's free and easy. It isn't always verbal; it can be written or nonverbal. If someone helped with a project, email your thanks. If you stood up against a bully and others stood with you, a smile or nod can show appreciation. If someone recommended you for a job or got you an interview, write a thank-you note. Gratitude is always welcome.

Let's see how our five fictional characters learned to advocate for themselves.

JACOB, 18

Jacob broke the water's surface, gulping air, desperately flailing at the arms pushing him under. The bell rang and the coach blew his whistle. "Everybody out of the pool!" Everyone else headed for the showers, but he was still shaking. "Out of the pool, Jacob, that means you!"

Jacob blinked up at him. "They were trying to kill me," he gasped out. "Didn't you see?"

"I saw a bunch of guys goofing off. No one was trying to kill you, drama queen. Shake it off! If you make a big deal, they'll never stop."

They'll never stop.

Those words echoed in Jacob's head as he dragged himself out of the water and found his towel, dripping wet and useless. If he was slow enough, maybe they'd all be gone when he got there. A tardy slip was better than a toe tag. Jacob dreaded the swimming unit in P.E. More than depressing, it was terrifying. How could a teacher ignore four boys ganging up on him? Even if they weren't actually trying to kill him, they were hardly paying attention to how long he was under or whether he had time to catch a breath between dunkings.

CHAPTER 14

Jacob was still shaky when he made his way to the office. His counselor's door was open, and she had time to talk, so Jacob poured out his story: tortured, held under water until his lungs burned, every single day. The coach saw, but let it happen. He wanted out.

It was too late to transfer, he'd have to stick it out, but she told him to write a letter to the coach and to bring it to her first. She wanted him to advocate for himself, but she'd have his back.

Jacob thought long and hard about what to write to the coach. That guy had clearly never been bullied; he was probably the bully of his high school. How could he understand? The next day he brought the letter to his counselor. She read it and arranged a meeting between Jacob, the coach, and the vice principal. She asked Jacob if he wanted his folks there, but he was an adult; he wouldn't ask them to take a day off of work, he'd do this himself.

Jacob sat in the office with the three adults, feeling small and nervous. The VP asked him to share his letter, and he nodded. Would they think he was a coward, or a crybaby? He read:

Dear Coach,
I want you to imagine a scenario for me. You are on your way to a staff meeting when four men—teachers you work with—grab you. They put a plastic bag over your head and hold it down, laughing at how funny you look. Together, they're too strong for you and they hold the plastic to your face, cutting off your oxygen, until you almost pass out. Finally, they take it off and slap you on the back, saying, "Man, you should have

seen your face! That was hilarious!" They walk off, waving the plastic bag at you, saying, "See you tomorrow!" As you struggle to catch your breath, you notice the principal; he saw what happened. You want to file a complaint, but he tells you to stop being so dramatic. After all, they were only joking, and they took the bag off your face soon enough, didn't they? Just be a good sport and don't make trouble. Now you understand that you'll be subjected to the same treatment every day, and no one will protect you. How will you go back to work, knowing that you'll be suffocated daily, your only hope that they don't miscalculate how long you can hold your breath?

Coach, this is how I feel every day when four guys hold me under water, and you just watch. Every day you let them torture me and you say they're only joking. This no joke to me, it's literally life and death. Do I deserve this? If not, how will you protect me?

The room was quiet; he was afraid to look up. Finally, Coach cleared his throat.

"Jacob, I want to apologize." His face was red and grim, and it clearly wasn't easy for him. "I'm sorry, I truly am. I had no idea. I thought you guys were horsing around together. I guess I didn't notice it was always you being dunked, four on one. It's not fair, and it's not going to happen again, not on my watch. You can count on that!"

"Thank you," Jacob murmured. Then he had a scary thought and looked up at his counselor. She seemed to be thinking the same thing, and she spoke up.

CHAPTER 14

"Coach, you remember from our bullying prevention training that if you confront the boys, they'll retaliate later. How can you stop the behavior without calling attention to Jacob?"

"Leave that to me, I'll be careful. Jacob, you can count on me."

The next day, Coach announced a schedule change. Instead of free play at the end of class, they'd swim laps so he could make notes for their grades. Everybody groaned, but no one realized the reason except Jacob. Later he left a note in his counselor's box reading, *"It's better now. Thank you. Thank Coach for me. —Jacob."*

For Jacob, getting support from his counselor and writing his thoughts in advance helped him self-advocate. He was proud, because even though he was scared, he stood up for himself.

EMILY, 22

Emily felt that twitchy feeling between her shoulder blades. Her peripheral senses were tingling; he was right behind her, wasn't he? She spun around, and there he was, her least favorite housemate, being all creepy and stalker-y again.

"Hi, Emily. Isn't this a coincidence, us both having breakfast at the same time? Again?" He smiled and stepped closer. "I couldn't help but notice we're both having cereal. We have a lot in common, don't we?"

"Not really. It's breakfast time. Excuse me, I need to get to the refrigerator—"

"—for milk, I knew it. We really finish each other's ... " he trailed off. Emily poured her milk and sat down. When he sat beside her, she moved to the next chair over. He moved right along with her, still talking.

"Sentences. We finish each other's sentences. So, anyhoo, I was wondering when you and I are going out on a date." Emily stopped chewing. A date? With him? How about never? She was silent, but that didn't stop him. "So, I was thinking, you're twenty-two, I'm twenty-two, we both eat cereal and live in the same place. Obviously, we're MFEO."

MFEO? Had he really said that?

"Yeah, we're totally made for each other. And there's no reason two people living in the same group home can't date. I asked. So what do you say? When are we going out?"

Emily's stomach hurt and she couldn't eat. She didn't know what to say. If she told him that she wouldn't date him if he were the last person on Earth, it would hurt his feelings. She hated conflict and wished he would just go away. No such luck.

"I was thinking Saturday night. The movie theater is right by the bus stop, so we'll ride the bus together, holding hands. I'll buy the tickets and you can buy the drinks and popcorn. That's only fair, right? Then we'll hold hands again during the movie, and we'll look at each other and laugh at all the funny parts. If it's a scary movie, I'll put my arm around you. If it's a romantic movie, who knows?" He waggled his eyebrows up and down. Emily felt sick, but he didn't notice. He seemed more comfortable with a monologue than a dialogue. "Later, after we walk hand-in-hand to the bus stop and ride home with your head on my shoulder, I'll walk you to your door like a gentleman, and only expect one, sweet kiss. After all, it'll only be our first date. The real romance comes after our third date, am I right?" He did that eyebrow thing again.

CHAPTER 14

Emily walked out, leaving her cereal untouched, and shut herself in her room. She paced, alternating between tapping her ears and super-speed jazz hands. Eventually she wound down and lay on her bed, eyes closed, imagining the *Hamilton* score in her head because she was too upset to get up and turn it on.

Knock-knock. If that was him, she was never coming out. Thankfully, it was Sarah, Emily's fave staff member, to tell her she'd left her cereal out. Emily poured out the story of her unwanted admirer. He seemed to have their whole romance planned out, but she didn't even like him. At all. She didn't know what to do.

Sarah said she never had to go on a date with anyone if she didn't want to. Just because he had ideas didn't mean she had to go along. However, he was telling everyone in the house that they were dating, so she should probably set him straight.

"What do I say? I don't want to hurt him, I just don't want to date him. Ever!"

"You can say no without being mean. You don't owe him an explanation, just tell him you're not going out with him. Clearly. And soon, before he announces your engagement."

Emily sighed. She didn't want to, but she knew she had to put an end to this. He was still in the kitchen, and the others quickly left when she walked in. Maybe they thought the two of them wanted to be alone together. Gross.

"So, are you excited about our first date?" he asked.

"No. The answer is no."

"What do you mean, no movie? How about dinner? Lady's choice, I'm easy."

"No, I mean no, we're not dating. We're not going out on any date at all."

"Why? Was it how I asked? I can change. I can be cooler. I can be at least 20 percent cooler."

"No, there's nothing for you to change, we're just not gonna date each other."

"But give me a chance. I have to know why, so I can fix it."

Emily realized anything she said now, he would say he could fix it and they should still date. Also, her reasons, though true, would sound mean. She didn't owe him anything.

"You know, whenever there are two people, and one of those people says they're not going to date, they are not going to date. That's just it." She almost said she was sorry, but she stopped herself. She wasn't sorry, and she didn't need to apologize for her feelings.

"I can't believe it. We're perfect together. I will win you over, I promise you that."

"No. Stop asking. If you don't, I'll file a harassment report with staff."

Emily left him blessedly speechless for once. She played that song about saying no to all those guys who ask girls for their name, or their sign, or their number. It was empowering. She danced around her room with Alpeggy, tremendously relieved. She did it, she stood up for herself and said NO! The next time she saw Sarah, Emily gave her a big hug and said, "Thank you. Everything's okay now."

What worked for Emily was knowing she could say no without apologizing for her feelings. Talking with a trusted staff member helped her find courage, but she did it on her own.

CHAPTER 14

"Oops!" Zach turned to see Aaron grin as soda streamed from his upside-down can. Aaron made a point of accidentally-on-purpose making a mess at every young adult group meeting. "Good thing Zacky's so good at cleaning up. I mean, that's your job, right, Zacky?"

Head down, Zach went to get a mop, but then he hesitated. He realized it would never stop unless he put a stop to it. Aaron was like a schoolyard bully. It was time to speak up.

"Actually, Aaron, it's not my job. I'm the caretaker, so I unlock the building for us and lock up afterward, but I'm not the custodian. The person whose job it is to clean this room is Mrs. Avirom. Isn't she a friend of your grandmother? Yeah, that sweet old lady is responsible for taking care of this room. I've been cleaning up after you as a mitzvah. She doesn't deserve to find the place looking like this." Zach had surprised himself, and he kept going. "I think you should take care of your own mess. There's the mop, help yourself."

There was a moment of silence, and then everybody told Aaron to quit being a jerk. Leah said Mrs. Avirom was a friend of her bubbe, too, and he should know better. Several people smiled and nodded at Zach, and Noah gave him a thumbs up. He was grateful for the backup.

When Aaron saw no one was taking his side, he begrudgingly got the mop. "I was about to clean it up. Can't a guy have an accident without everybody making a federal case out of it?"

Zach ate a cookie while Aaron mopped. For so long, it seemed easier to clean it up himself to avoid confrontation. He was glad he finally said something and kept his cool. He never got an apology, but he hadn't expected one. The best part was he stood up to a bully, and the bully backed down. From that day on there were no more "accidental" spills. Aaron was still a sarcastic jerk, but he spread it around instead of dumping on Zach. It felt great to self-advocate.

MARIA, 45

Oh, dear, it was happening again. It started a few months ago when Maria's friend, Sofia, had to stay late for a committee meeting, so Maria stayed with her. Now she was on that committee, and somehow in charge of the spring fundraiser. There were supposed to be at least eight on the committee, but most of the time they didn't show up. Everybody had jobs, or children at home, or aging parents to care for, or dogs to walk. It was always something. They'd say, "Call me if I can help," but Maria was never going to call anybody. When they didn't come to the meetings, everything fell on her shoulders.

It reminded Maria of high school. They're called group projects, but in every group she was in, everyone else had something better to do. Everyone except Maria, so she did it all.

Father Gonzales was counting on this fundraiser to meet the annual budget. The stress was intense. Maria wrung her hands and pressed them to her face, but she couldn't calm down. She imagined Father Gonzales' sad eyes. She didn't want to let him down.

After stressing for an afternoon, Maria made lists of everything that had to be done. She emailed the parish secretary to get email addresses for all the people on her committee. She sent them each an email with a list of jobs, asking how many they would do. When the replies started coming in, Maria organized them. There were very few jobs unclaimed. She contacted the people who didn't reply to her first email and assigned those tasks to them. If they wanted first pick, they should have answered sooner.

Now all the jobs were assigned, and it was up to Maria to manage them. She kept calendars of what had to be done by when, and made alerts to email each person twice to remind them of their commitment. By the day of the fundraiser she was able to stay behind the scenes and out of the spotlight, which was how she wanted it.

Once it was over and they'd met their fund-raising goal, Maria made a resolution. She was not going to say "yes" any more. It wouldn't be easy, but she would learn to say "no."

She got her first opportunity the next Sunday after mass. One of the ladies complimented her on what a good job she'd done on the spring fundraiser, and suggested she'd be perfect to organize the parish graduation party.

Maria took a deep breath and closed her eyes for a moment. She straightened her shoulders and looked the woman almost in the eye. "I'm sorry, but I won't be able to chair the event. After you find your chairperson, please let them know they may email me if they need me to bake something, but I'm afraid I can't do more than that." She braced herself, but the woman just thanked her and moved on to ask someone else. Saying no was easier than she feared.

For Maria, self-advocacy meant communicating in a way that worked for her, emailing rather than telephoning, and learning to say no to future commitments.

ROBERT, 62

"That's it, Robert. Stop this car. Now." His wife was usually calm, but her voice had a serious note he couldn't ignore. He pulled off the freeway.

"What's wrong? Do you need a rest stop?"

"No, I need you to stop being an old fool. You won't admit you're lost. I've been telling you we're going the wrong way for the last half hour, but you won't listen."

"It's right around here somewhere. Don't you trust my Daniel Boone scouting skills?"

"It's not your skills I have a problem with, it's that you won't 'fess up when you need help. Why can't we use the map on my phone?"

"I don't trust those crazy things. That weird voice makes my skin crawl. Are we being taken over by robots? What's next, a toaster that cooks your eggs?"

"Actually, you can buy a toaster that also cooks eggs, so I guess we live in the future. Now, either follow the GPS directions, or let me drive."

Robert fumed. The only thing worse than asking for directions was being a passenger in his own car. He knew the old jokes about women drivers were a bunch of malarkey, but he was too old-fashioned to sit back and let his wife drive.

"Okay, okay, if you've gotta use your robot, fine. But I would've gotten us there."

"I know this isn't easy for you, and I appreciate it. If you don't like the sound of the voice on my phone, I can change it." They listened to the voice options, giggling at how silly some of them sounded, and finally agreed on an Irish woman's voice.

CHAPTER 14

Once their destination was typed in, Robert got back on the road, guided by the phone. It was a bit annoying, but it turned out he'd been going the wrong way for quite a while. His wife never said, "I told you so," even though it was deserved, and Robert was grateful for that.

That night she asked him why he always had so much trouble asking for help.

"What do you mean 'always?' I got lost, it could happen to anyone."

"Getting lost isn't the problem, not asking for help is. And it's not just directions, it's assembling things, or learning how a new gadget works. You never read the instructions, or find an online tutorial, or ask anyone for help with anything. Ever."

"But I'm a guy, we don't ask for directions."

"Plenty of men know how to get help when they need it. Remember when your buddy from the diner asked you to help him with his mother's old TV set?"

"That was a real antique, a beauty. But it was never going to work again."

Robert smiled, thinking about how good it felt when his friend asked him for advice.

"He didn't know anything about old TVs, but he knew you did. So he asked you for help. It's a thing guys do. Most guys, but not you."

"Really? I never ask for help?" He thought back, trying to come up with an example he could use to show her she was wrong about this, but he couldn't think of a single one.

"I think it's related to your autism. You know, Bobby never used to raise his hand when he got stumped, he had to be taught to ask for help. But he learned, and you can, too."

"I guess I can, I never thought about it." Robert knew he could do this himself. Then he thought again. Maybe he should ask for help. That was the whole idea, right?

"Next time we head off on another day trip, could we ask your phone for directions?"

"Of course. You only have to ask."

It sounded simple enough, but it took him a while to get used to asking. His standard operating procedure was to keep trying on his own, and then complain about it loudly until someone offered to help. Wouldn't it save time and misery to just ask for help in the first place?

A few months later, Robert's old computer died and he had to get a new one. He asked his daughter and wife to help choose the right one. At the big box store, he asked an employee directions to the computer section. When he got home, he asked his daughter to help him set it up. He even asked Bobby to show him how to play games on it. Each time, he asked politely and thanked the person who helped him. He remembered how good he'd felt when his buddy asked him for help. Robert's view was that he was actually helping others when he gave them the chance to assist him. The more he practiced asking for help, the more comfortable he got, until he could accept help with gratitude rather than with annoyance or embarrassment.

For Robert, self-advocacy meant being aware he needed assistance, asking for it politely knowing that people enjoy being helpful, and accepting help graciously.

CHAPTER 14

SPEAKING FOR OURSELVES

"When I found out I had autism in college, it opened the door for me to ask for clarification without feeling embarrassed. It meant there was a foundation of understanding if I was a bit out of step. I needed my professors to understand that my brain worked a bit differently. That could be an asset, but there might also be times when I would need things explained differently. Knowing about my autism helped me learn to advocate for myself."

— *Cat, autistic adult*

CHAPTER 15
DISCLOSURE

(To Tell or Not to Tell?)

Disclosure means sharing private information. When you're diagnosed with autism, some people will already know, like your family, your IEP team in school, whoever diagnosed you, and anyone you've already told. As an adult, you decide who else to tell and who not to tell. You can make your disclosure decision easier by thinking CUPS: Closeness, Understanding, Professionalism, and Support.

Closeness

The first thing you should think about before disclosing is closeness. How well do you know this person? If you have friends or extended family members that you see regularly at social events, you might choose to confide in them. Because you'll see each other often, it may help them understand you. If you ride the same bus with a person but don't see each other socially anyplace else, that person would not usually be considered a close friend. You probably won't want to disclose your diagnosis to them. On the other hand, if you two have been riding the same bus for years, and you now sit together and chat about your lives, that's another story. If talking to them usually makes you feel better about yourself and about life in general, it may feel right to share your diagnosis. However, if they're negative and often critical, disclosing to them could be risky.

It's rarely wise to disclose with strangers or casual acquaintances, because you don't know how they'll respond. Will they use the information against you, like a bully uses a weakness? It may not be safe to share private information with them. Still, it's always your choice as an adult to make your own disclosure decisions.

Understanding

One of the important reasons for disclosure is to increase understanding. If people close to you don't realize you're on the spectrum, they may be confused if you react unexpectedly to things they take in stride. Some neurotypical people assume everyone sees things the same way they do. If certain smells, sounds, textures, or other sensory experiences don't bother them, then they don't see why anyone would be bothered. If they find big parties fun and loud concerts exciting, then there must be something "wrong" with those who don't. It doesn't sound very accepting, does it? Of course, not all neurotypical people are like that. Many are open to learning and will understand you better if you disclose your diagnosis.

CHAPTER 15

Professionalism

This next section is about professionalism, at work or at school. If you were hired for a job that you are fully qualified for and capable of doing with no workplace accommodations needed, then there may be no reason for you to disclose your autism to your employer. You might fear that they will treat you differently than they treat your co-workers, or overly scrutinize your work performance and your workplace behaviors, looking for problems if they know you have a disability. If your autism has no effect on your ability to do your job, including the social expectations, it might be wise not to disclose.

On the other hand, if you need workplace accommodations which are protected under Americans with Disabilities Act (ADA), then you will need to disclose your disability. An autistic employee may receive a range of supports, such as modifying schedules for consistency, allowing flex time or work from home, delegating a stressful customer interaction to a supervisor, or providing a quiet, non-distracting work space. If your employer has no idea that you have a disability, you won't be given accommodations. You can learn more about this online at website of the Office of Disability Employment Policy section of the United States Department of Labor (https://www.dol.gov/odep/topics/Autism.htm).

Similar to workplace disclosure decisions, if you are a student you are not required to disclose your disability unless you want special help, accommodations, or modifications. If you feel that your education will be enhanced if you let your professors or teachers know about your autism, it's your choice. Your school should already have policies in place about rights of students with disabilities. Don't expect an IEP from high school to carry over to college, though. Once a student with a disability graduates from high school or ages out, the IEP is no longer valid. You will need to advocate for yourself to receive accommodations in college.

In professional situations, whether at work or at school, disclosure is always your choice. It should be based on your need for understanding or accommodations related to autism.

Support

If you need special support because of your autism, whether it's social, environmental, community, or legal, you'll need to disclose your disability. Do an honest self-examination, asking someone you trust for input, to determine if you need any support. Maybe there's nothing you need right now, but you might require support in the future. You can research what's available where you live and find out if you're eligible, and how to access services. There have traditionally been more services available for children with autism than for autistic adults, and more services for those severely handicapped by their disability than for those who are considered "high functioning."

While we're on the subject, the idea of "high functioning" and "low functioning" is neither descriptive nor accurate. Everyone has areas in which we excel and could be called "high functioning" while at the same time we all have weaknesses, or areas of "low functioning." Not only that, but we can be "high functioning" when stress is low, but "low functioning" when stress is high. Functioning labels are not useful in real life; people are far too complex. Still, services are often distributed based on the appearance of functioning. Whether or not you disclose your disability in order to access support services is a personal decision.

Disclosure is a complex issue, isn't it? You get to decide if you want to disclose, based on your CUPS. Let's see how our five fictional characters made their disclosure decisions.

JACOB, 18

Jacob usually loved his advanced placement (AP) computer science class, but he was dreading today. They were supposed to do a partner project, which he hated. Why couldn't he do the work by himself? He didn't need a partner. Luckily, the teacher was assigning teams so he wouldn't have to be the last one picked. That was the worst.

He got paired up with a girl named Hannah. That made it worse, because Jacob got nervous around girls. Hannah was kind of quiet and cute. She seemed smart and answered questions in class, which he never did. He wondered if she was disappointed to be paired with him, but if she was, he couldn't read it in her facial expression.

The rest of the period was for project planning. Jacob knew he didn't work well in groups. He introduced himself to Hannah, and wondered what else he should say. Should he tell her that he was on the autism spectrum? He couldn't bring himself to do that, but he also didn't want her to think he was a jerk if he stumbled socially. He decided to compromise.

"Um, I guess I should tell you that I'm sort of awkward. When it comes to computer science, I really do know what I'm doing and I won't let you down on the project, but I'm not too social. If it seems like I'm trying to take over the project, it's just that I really love this stuff and I get excited about it. Just remind me that this is not a one-person thing. Oh, and also, if I say or do something that seems rude, I hope you'll tell me, because I never mean to be a jerk. I guess when it comes to social stuff, I'm clueless, but not when it comes to computers. Sorry you got stuck with me."

To his relief, she seemed to take this in stride, and said it was no problem. Then she said that she had a cousin on the autism spectrum, so she was cool with socially different people. Jacob wasn't sure if she meant she thought he was autistic, too, but he decided to let that comment go by. He wasn't ready to tell a girl he just met that he was autistic like her cousin. Maybe her cousin was one of those kids who couldn't talk, or who flapped his hands all day. Then Jacob realized he was stereotyping autistic people, and he was one, himself! Obviously, not everyone with autism was the same. Still, he didn't know Hannah well enough to share more. For Jacob, describing some of the characteristics of his autism that might affect their project, without sharing his diagnosis, was the right level of disclosure for a classmate he'd just met.

EMILY, 22

Emily got on the bus, fumbling for bus pass while telling the driver about a *Hamilton* meme. It was so funny! She described the photo taken from the musical, and the hilarious caption. The bus driver stared straight ahead, and said, "Bus pass," again.

CHAPTER 15

"I do have a pass, it's right here in my backpack. I just have so much stuff in here. Hey, here's my favorite button! I thought I'd lost this one! Look, it has an alpaca on it, but it says, 'No Drama Llama.' With an alpaca! What were they thinking? Crazy, right?"

"If you don't have the fare or a pass, I'm going to have to ask you to step down and let other passengers board." His mouth was turned down at the corners. Emily stepped off of the bus, confused. Was he mad at her? Luckily, she found her pass and got on. While she rode, she thought about what happened. Emily was naturally friendly, and she assumed everyone else was the same. The driver usually smiled, but not today. What was different? Maybe it was the line of people. Maybe he was late and she was making him later. She wasn't sure what to say to him.

By the time they got to her stop, the bus was nearly empty. She paused at the door. "I'm sorry for talking so much before. Sometimes I get overexcited and run off at the mouth. I'm autistic, and I don't always pick up on social cues. If I start to ramble on again, just tell me to be quiet, and I will. I don't want you to be mad at me or kick me off the bus."

The driver smiled and said, "Aw, it's not a big problem, I was just running late today. You know, my sister's kid has that 'artistic' thing. I get it. I'm not mad at you, and I'm not kicking you off the bus. You just need to keep your bus pass where you can find it, okay?"

"Okay, I'll do that. Thank you." Emily was so relieved she almost skipped down the bus steps. "See you next time!" she called back over her shoulder.

Emily had made a spur-of-the-moment decision to disclose her disability. She rode with this bus driver regularly, so he was familiar and it felt natural for her to talk about herself. Although they weren't close, she wanted him to understand her better. Most people don't disclose personal information with bus drivers, but sharing was Emily's style and her choice.

ZACH, 33

"Zach, I need to talk to you. Can you sit down with me for a moment?" The rabbi gestured to a bench. Zach sat, wondering what was up.

"Some of the ladies tell me you're rude when you unlock for their meetings."

"Rude?" Zach was confused. "I never say anything rude, I never even speak to them."

The rabbi nodded. "Yes, that's what they said. You unlock the door looking down, and when they greet you, not a word. They find you standoffish, too much inside yourself."

"I didn't mean to be, I don't want to be rude." Zach felt his face grow warm as he realized he hadn't even glanced at their faces when he opened up for them.

"It didn't sound like you, but this is what they told me. Whenever I see you, you look at me and greet me. Why not them?"

"I've known you since I was a kid, so I guess I'm comfortable, but I don't know them."

"Is it so difficult for you to treat them as you treat me?"

"Actually, rabbi, it is difficult for me, but I can do better. I don't know if you're aware that I'm on the autism spectrum. It's what makes it hard for me to talk with people I don't know well, or to look them in the eye." He worried that he might lose his position and apartment. "Maybe I should have told you before,

CHAPTER 15

and I'm sorry, but I really can learn. Sometimes I need someone to tell me when I've been rude, because I don't notice."

"I thought there might be something when a healthy young man your age needed this kind of job, but I was grateful to have you here. Thank you for sharing this with me."

"Will I lose my job?" Zach could hardly get the words out, but he had to know.

The rabbi looked at him with both his eyebrows raised and his mouth slightly open. It was a surprised look, Zach realized. "Of course you won't lose your job!" the rabbi said. "Why would you? It's just that the ladies would like it if you look up and say 'good morning' when you unlock the doors for them, that is all. You can do that, yes?"

"Yes, of course! You can count on me."

"One more thing. Can you recommend a book about autism? I'm sure you are not the only person in our faith family who is on the spectrum, and I would love to learn more."

"Sure thing, rabbi. I'll find one to recommend and email you the title and author."

"Thank you, Zach, that would be a mitzvah."

Zach had several feelings at once, which he sorted out while walking around the block to clear his head. He felt embarrassed that the ladies thought he was rude. He was relieved that he wouldn't be fired. He felt surprised and happy that the rabbi wanted to read more about autism. He was determined to show everyone that he could be socially appropriate rather than withdrawn. Finally, he felt confident that he could do so now that he was aware of how others saw him. For Zach, disclosing the truth about his diagnosis led to improved understanding.

MARIA, 45

"I don't know if I can go to mass this week," Maria told her friend.

"But whyever not?" Sofia asked. "Are you sick?"

"No, I'm not sick, I just have to go to that fundraiser planning meeting on Saturday and I have a doctor's appointment on Monday."

"How do your Saturday and Monday plans mean you can't go to mass? It's on Sunday."

"I just ..." Maria started to wring her hands, and then locked her fingers together to still them. "I can't go to social events three days in a row. I simply can't."

"But, how are a committee meeting, mass, and a doctor's appointment all social events? And why can't you do three days in a row? I don't understand." Sofia looked confused, with one eyebrow slightly higher than the other and a small crease between them.

"I don't know." Maria sighed. She preferred to guard her privacy, but this woman had been a friend to her. She took a deep breath and looked down at her hands. "I'm on the autism spectrum. Anything that involves other people is a social event for me, and it's exhausting. I just can't handle three days in a row. I'm sorry."

"Oh." Sofia drew out the syllable. "I had no idea. I thought you were shy, or quirky. I didn't know women could get the autism."

"So now you know. I hope you don't think less of me."

"Of course not. We're friends. I'm glad you told me, so I can understand better when you say no to some of my invitations."

CHAPTER 15

"Thank you. I actually feel a lot better now that you know. I was trying so hard to act normal, it was tiring me out."

"I hope you don't feel like you have to pretend when you're with me, Maria. We're friends, and friends always have each other's backs."

For Maria, telling Sofia about her autism was a tremendous relief. If she had to turn down a social invitation sometimes, now she wouldn't worry about what her friend would think. It felt good to have a friend who knew and who believed her without questioning whether it was really autism. Disclosure had been a good idea in this situation.

ROBERT, 62

Robert got in his car and headed to the cafe for another meeting of the OGC—the Old Geezers' Club. He thought back to that day when Cliff had gotten so mad at him, and he'd ended up telling everyone that he had autism, like his grandson. It was such a relief to know that they knew. Nobody ever acted weird about it, either. Cliff even brought in an article he had read about autism being diagnosed more often in adults. Even Robert used to think it was a kid's thing, until he realized he had it, too. Ever since he told them, any time he said something awkward or rude-sounding, somebody in the group would let him know—usually by smacking their rolled-up cap against the back of his head. It was always good-natured, and he wasn't the only one in the group who got the cap-to-the-head treatment, either. It felt great to have a group of pals who knew him and liked him, anyway. Disclosure had been the right decision for Robert.

SPEAKING FOR OURSELVES

"Disclosing a diagnosis is a personal decision everyone has to weigh based on the situation they're in. I'm very open about the fact that I'm autistic, as I have no reason not to be. When I was diagnosed in college, the disability office wasn't set up to offer very many accommodations, certainly not for the kinds of things I might have struggled with. I let my professors know, and while not everyone understood what that meant, they were all ready to work with me if I came to them with struggles I was having. I learned that one of my professors was also on the spectrum, which was something we were able to connect on. At that time, it was helpful to be open about my diagnosis."

— Cat, autistic adult

PART IV
RECREATION

———⊰❦⊱———

Sometimes It *Is* All Fun and Games

"We don't want your judgment
and we don't need your pity.
This is where I want to be,
Hanging out with cats at parties."

— *"Cats at Parties"*

Lyrics by The Doubleclicks

CHAPTER 16
CLUBS AND GROUPS

(Playing Well With Others)

Recreation is an important part of adult life. Having work you enjoy is great, but recreation—doing things for pleasure—is vital for balance. What do you do to amuse or refresh yourself? Many people have hobbies they love, and they like to meet others who share their passion.

If you've always said, "Groups and clubs are not for me," you may be right. On the other hand, maybe you haven't found the right group yet. When you find like-minded souls who are passionate about your hobby, a club can be a great way to share your interests.

How do you find your people? Start online. Search for your area of interest and see what comes up. You might find people you can meet in your local area, or an online forum of people from around the world. Trust your instincts and your comfort level to find your tribe.

If you love to be outdoors hiking, cycling, or bird watching, you might find an activity-based group where chatting is a low priority. When you do stop to rest, conversational topics come up naturally, like the weather, landscape, birds, and wildlife.

Do you enjoy artistic or crafting hobbies? Getting together to knit, draw, quilt, or scrapbook provides obvious conversation starters, like asking about each other's projects.

Perhaps you enjoy playing board games, card games, video games, or roleplaying games like Dungeons & Dragons (D&D). You'll find others who enjoy them, too. It's easier to talk over a game than to make idle chit-chat. Also, playing a role lets you pretend to be someone you're not.

There are conventions, or "cons," for just about any interest from comics to sci-fi and beyond, and the internet will tell you where and when they are. You may meet someone at a con who shares your interests and who wants to get together locally between cons.

If you don't find a group in your area that resonates with you, start one yourself. Start with the WH questions: Why start a club? Who might be in the club? Where and when will we meet? What will we do at the meetings? Ask the internet for tips on starting a club.

In addition to groups and clubs based on interests, many people find support groups enhance their personal growth while connecting with people who share their challenges and celebrate their triumphs. Jerry Newport, in his book *Your Life Is Not a Label*, includes a section on how to start your own support group.

Whether you find your people in an existing club or start one of your own, being part of a group of people who share your interests can be invaluable. Read on to see how each of our five fictional characters found groups where they felt they belonged.

CHAPTER 16

Apparently, no one cared about the environment at Jacob's school. Every time he tried to talk about global warming and the effects of fossil fuels on the Earth, people walked away or told him to shut up. Didn't they realize how vital this was to the future of the planet? He was tired of being blown off. There must be other kids who cared. Where were they?

Jacob stayed after class to talk to his science teacher about his concerns and his desire to share information with other kids. They decided to start an environment club to meet weekly during lunch in the science lab. His teacher would be the sponsor, and Jacob would lead the first meeting. They wanted to make a difference, not just complain about the way things were.

Three people showed up to the first meeting. At first Jacob was disappointed, until he realized that this was just the beginning. These kids shared his strong feelings about their planet. They watched a video of Greta Thunberg, an autistic teenager, speaking powerfully on behalf of climate justice. It sparked an animated conversation. By the end of the first meeting, they'd all committed to reduce their use of fossil fuels by walking or biking to school. It wouldn't be convenient, but it made sense to start making a change immediately, right where they were.

After the meeting, Jacob felt super charged and excited. It had been exhilarating to talk about his passion with others who shared his feelings, and to feel like they could make a difference. The next day, the group members found each other at lunch and continued their conversation. Over time, the group grew slowly as others who shared their commitment heard about them. It didn't matter to Jacob if the club were small or large, as long as the people in it could share a common interest and look for ways to make a difference.

EMILY, 22

No one ever got Emily's hilarious *Hamilton* references. Even when she explained the context, how a particular meme related to one of the songs in the musical, no one cared. Finally, she got fed up. She went in search of Hamilfans online and found a group that felt right to her. The members shared her extreme love for all things *Hamilton*, and like her, knew all of the lyrics and the cleverest ways to work them into conversation. They got her, and she got them. Having an online group was perfect for Emily; she met like-minded people from around the globe. It was awesome! Wow! This chat room was the room where it happens, and she was in it. Being part of the group made her appreciate how lucky she was to be alive right now.

ZACH, 33

Zach had two groups that were important to him: the young adults group at his temple, and the volunteer group for his political party. Each group was different, but each fulfilled a different need for him. In the temple group, he got to hang out with other people his age. In his political volunteer group, although some of the members were older than he was, they all shared the same ideals and passions about making a difference in the world. He loved the discussions they had, where he could go on and on

CHAPTER 16

because he knew they were interested. Of course, that meant he also had to listen when one of them went off on a tangent, but that was okay. For Zach, having two different in-person clubs or groups was just right.

MARIA, 45

"I'm sure you'll love it once you get to know everyone. The meeting's at 3:00 PM Wednesday, so I'll pick you up at a quarter to. And don't worry, you don't have to read the book before the meeting. You can just listen."

Maria watched the trees going past the window as Sofia drove her home from church. She blinked hard as she finally realized that her friend was talking about something specific, not chatting aimlessly as she usually did. What was that she said about picking her up at 3:00?

"Uh, I'm not sure ..."

"Don't worry about a thing! This is a low-key book club. No one will put you on the spot or anything. Anyway, it'll do you good to get out of the house." Sofia pulled up and stopped in front of Maria's house. "I'll be right here at quarter to three Wednesday. See you then!"

Maria wondered how she could get out of it. She didn't want to join a book club, but what could she do? There seemed no escape, short of calling Sofia on the phone, and that wasn't going to happen. So, here she was, her purse clutched in both hands, peering out the front window. As soon as the car pulled up she hurried out, but she was so anxious she hardly said a word. Fortunately, Sofia was fine carrying on a conversation by herself.

When they arrived Maria was nervous, but after introducing themselves the other club members chatted amongst themselves and let her sit quietly. She could see a cat in the corner; she hoped it would come and sit with her. By the end of the meeting, Maria felt much more comfortable, having succeeded in attracting the cat to her lap. Maria knew that next time the people would not be strangers, making it easier to come back. Having a friend encourage her and pick her up for the meeting made it possible. Knowing she could spend time with the host's cat was an added incentive. On top of all that, she loved having a new book to read each month, one that was already picked out for her.

ROBERT, 62

For Robert, the OGC—the Old Geezers' Club—was the only group he really cared about and felt comfortable with. Sure, he went to church with his wife, but not to socialize. When he showed up at the diner and saw his old cronies already there with their cups of coffee, waving him over and making room for him to sit, it felt right. He had learned that, even with old friends, you still had to think about what you said, and he'd put his foot in his mouth more times than he'd care to admit. Still, they accepted him as he was, warts and all, and that was a good feeling.

CHAPTER 16

SPEAKING FOR OURSELVES

"A lot of the friends I've made have been through Dungeons & Dragons groups, first in high school and college, and later as an adult moving to a new city where I didn't know anyone. Even though D&D isn't about socializing, socializing happens—it just happens in a way that has less pressure than a purely social meet-up."

— Cat, autistic adult

CHAPTER 17
SOLITARY PURSUITS

———⟶✦⟵———

(Who Says Fun Has to Be a Team Sport?)

People may tell you to stop wasting your time playing video games alone. If they want you to quit doing something that you love, ask them why. Do they fear you're addicted to video gaming or internet surfing? Do they think your self-care and career are suffering? Are they worried you're cutting yourself off from people? Listen to their concerns with an open mind. After all, these are people who know and care about you.

Once you understand where they're coming from, be honest with yourself. Do they have a point? Would your life be better if you cut down on some of your favorite things? As an adult, it's up to you to decide whether or not your interest has a negative or positive impact on your life.

When you examine your use of solitary activities to see if they help you or put up a road block, think WASH. Are you Wasting time? Are you Addicted to your passion? Does it get in the way of your Social relationships? Does it impact your Health? Consider wisely.

Are you WASTING time?

If you're accused of wasting your life obsessing about your interest, take some data to find out exactly how much time a day you spend on it. Use an app or write down when you start and stop. Do the math: how many hours a day do you actually spend on it? You get to decide if that's too much time, or if it's what you need to cope. If you miss meals, sleep, work, or appointments because of it, you have a problem. If not, giving it up might increase stress. You control your use of your interest; awareness is key to control.

Are you ADDICTED to your interest?

If your people believe you're addicted, take them seriously and do some introspection. Ask them why they believe you have an unhealthy addiction. Is it hard for you to stop? Do you become loud, belligerent, argumentative, or even violent when someone interrupts you or asks you to turn your game off? When a child throws a tantrum it's inappropriate, but when an adult throws a tantrum it can be scary, dangerous, or even illegal. If this is you, admit it and look for support in managing your emotions or addictions.

If you are addicted, re-read Chapter Thirteen, "Self-Management." You can create a plan that will help you make the changes you want to make in your life. Get help from a counselor, case manager, coach, or behavior specialist to put you on the right road.

If you learn that your interest is not an addiction, share the difference between addictions and interests to your well-meaning friends and family. Tell them why you don't meet the criteria for addiction. Show them you can walk away when needed. Continue to self-monitor to ensure that your passion doesn't cross the line into addiction and use it as a positive stress reliever.

Does it get in the way of your SOCIAL relationships?

Are you accused of shutting people out to play your games or focus on your interests? Find out what they mean. Do they feel disrespected if you use your cellphone when you're with them? Do they feel that you only play games alone and never include them in two-player games? Do they say that you turn down their invitations to go out because you'd rather stay home and do your own thing? Or that you never talk to them unless it's about your interest? Listen to their concerns. You may not realize people want to hang out with you. Focusing on your phone or game when you're with them hurts their feelings. If this is true for you, find ways to let your people know that you care. Even though you need some alone time to de-stress, that doesn't mean you don't want their companionship. If you plan to spend undistracted time with them, they needn't take it personally that you also need solitude sometimes.

Does it adversely affect your HEALTH?

Some people are so passionate about their games, hobbies, or interests that they can completely lose track of everything else, including their own needs. Do you ever forget to eat, or get dehydrated? Do you hold your urine for hours rather than leaving your game to go to the bathroom? Have you missed school, work, parties, or family meals because you get so caught up in your passion? Do you stay up late playing or reading? Don't underestimate how much sleep adults need; check out the research online and get enough sleep every night.

Any of these could be a sign of an unhealthy level of interest. That doesn't mean the interest is unhealthy, just that it's taking over your life so much it can affect your health. You don't need to give it up, but you do need to make your health a priority. If you can't control it, you might be addicted; go back to the previous section, "Are you ADDICTED to your interest?"

Read how our five fictional characters kept their need for solitary pursuits in balance.

JACOB, 18

Jacob was dimly aware of an annoying buzz behind him. His mom was talking, probably had been for a while. Reluctantly, he pulled his attention away from his game and turned around.

"You have to quit playing that game, get rid of it. You're eighteen years old and you'll be out of school soon. You can't keep playing games when you're an adult, you know." This surprised Jacob. He knew for a fact that grownups played video games too, not just kids.

"Why do you want me to quit my game? I love it. I don't care how old I am."

"Well, you're not a little boy anymore. You're going to have to put away childish things. Honestly, I think you're addicted. Just quit cold turkey, so you can have a life."

CHAPTER 17

After his mother left, Jacob thought about what she said. He felt anxious and short of breath. He'd never dreamed of giving up his gaming. Why would he? He wasn't addicted to it. Was he? Just because he didn't want to quit didn't mean he was addicted, right? Jacob looked up video gaming addictions online. Was he an addict? He had to know the truth.

In his search, Jacob found a site for gamers, and somebody had posted they thought they were addicted to games. The comments were unhelpful, negative, and often brutal. He left that site quickly and kept searching. A couple of places had quizzes you could take to see if you were addicted. After taking them, Jacob came to three conclusions:

1. He was not actually addicted to video games, he just loved playing them

2. Playing video games in moderation was useful for him in reducing stress

3. He could balance his gaming with the rest of his life

Jacob told his parents what he'd learned, and how helpful his games were for decompressing after a stressful day. He assured them his schoolwork and chores would be a priority. They agreed to stop trying to make him quit gaming. He was an adult who could manage his own use of video games without parental guidance.

Emily pulled out her felt squares and embroidery thread, looking for the perfect color combination. Then she took out Ichabod, her rose gold scissors shaped like a crane. Every time she saw those scissors, she smiled. Life was good when you could surround yourself with cute things that had faces and names. She cut pieces of white and pink felt, sewed them together with pink thread, and added purple beads for eyes and loops of pink, purple, and white floss for fluffy hair. She sewed on tiny pre-made wings and glued a tiny cone-shaped horn to the forehead. After stuffing her creation with cotton batting, she stood it up and looked at it from all angles. A perfect little alpacorn. "I'm going to call you ... Butterfly Sparkle Horn! You can live here, between ChewPaca and Alpuccino." She set the white alpacorn gently between the two brown ones and stepped back to survey her display. One hundred forty-nine. She counted again. Still 149. She got to work to make it an even 150. The knock startled her.

"Emily? Are you okay?" It was Sarah, her favorite staff member.

"Sarah! Come in!" she sang out. "Of course I'm okay, why wouldn't I be?"

"Well, you haven't come out of your room all day, and it's after 4:00 in the afternoon. Did you eat breakfast or lunch?" Emily was shocked. The day had disappeared while she was enchanted by her felt creations. Suddenly, she realized she was starving.

"I was making my alpacorns," she called. "I'll be right out to get something to eat."

CHAPTER 17

Emily ate a snack to tide her over until dinner, and Sarah sat down with her.

"I'm concerned about the amount of time you're spending alone in your room. We worry that you might be depressed or sick. Are you sure you're all right?"

"Yes, I'm fine. I was just sewing my alpacorns and I lost track of time." Emily gulped down a glass of water. She hadn't realized how thirsty she was.

"It's important to have alone time, and time to be creative, but you have to take care of yourself. Also, people like it when you come hang out."

"I guess I could set alarms on my phone to come out for meals. That seems do-able."

"That sounds like a great idea. See you at dinner."

Emily was grateful to have people who cared about her but weren't as pushy as parents could be. She wanted to avoid getting carried away with her art and missing meals, because that could affect her health. The phone alarm system sounded like it would help her keep a balance between her alone time and coming out to eat meals and socialize.

ZACH, 33

As soon as Zach had locked up the building after the young adult group, he went straight to his room and closed the door. He liked hanging out, but being social for hours was exhausting. He threw himself onto his bed and picked up the remote, clicking through to find episodes of the pony friends cartoon. He only watched it when he was alone. He'd be embarrassed if anyone knew, but it relaxed him. The soft colors, the music, the way the ponies always solved their problems in less than a half hour and learned a valuable lesson about friendship—everything about it was pleasant. He knew that the ponies would replenish his sapped energy.

Zach knew he needed time alone every single day. If he tried to push himself too far, it took a toll. He wasn't wasting time when he isolated himself, this was vital to his well-being.

MARIA, 45

Book club was over, and Maria waved goodbye to Sofia. Although she enjoyed the group now that she was used to it, she still felt utterly exhausted after three hours in a social setting.

She watched her friend drive away, then closed the drapes and got out a hobby store bag. She took out a model kit of a giant robot made of smaller robots as the arms, legs, and torso. There was even a tiny pilot that fit into the head. She gazed lovingly at it. The clerk at the hobby store assumed Maria was buying models for a son or nephew, and she never corrected him. Why should she? It wasn't his concern.

She examined the picture on the box, peering at it from various angles and marveling at the intricacies. Then she turned it over and read the list of all the tiny parts inside. She read everything twice, smiling all the while, anticipating the task before her.

Next, she opened the box and laid out each sprue or frame of model pieces. She also got out her hobby knife, file, and glue. She wouldn't need paints or brushes today. Maria used the knife to carefully cut each tiny plastic piece out of the sprue and then filed the rough edges. She arranged all of the pieces in order. What immense satisfaction she felt looking at everything! In her mind's eye, she could clearly imagine all of the pieces moving, joining, and fitting together to form the gigantic, powerful robot. If she were the pilot controlling such an elegant creation, she would never be afraid of anything.

The sound of a robotic voice gibbering brought her out of her reverie. It was her phone alarm, telling her to fix dinner. The gluing would wait until tomorrow. This was fine with Maria, because it extended her enjoyment. For Maria, working on her hobby in solitude was relaxing and pleasurable. It didn't get in the way of her social life. After a social event, which was stressful even if enjoyable, she needed her project and her privacy more than ever.

ROBERT, 62

Robert recognized the timid tapping at his study door. "Not right now, Bobby, Grandpa's busy with breakable stuff." He turned back to the boxes of cathode ray tubes. In the background, the familiar sound of his science fiction TV show droned on. He didn't have to look at the screen, he knew each episode by heart, but having it on was soothing.

Robert picked up and examined each tube, looking for possible defects. He wore protective glasses and disposable gloves. He hadn't broken any of his pieces yet, and he didn't intend to, but he was careful. That's why Bobby couldn't come in yet, but Bobby wasn't interested anyway. Why should he be? It was a weird fascination, there was no getting around that, but it made

Robert happy. And wasn't that the reason to have a hobby in the first place? He completed his inspection and returned the box to the top shelf.

"Okay, Bobby, come on in!" he called out. "Do you want to watch the spaceship show?" Bobby wanted to watch cartoons instead. Robert was happy to change the channel and hold his grandson on his lap as they watched a show about talking trains. After some uninterrupted alone time, he could really enjoy spending time with his little locomotive-fan. He guessed Bobby loved trains as much as he loved cathode ray tubes and his sci-fi show. Different strokes for different folks, right? Robert figured there was nothing wrong with that, nothing at all.

SPEAKING FOR OURSELVES

"I need time to myself every day that is not social or work-related. Collecting cards for the art and stats, without needing to play the card games with others, is a good hobby for me. Arranging and organizing them is calming, learning the statistics is interesting, and appreciating the artwork on each card is soothing. Spending time alone with my card collection can regenerate energy that has been depleted through too much time spent in the company of others."

— *Noel, autistic adult*

CHAPTER 18
FRIENDSHIP

———◄►●◄———

(The Rules of Friending)

What is friending? Today, people think of social media, but in ancient times, friending meant to befriend. Friendship can be a strong and happy alliance between like-minded individuals. Someone who knows your faults as well as your strengths and still likes you is precious.

There are all kinds of friends. Some you may have known since early childhood. Others you know from work or choir, or you met at a convention and just clicked. Family members can also be friends, and even animals; ask any pet owner. Online friends may never meet in person, but still share common interests.

Not everyone you know is a friend. Some are acquaintances you've run into a few times but don't know well. Others you see at the office or school, but not socially. Just because you see someone every day, like your barista or bus driver, that doesn't mean you're friends.

One of Temple Grandin's and Sean Barron's *Unwritten Rules of Social Relationships* is "Not Everyone Who is Nice to Me is My Friend." People can be polite on the surface without wanting to be friends. If you already have a good and trusted friend, you are fortunate. If you're looking for a friend, start with PAL: Play it cool, Ask, and Let it be.

Play It Cool

You won't find or keep a friend using a choke hold. Anyone who tries too hard can become intrusive, and others are put off by their smothering ways. Daniel Tammet, author and autistic savant, wrote, "I had eventually come to understand that friendship was a delicate, gradual process that mustn't be rushed or seized upon but allowed and encouraged to take its course over time. I pictured it as a butterfly, simultaneously beautiful and fragile, that once afloat belonged to the air and any attempt to grab at it would only destroy it." Be patient.

Why do you want a particular person to be your friend? Be honest with yourself. If it's because they're popular and you want to gain acceptance by association, reconsider. No one wants to be used, even popular people, and this kind of connection is rarely equal or reciprocal. Sometimes, an unpopular person is accepted as a fringe member of clique so the others have someone to look down on or boss around. This is not a happy position to be in.

Rather than trying too hard or fawning over a popular person, look around for someone who likes the same things you like and who could be a friend on equal footing. Shared interests start many friendships. You might meet someone in a class about your favorite subject, where it's natural to strike up a conversation. Talking about things you both like is a good way to lay the groundwork for friendship. Remember to play it cool and don't try to push it.

CHAPTER 18

Ask

If you always wait for the other person to initiate, you could wait a long time. It may not be easy, but if you want to be friends with someone, you may have to ask. Think of something low key, like hanging out after work or attending a lecture about the interest you share. Don't try to impress them with expensive, hard-to-get tickets for a concert or big game. If they say yes, it should be because they like you, not because they couldn't resist the temptation of the event. Don't try to purchase friendship; it's never a good buy.

If you ask a friend to join you in a social event and they say no, don't immediately jump to offering a different day and time, pressing them into a corner. Just say, "Okay, maybe another time," and back off for a while. Another time, try inviting them to a different kind of activity. If they say no to a second invitation, check out their facial expression and body language. If they seem to be in a hurry to end the conversation, glancing away and checking their phone, don't ask again. If they really want to hang out with you, they can ask you. On the other hand, if they appear genuinely disappointed that they have a conflict, try inviting them one more time. After a maximum of three invitations and three "no" answers, it's time to move on. Play it cool.

Let It Be

If a friendship you hoped for didn't work out, don't obsess over the person and keep badgering them with invitations. Pushiness gets annoying fast, and they will avoid you. Just back off and quit asking. Not everyone you want to be friends with will become your friend. That doesn't mean there are no friends for you, just not this one. Let it be and look elsewhere.

Each of our five fictional characters learned from their friendship experiences.

JACOB, 18

Jacob wanted friends. It's not that he didn't have any. He had online friends who shared his interest in the mining-crafting video game. They had great discussions, not just about the game, but about life. He often felt they were more real to him than his friends at school. Still, sometimes he wanted someone to do things with in person.

He ate lunch with guys from his environment club, but he never got invited to hang out on weekends. He'd hear about their plans to go to the mall on Saturday, and Mondays they'd talk about how much fun they'd had. It hurt his feelings that they never invited him.

Finally, Jacob got up the courage to ask one of the guys about it. They had a class together and were both early, so he asked why he never got included in their weekend plans.

"What are you talking about?" his friend asked.

"You guys do fun stuff on the weekends, and I wondered why I'm never invited."

"Were you waiting for an engraved invitation? We just talk about it, and then we do it. You never show up, so I figured you just didn't want to hang out with us."

"But nobody ever said that I was invited."

"Nobody ever said that I was invited, either. It's not a formal event. If we talk about hanging out at the mall on Saturday, then you show up at the mall on Saturday. That's it."

Jacob was stunned. Was it that easy? "You mean, it would be okay if I show up?"

"Of course. That's what we all do. Don't make it weird."

The next weekend, Jacob showed up at the mall the guys had been talking about and they hung out in the food court and then caught a movie. No one was surprised to see him or questioned his being part of the group. It felt great to feel accepted and was a lot more fun than sitting at home playing his game. Not that he didn't play once he got home to unwind after being social all day, but he liked spending a Saturday with friends. Jacob was glad he'd asked.

EMILY, 22

"So, are you making any friends at the group home?" Emily's mom asked.

"Of course I have friends."

"Wonderful! So, tell me about them. What are their names?" Emily rattled off all of their names alphabetically. "It sounds like you just told me the names of every single resident and staff member," her mother said.

"Yeah, so?"

"Well, they can't all really be your friends, can they?"

"Why not? They're all nice." Emily didn't understand what her mother was getting at.

"Remember the 'circles of friendship' chart your teacher made for you in your social skills class in school? You were at the center of the circle, then family, then close friends that you could trust and share your feelings with, then acquaintances like teachers or classmates, all the way out to strangers. Don't you remember?"

"Sure, but I'm an adult now. Anyway, I got an A, so I'm excellent at social skills."

Her mother sighed. "Everyone keeps learning all their lives. Just because you got an A doesn't mean you're finished learning social skills. And the same concept in the 'circles of friendship' chart still applies, only with housemates and staff members rather than classmates and teachers." She got out a paper and drew a series of concentric circles, like a target. "Let's make a new one. Here's you in the middle, and then here's your father and me. Out here are strangers at the very outside, and acquaintances like staff members and bus drivers a little bit closer. Now, here's a circle between family and acquaintances. This is for special friends you share personal things with, more than the others. Do you have any friends like that?"

Emily looked at the circles and thought. She picked up the pen and wrote Alpeggy, the name of her stuffed alpacorn, in the "friends" circle, then she crossed it out and wrote it in the "family" circle. She wrote Sarah in the "friends" circle. She loved Sarah. Then she circled the name and drew an arrow out to the "acquaintance" circle, because Sarah was staff. She squinted at the paper and tapped the pen lightly against her ear. "I don't know," she admitted. "I like everybody. I don't know who goes in the 'friends' circle, if staff and housemates are acquaintances."

"That's okay," her mother said. "It gives you something to think about this week. Maybe you'll notice someone that you'd consider a closer friend."

CHAPTER 18

"Hmm ..." Emily thought about that. "Maybe."

The next week, she did think about it. Who did she eat breakfast with? Who did she watch TV with or go to the mall with? Emily noticed a pattern. She spent more time with Ashley than with their other housemates, and they seemed to laugh at the same jokes. Sometimes they got really silly, giggling about a play on words that tickled their funny bones. She started to go out of her way to sit with her at meals and to do other things together.

The next weekend, Emily had a name to put in the "friends" circle: Ashley. It wasn't that her life was completely different because of this change. She already enjoyed spending time with Ashley, even though she hadn't categorized her as a closer friend. It did make her mother happy, and when she thought about it, it made Emily happy, too. She made a felt alpacorn to give Ashley. It had curly brown hair like hers, and a laughing face, which came out a little off-center and silly-looking. Ashley loved it and hugged it tightly with a big grin. They decided to name it Angelipaca, Alpeggy's sister. It felt good to realize Ashley was a good friend.

ZACH, 33

Zach wondered why no one at his political party office ever went out after their shift. The office was right next door to an upscale microbrewery. It would be so simple to continue their discussions over a beer, but no one ever brought it up. He wished somebody would.

Then Zach realized, he was somebody. He could be the one to ask if anyone wanted to grab a beer at the end of the shift.

Why not? Well, Zach knew why not. Because probably no one would want to join him, and he'd feel like a loser for asking. So he never said anything.

Several more volunteer shifts went by. Finally, Zach decided to ask. Sure, he'd feel bad if everyone turned him down, but if he didn't try, he'd never know. He went for it.

"Hey, anyone want to grab a brew next door after we lock up?" He almost held his breath, waiting to see if he'd be left hanging. Some said they had families to get home to, but three people said yes. Zach had hoped Crystal would join them, but she left. Singling her out to ask might seem too pushy. He decided to play it cool, and if she wasn't interested, he'd just let it be.

The group of four had a beer together, talked some more about their political candidate of choice and the opposition, and then went on to share about their lives, jobs, and families. Zach felt great. He'd spoken up even though he was afraid of looking stupid, and he ended up getting to know some of his fellow volunteers a little better. He hoped that they'd do this every week. He didn't want to push it, but he liked moving from acquaintances to friends.

MARIA, 45

Maria was glad Sofia knew about her autism so she could understand that sometimes Maria couldn't socialize, while other times she could. Still, it seemed as if Sofia was always the one to initiate going out for coffee or lunch, never Maria. Should she be calling Sofia to get together? Maria hated phoning, but it didn't feel fair for one friend to do all of the inviting.

CHAPTER 18

She came up with an idea she thought would work. Maria suggested that they have a standing date on the third Thursday of every month at 3:00 PM at their favorite coffee shop in the mall. Maria liked the alliteration of "third Thursday at three." It was fun to say, and it helped her remember.

Sofia liked the idea. She said that if ever Maria didn't feel up to it she could always cancel, but Maria thought she probably wouldn't need to. Having coffee at the same time, same place, and with the same person was a routine she could find comfort in.

After a couple of months of meeting for coffee, Sofia suggested adding another meeting for lunch once a month. Maria suggested the first Friday of the month. She thought about "first Friday at four" because it was also fun to say, but 4:00 PM would be too late for lunch, so they made it noon. Having plans on the calendar without having to initiate was perfect for Maria.

ROBERT, 62

"Honey, do you remember the barbecue we went to last month with the whole family?" Robert's wife asked one morning over coffee.

"Of course I do. We had a great time, as I recall." One of his cronies from the OGC had hosted a big backyard bash and invited all the geezers and their families.

"How many times have we been invited to parties by your friends from the diner?"

"More times than I can count, I guess. Good friends, good times."

"And how many times have we invited them over here?"

That had him stumped. "I don't rightly know."

"Never. We've never invited them over here. Why do you suppose that is?"

"No idea. Do you want to invite them over? I'm sure they'd love to come."

"Robert, they're your friends, not mine. You should invite them. You can't keep going over to their homes and never invite them here. It's not fair."

Robert bristled. "But, can't you do it? You're good at all that party stuff."

"We'll help out, but this event should be yours. What kind of party would you like?"

"Hmm ... a picnic and barbecue sounds good. Burgers on the grill, beans, potato salad, watermelon, stuff like that. Can't you do it?" Even as he asked, he knew it wouldn't be fair to put this all on his wife. He was retired now, so he had plenty of time.

"You pick a date and invite them. Just check the family calendar before you do. Then we can talk about whether it will be a pot luck or if we'll provide all the food. We'll handle the details later, but first make sure your friends can join us."

Robert brought the family calendar with him to the diner and found a date they could agree on for a barbecue. They were excited to be invited and offered to bring side dishes. His wife and daughter helped him with the logistics and cooking, although Robert did all the grilling himself. The planning wasn't too stressful once he had a date on the calendar. Everyone seemed to have a great time. Robert wondered why he hadn't thought of inviting them over sooner.

CHAPTER 18

"I find that the easiest way of making friends is through a shared interest. Whether online, joining forums, blogging communities, or chats, if our first connection is based on a shared interest, then I know there's one thing I can talk to new people about. Often when I click with someone because we have the same favorite book, show, movie, or hobby, I learn we have other things in common, too. Sometimes it's a second shared hobby or interest, sometimes it's a similar mental health journey, sometimes it's some other facet of shared identity. Some friends I met through one interest have jumped to other interests with me, and me with them. I know certain people very deeply even though we met as 'fandom friends.' The same is true of IRL (in real life) friendships."

— Cat, autistic adult

CHAPTER 19
DATING AND ROMANCE

(It's Not Like the Movies)

Movies make it look easy. Two attractive people meet in some cute way, they start out disliking each other, survive several comedic misunderstandings, and then fall madly in love by the closing credits. Nice and neat, right? Of course, real life is never so predictable, and happy endings are not guaranteed. Still, it is possible to find love if that's what you hope for in your life.

Being in a couple is not required, regardless of how romcoms make it seem. Some people prefer solitude rather than navigating obstacles along the sometimes-rocky road to relationship. There is no law about what a relationship should look like, either. An online or long-distance romance is just as valid as dating someone who lives around the corner.

Some autistic adults, more than in the typical population, identify somewhere on the LGBTQIA+ spectrum as well as the autism spectrum. (The letters LGBTQIA stand for Lesbian, Gay, Bisexual, Transgender, Questioning and/or Queer, Intersex, and Asexual.) Homosexuality, being attracted to your own gender, includes gay men (who are attracted to other men) and lesbians (women who are attracted to women). Bisexuals are attracted to both men and women. Transgender or trans individuals could be men who were assigned female at birth or women who were assigned male at birth, based on external genitalia. Some people identify as asexual or ace (people who tend to have little or no sexual desire) or aromantic (no desire for nonsexual romance). Some people are non-binary and don't feel strongly that they are either male or female, but just themselves. Others are genderfluid, and may at different times identify as male, female, or other without having one consistent gender. Fewer people are intersex, which may mean they have internal sex organs, external genitalia, and/or chromosomes associated with both genders. Most people are cisgender (identifying with the gender they were assigned at birth) and heterosexual, or straight (attracted to the opposite gender). The umbrella term "queer" includes all sexual and gender minorities, and "questioning" means being unsure whether or not they're on the LGBTQIA+ spectrum. That's okay. You don't need to align with the majority if that's not who you are. Trust your own understanding of yourself, and don't try to be anything you're not.

Regardless of your sexual orientation and gender identity, when it comes to finding someone to go out with, there are a few things to think about.

Choose Wisely

First, choose wisely before you ask someone out on a date. You may have heard the phrase, "She's out of his league," meaning that she's too beautiful, popular, wealthy, or intelligent for him. The phrase implies that she wouldn't go out with someone who's less attractive, less popular, poorer, and less intelligent. This goes both ways; he may be out of her league if he has more of those characteristics, however shallow they may seem.

If you think this is old fashioned, you're right. Unfortunately, it often still applies. If you're a guy and you want to date the most beautiful woman you know, ask yourself, why her? Is it because of her looks? That's no way to judge compatibility. It's smarter to find someone who shares your interests. If you love to hike and camp, and she hates the outdoors, it'll be hard to find things to do together. Getting to know someone's likes, dislikes, and favorite activities is a good way to find out if you'd have fun dating.

Interpret Their Interest Level

How can you tell if they are interested in you? Pay attention to their nonverbal cues. Do they glance your way often? Even if they don't like to make eye contact, they'll probably orient toward you if they like you. If they turn away, it could mean they're not so interested.

When you're chatting, do they reply to your comments and share the load of keeping a conversation going? That's a sign of interest. Do they only say "uh-huh" or drop the conversational ball when there's a pause? If they don't hold up their end of a conversation, maybe they're not interested in what you're talking about, or maybe they're not interested in you. Find out which by bringing up subjects they are interested in.

Do they check their phone and look around often? They might want to escape. Do they look at you, lean in, smile or laugh at jokes with you, and seem happy to be with you? They might like you, either as a date or a friend. Either one is a good thing.

First Date

A romantic candlelight dinner or expensive evening at the theater for a first date could be your ticket to disaster. This kind of formal date is best after you've been together a while and have acknowledged romantic feelings. It's too much pressure for a first date. Try a group activity around a shared interest, a double date with friends, or just coffee and a chance to talk.

Who Pays?

Long ago, when most men had careers and most women didn't, the man traditionally paid for dates. Today, while there is still a gender pay gap (men are paid more than women in general), women are as likely to be able to pay as men. It's not necessary to stick to archaic practices, but it's also wise not to make assumptions. This is one reason why coffee is such a good idea for a first date; it's inexpensive, so if one person pays for both, it's no big deal.

You could ask for separate checks, so each person pays only for what they ordered. Many couples prefer to take turns treating one another. That way, the one inviting has the freedom to choose activities they know they can afford. In any case, it's a good idea to talk about expectations so you're both on the same page and to avoid awkwardness when the bill comes.

CHAPTER 19

Safety First

Regardless of gender, be careful when meeting someone new. Many autistic adults are trusting and open, which is admirable, but this may also make them vulnerable.

Many people today find their matches through online dating sites. While this can open up a world of new people you may not otherwise have met, it can also be dangerous. Scammers prey on trusting people. Dating sites that charge a fee are less likely to attract con artists, because they don't want to pay, they just want to get your money or personal information. Some of them write beautiful, flowery declarations of love, hoping someone will fall for them since people in love might send money to buy a plane ticket so they can be together. Do not send them money. These are made up stories to trick people. Others may try to get confidential information. They say they want your birth date and address to send you a card, but they use it for identity theft. In the absolute worst case, rapists or killers may use the internet to find their victims.

If you're interested in someone you met online, make sure they really are who they say they are. If they'll meet you for coffee in a public place, they are less likely to be part of a scam. If, on the other hand, they've been declaring their feelings for you but they can't meet IRL because they're out of the country, a gemologist visiting a diamond mine, or on a secret government mission, be suspicious.

If you do meet, be sure that your first few dates are in public places where you feel safe and other people are around. Many people on the autism spectrum know they're not good at judging people's intentions and tend to give everyone the benefit of the doubt. If this sounds like you, consider inviting a more intuitive friend to meet them and see if they get a good or bad feeling. It's smart to take precautions. Text a friend or family member where you're meeting and when you expect to be home. Be aware someone could put something in your drink while you're away from the table. It's not rude or untrusting to be safe, it's your number one priority.

If you choose to be in a sexual relationship, safety first means being careful about sexually transmitted diseases and the possibility of pregnancy. You can ask your doctor about being tested, ways to prevent disease (like condoms), and birth control options. An IUD will not protect you from herpes. And don't think that if you can't get pregnant yourself, you're off the hook. It takes two, and both need to be responsible.

BANANA

Since the #MeToo movement, awareness has increased about people's rights related to their bodies. Just because you're on a date doesn't automatically give you the right to hold hands or put your arm around your date. A kiss good night is not guaranteed and needs to be shared only with permission. This doesn't mean that you'll always have a hands-off relationship, of course, but permission is required at every point along the path to intimacy. Think BANANA: Behave Admirably, Need to Ask, Never Assume.

Behave Admirably

Regardless of gender, it is your responsibility to behave admirably. This means being polite, courteous, and respectful. Taking liberties that have not been granted, such as trying to steal a kiss or cop a feel, is not behaving admirably.

Need to Ask

You need to ask before the first kiss or going further toward a sexual relationship. Even if it seems the other person is on board, it's important and respectful to ask before each new intimacy. You may feel awkward asking, but that's better than finding out afterward that your advances were unwelcome. Plus, many find it endearing to be asked rather than taken for granted.

Never Assume

Never assume your partner wants to do the same things sexually that you want to do. Never assume that because you have done things in the past, you have lifetime consent. Never assume that because you started an amorous encounter, it will be completed. Everyone has the right to change their mind at any point in a sexual relationship, and they may say "yes" at first and "no" later. Communicate your feelings and desires, listen to your partner's wishes, and be prepared to take "no" for an answer. This means you have the right to say "no," too.

Read how our five fictional characters handle romance and dating in their lives.

JACOB, 18

Jacob stuck his head into his counselor's office. "Do you have a minute?" he asked.

"Sure, what's up?" Jacob was glad; some things he wasn't comfortable asking his parents.

"I decided to ask Tiffany to the prom. I'm going to make a big poster for a viral promposal. If I use enough glitter, do you think she'll say yes?"

"Tiffany, from the cheer squad? Are you two dating?"

"Not yet. I used to be really shy around girls, but I'm trying to get over it. Tiffany's so beautiful, naturally she's my first choice for prom. Why not? It's a free country, right?"

"Well, you can ask anyone, but that doesn't mean they'll accept."

"That's why I'm planning so early. If I ask her first, she'll have to go with me, right?"

"No, the prom is not first come, first served. If she doesn't want to go with you, she'll say no and wait for someone she knows and likes to ask her."

"Why wouldn't she want to go with me?"

"Instead of asking why she wouldn't, ask why she would. Does she know you?"

"We have English together, but I sit in the front and she sits in the back. We've never actually had a conversation, but we could get to know each other at the prom if she says yes."

"Is a girl likely to say yes to a guy she doesn't know and has never talked to?"

"I never thought about that. I was just thinking how much I'd like to go with her. I mean, it doesn't bother me that we don't know each other yet, but ..." Jacob sighed. "I guess she'd probably rather go with one of the football players rather than a stranger. Hot girls are like that."

"Everyone's 'like that.' So, who do you know and like,

someone who knows and likes you, too, that you could ask to the prom instead?"

Jacob thought. "Hannah, I guess. She's smart and she laughs at my jokes."

"That sounds promising. But, can I give you one more piece of advice?"

"Sure," said Jacob.

"Don't surprise her with one of those big promposal events if you don't know for sure she'll say yes. I've seen too many of those end badly. First, talk to her about the prom and ask her if she'd say yes to a promposal from you. Then you can make it as fancy and public as you want, because you'll already know she'll say yes."

That sounded smart to Jacob. The next day in lab, he got his courage up to talk to her about the prom and he learned that she would kind of like to go, but she didn't have a date. He asked her if she'd say yes to a promposal from him, and she smiled and nodded. What a relief!

By the next day, Jacob had created a poster covered with silver foil and glitter and pictures of computer-robots, one in a tux and one in a gown with a corsage, inviting her to the prom. She said yes, and everyone cheered.

Jacob and Hannah had a great time at the prom. His father drove them, and even wore a chauffeur's cap like a limo driver. They danced and joked around with their classmates. Later, when he walked her to her door, Jacob got nervous. He wanted to kiss her, but he was afraid she'd pull away. After an awkward silence, he asked her for a kiss. To his surprise, she leaned up and kissed him quickly, then in a swish of chiffon she was gone. Jacob smiled all the way home.

EMILY, 22

Emily couldn't wait to see her favorite staff member, Sarah. Being with Sarah always made her feel happy and excited. She got to the breakfast room as the staff changed shifts, but was surprised to see a new person, and no Sarah. The house head motioned Emily into her office.

"Where's Sarah? Is she okay?" Emily asked breathlessly.

"She's fine, but she's been transferred to another group home."

"But why?" Emily wailed. "She wouldn't go without saying goodbye to me!"

"Actually, you're the reason she moved. She felt your relationship with her was at risk of becoming inappropriate, and she was uncomfortable."

"What do you mean 'uncomfortable?' We're like, best friends!"

"No, Emily, you're not best friends. Sarah was a staff member and you're a resident. Sarah felt you were getting too attached, too affectionate, and hanging all over her. It started to seem like you were romantically attracted to her. Now, if you're a lesbian, there's nothing wrong with that, but a relationship with a staff member would be out of line."

"A lesbian?" Emily wondered where that idea came from. Was she a lesbian? She thought about Sarah. Would she like to hold hands with Sarah, or even kiss her? Maybe. Did she want to have sex with Sarah? No. What about with a guy? No! "I don't think I'm a lesbian. I'm not sure. I just really, really like Sarah. What's wrong with that?"

"Only the fact that she's a staff member and you're a resident. There are professional and ethical guidelines about staff-resident relationships, and Sarah felt you were becoming overly attached, so she asked for a transfer."

Emily was stunned. Had she completely misunderstood her special friendship with Sarah? She wandered back to her room in a daze.

Later, Ashley came looking for her to see if she was alright. Emily told her about Sarah leaving because of her, and how awful it felt. Ashley shared about her crush on a guy on staff when she first moved here, but she'd been so shy no one knew. Eventually, she got over it.

"So, you like guys, right?" Emily asked.

"Yeah, sure, I guess so. Don't you?"

"I really don't know. I don't want to fall in love with anyone and get all mushy. I just want to like everybody and be happy. I'm only in love with Alpeggy."

"Alpacorns. Who wouldn't be in love with them?" Ashley and Emily laughed and brought Alpeggy and Angelipaca down to sit at the breakfast table between them. She would have time to sort out her feelings later; there was no rush.

ZACH, 33

Crystal, in Zach's volunteer group, never went out for a beer after their shift. Zach realized he was disappointed each time she turned and walked to her car. The more time he spent with her, the more he respected her. She was smart, knowledgeable about issues, and she really cared about the country and the planet. That meant a lot to Zach. Why wouldn't she join them for a brew at the end of the evening?

Maybe she didn't drink, he thought. Maybe she'd been an alcoholic and couldn't be around beer. Or maybe she was an airline pilot for her day job and she couldn't drink when she was on call. Or maybe she hated beer. Or maybe she hated him. No, probably not that last one. Just because she didn't grab a beer with the rest of them didn't mean she hated Zach. He decided to ask her out for coffee to see if they could get to know each other better.

At their next volunteer shift, Zach found an excuse to go to the copier when Crystal was already there. He was careful to keep his distance so she wouldn't feel trapped. No need to creep her out or make her think he was a stalker or anything. He took a deep breath and went for it.

"Hey, Crystal. Do you want to grab a cup of coffee with me after we're done here?" There, he'd said it. He made it clear he was talking about coffee, not beer, and that it was an invitation to go with him, not a group thing. He let out his breath, waiting for her reply. She was quiet long enough for him to get even more nervous.

"Just coffee? Just the two of us?" she asked.

"Yeah, I was hoping to get to know you a little better, and you never join us for a beer."

"I don't like beer." She wrinkled her nose. "I don't really like coffee, either."

"Hot chocolate? Or soda. Whatever. But not beer. Or coffee." Zach started to stumble over his words, but he reined himself in and tried to breathe more slowly.

"Sure, hot chocolate sounds good," she said. "There's a place across the street. After our shift we can walk there together."

"Great, thanks, that will be great."

CHAPTER 19

Zach managed to get back to his station without falling over his feet. He was excited and surprised that she'd said yes.

They had a good time talking and laughing into the evening, and then he walked her to her car. She even suggested that they do this again, which he was already looking forward to.

MARIA, 45

Sofia kept showing Maria pictures of men from online dating sites. Maria couldn't care less, but she hated to be rude. Her friend was ready to meet someone and she thought Maria should, too, but Maria wasn't interested. She told Sofia to be careful, but Sofia knew all about internet dating safety. She wasn't about to meet someone at their place or invite them home. She met her dates at busy coffee shops. She even had a three-part exit route to make sure she wasn't followed: get on the freeway, get off to put gas in her car, and then back on the freeway heading for home. She tried to convince Maria to join her on her online dating adventure.

Maria had never been excited about dating in high school, and then she married her husband after a whirlwind courtship. She didn't really understand what anyone saw in the act of marital congress. It seemed embarrassing, undignified, and messy. The twins were her excuse to withdraw from the marriage bed. They needed her all the time, so she slept in the nursery. She was relieved when he stopped asking for sex and secretly glad when he finally filed for divorce. She only wondered what took him so long.

As she listened to Sofia share her excitement about meeting new men, Maria realized that not all women felt the way she did about such things. Perhaps she was simply asexual. No desire, no interest, no regret. Yes, asexuality suited her, and she wouldn't have it any other way.

ROBERT, 62

"Congratulations!" The room was crowded with family and friends, all helping them celebrate their anniversary. Robert clinked his champagne glass against his wife's and put his arm around her. How had he been so lucky? He could hardly remember his life before her.

When they met, she'd been the one to ask him out. Smart of her, he probably would've taken years to find the courage. Although she seemed shy, she was the one to smooth things out for him. Anytime he felt out of his depth at a party, feeling the warmth of her standing next to him, her hand on his arm, calmed him. She seemed to know when he needed to get out of a situation and helped them make a graceful exit. When their grandson had been diagnosed with autism, she didn't say a word about Robert having it, too, but she left plenty of books on the subject around the house. Of course, once he read about it, he knew that was him, too. She must have known. Now that he was diagnosed, they both seemed a bit more open. In the past he pretended he didn't need any help, and she pretended she wasn't helping. Sure, there were bumpy times when he misunderstood or overreacted to things and when her support felt like nagging, but they were doing okay. Maybe better than okay.

Sometimes he loved her so much, it was all he could do to keep from saying it out loud.

CHAPTER 19

"You look a million miles away. What are you thinking?" she asked.

"Me? Nothing," he said, and smiled. She smiled back, and the room erupted in applause as she stood on her tiptoes to give him a big kiss.

SPEAKING FOR OURSELVES

"When I was young, I was told that I was ugly and stupid, and no woman would ever want me. (I didn't know I had Asperger's back then.) I grew up feeling inadequate, so I didn't approach women at all. Eventually I met a young woman at church, the most beautiful woman I had ever seen, but I was too shy and nervous to approach her. One time she found out that I thought I was ugly. She scolded me and told me to stop putting myself down and believing what other people said. We started hanging out, and soon our friendship blossomed into a romantic relationship. After a year of dating, I proposed, she accepted, and we got married. It doesn't matter if you have a neurological disorder like I do. If God has someone for you, then it's meant to be."

— *Kato Foxx, artist and performer with Asperger's*

PART V
EMPLOYABILITY

—◦◦◦—

Bringing Home the Bucks

"Don't be afraid to be unusual because the skills unusual people have are often highly sought after."
— *Gavin Bollard, author, parent, and blogger with Asperger's*

"Skills make dreams happen ... They are constantly, and I do mean constantly, looking for people with the right skills. People that can get the job done."
— *Emi Iyalla, author*

CHAPTER 20
READY TO WORK

———

(Everybody Wants Somebody with Skills)

If you want a career you love, you'll need to develop the right skills for the job. Think SPACE: Self, People, Authority, Communication, and Employment. Master these to be on the right path.

Self-Skills

The self-skills you'll need include self-awareness, self-presentation, and self-control.

Self-Awareness

When you have self-awareness, you think about yourself and how others see you. At home, you might do your best thinking while lounging with your feet on the desk, but if you sat the same way at work, you'd look lazy or disrespectful. One of Temple Grandin's and Sean Barron's ten unwritten rules of social relationships is "People Act Differently in Public than They Do in Private." People with self-awareness skills know the difference and act accordingly.

You can develop your self-awareness skills by consciously asking yourself what other people might think about you based on what you do or say. What kind of a first impression do you make? Are you sending signals to show you're open to conversation, or are you turned away? Slouching with your head down and arms crossed may ward off strangers on public transportation, but the same posture at work looks uncommunicative, like you're not a team player. Becoming more aware of yourself and how others see you is an important skill to develop.

Self-Presentation

Self-presentation is crucial. If you, your clothes, or hair are unkempt, it won't matter if you're good at your job. Nobody wants to work next to someone who stinks or has hair like a greasy rat's nest. Another of Grandin's and Barron's unwritten rules is "Fitting In is Often Tied to Looking and Sounding Like You Fit In." When you fit in visually, people are more open to what you have to say. You might think, "They should listen to me because I'm smart and I have great ideas." Ideally, sure, but people seldom respect those whose presentation is too far outside the norm or who look or smell dirty.

One way you can develop self-presentation skills is to notice how coworkers present themselves. Model your own presentation on those around you. If there's a range of styles from blue jeans to suits, don't go straight to the most casual look. Dress for the job you want and choose a presentation that is slightly above your level without being extreme. If your co-workers in the mail room wear jeans and your supervisor wears slacks and a buttoned shirt, don't wear a suit and tie. Dress like the person just one step above you in the chain of command. That doesn't mean you can't be comfortable or have your own unique style, just avoid being extreme.

Self-Control

Self-control may be the most important self-skill of all. If you raise your voice or argue when your supervisor corrects you, it shows a lack of self-control. If you melt down, cry, or freeze when something unexpected happens, you could be replaced. If you lose your temper easily, failing to control yourself could get you fired. Someone who can't function under stress will not be seen as a valuable worker. The risks are too great for most companies to keep an employee who is seen as out of control.

If lack of self-control has been a major problem in your life, consider seeking help. Talk to your doctor. A counselor, behavior analyst, or anger management coach can help. If you don't have a serious problem, go back to Chapter Thirteen, "Self Management," and create your own plan.

People Skills

In addition to self-skills, having good people skills is vital in any career. Getting along with colleagues and customers will help you get and keep your job. This includes practicing common courtesy and tact. If you pride yourself on your brutal honesty, learn to be truthful without being brutal. For instance, if a co-worker shows you an ugly baby picture, be kind. Words like "precious" or "priceless," mean of great value, and "adorable" means able to be adored, which is certainly true. Keeping negative thoughts to yourself is an excellent people skill.

Another people skill is to avoid commenting on anyone's body. Even complimenting a woman on her blouse calls attention to her chest area, which is inappropriate. If you want to give a compliment, stick to their talents and abilities, not their physical attributes. Beware if someone asks, "Do these pants make my behind look fat?" Under no circumstances should you say, "Of course not. It's your behind that makes the pants look fat." Funny does not excuse rudeness. Try a noncommittal response, such as, "You always look fine," then return the topic to work.

Put yourself in someone else's shoes to see their perspective. You can practice while watching TV by imagining what each character is thinking. What's their motivation? Do their words match their feelings? Any underlying nonverbal cues? Practice improves people skills.

Authority Skills

Unless you're self-employed and have no supervisors or customers, you need to respond respectfully to authority figures. Some people find it difficult to work with a supervisor who's not as smart as they are. If you're highly intelligent, it'll be difficult to find a job working for someone you recognize as your intellectual superior. However, it's not at all smart to let people know you think you're smarter. Don't patronize or imply they won't understand. Don't purposefully use big, pretentious words, but don't talk down to them, either. Always be respectful. If a supervisor says something you think is wrong, don't call them out in front of others. If it's important, speak to them privately later. If it's minor, like saying, "Around the beginning of the month ..." don't correct them with, "Actually, it was on the twelfth of the month." Nit picking will make you look like a jerk, and you're not a jerk, are you? Knowing when to keep your opinions to yourself is an important skill, especially when dealing with those in authority.

This is a vital skill in all of life, not just at work, but also when interacting with law enforcement. Be mindful of how they may perceive your attitude. Some people act like nonverbal expressions of exasperation or contempt are not real communication and that they should be judged on their words alone, but this is not the case. If you sigh heavily, roll your eyes, and use a sarcastic tone of voice when talking to someone in authority, you will be judged harshly. Work on curbing these signals. When you show respect, you're more likely to be respected.

Communication Skills

In their book, *Autism and Employment*, Lisa Tew and Diane Zajac wrote, "Strong social-communication skills help individuals to interact productively and positively with others for any job." All communication has a social component; it doesn't happen in a vacuum. Good verbal and nonverbal skills are necessary. If your boss gives you a project and you walk away without replying or making eye contact, they may assume you're ignoring them and refusing the assignment. Sure, you were already planning a thousand brilliant ideas in your head to make the project successful, but it won't matter if you get fired before you even start.

When your boss gives you an assignment, first make (or fake) eye contact.

Second, reflect back what you think they said, such as, "I see, you want me to (summarize assignment), and you need it by (due date). Is that right?" Understand their expectations. Later, send an email recapping the conversation so you'll have a written record.

Third, let them know that you'll get right to work on it. This is also the time to share your excitement if you think it's a great project, and/or to let them know if you might need support to get it done. This is not the time to make general negative or pessimistic remarks; give it a chance. If you encounter problems, present them with possible solutions. Don't badmouth the project without offering strategies to make it better.

One of the most difficult types of communication at work is when the boss gives you constructive criticism. This can be hard to take, but it's important to accept it well. Put yourself in your employer's shoes. Would you rather have a worker who listens and tries to improve, or one who's stubborn, argumentative, and can't take correction? Be the one who accepts criticism graciously and you'll make your boss's job easier.

Employment Skills

The employment skills you need depend on the job you want. Whatever the field, it's up to you to get those skills. Some careers require a high school diploma, a college degree, or special training. Check out colleges, adult education courses, and online courses. Don't invest in a school unless you're sure it's reputable. Be smart and check your options before committing.

Another way to get employment skills is to volunteer or intern in your field. You'll not only gain valuable experience for your resumé, there's a chance you may be offered a job. There's no guarantee, but an internship lets the employer see first-hand what kind of an employee you'd be. If you do an exemplary job with a positive attitude and strong work ethic, you might get hired.

Not all of your skills may be marketable or may be difficult to monetize. Everyone wants a job testing video games or writing comic books, but those jobs are rare. Your personal passion may be better used as a side hustle for extra pocket money or for stress relief, while your day job supplies steady income and, hopefully, benefits.

Whatever your dream career, learn the skills and get the training you need.

Now that we've explored SPACE, read how our five characters worked on employability.

JACOB, 18

"You're wrong. Learn English!" Jacob didn't raise his hand, he just called his teacher out.

"Excuse me, Jacob, but in this class we raise our hands to speak."

"No, 'we' don't. You never raise your hand. And you're wrong when you use 'they' for one person. 'They' is plural. If you don't know the basics of the English language, maybe you shouldn't be teaching." Jacob fumed all the way to the office, referral slip in hand. He was still mad when he got to his counselor's office. "He should be thanking me for helping him do his job, not sending me to the office! What an idiot!"

"That's never going to happen, Jacob. You were in the wrong here."

"But I was right! 'They' is plural, and he was using it in the singular!"

"Actually, he was correct. The singular 'they' as a gender-neutral option is accepted usage going back to the Elizabethan era. But the important thing here is your behavior. You're not that teacher's supervisor, you're a student. When you call him out, it's not only rude and inappropriate, it is insubordination."

"Well, maybe he shouldn't be teaching if he can't handle students telling the truth."

"It's not for you to decide who should be teaching. Your teacher, on the other hand, does get to decide who stays in his classroom, and you're out."

"That's not fair! He can't kick me out, I need that class to graduate!"

"Teachers can suspend a student for disruption. Tomorrow, instead of going to his room, you will report here and do the work for the day independently."

"Just one day?"

"As of now, just one day, but you need learn to control your outbursts. If you disagree with a teacher, write a letter, don't insult someone who's grading you in a required course."

"I didn't think about that."

"Your case manager will work with you on self-control with authority figures."

"I don't need that. I already took social skills, I got an A. It's one of my strengths."

"Not according to your behavior, it's not. If you pulled this at work, you'd be fired."

Jacob never thought about that. What if he had a boss as stupid as this teacher? Would he mouth off and get fired? He decided he'd better learn to control himself with authority figures.

CHAPTER 20

Emily was proud to have an artist's table at the local crafts fair. She'd made so many alpacorns she didn't have room for them all, and when someone suggested she sell them, she was flattered. If she sold some, she'd have room for all the others she wanted to make.

She rearranged them again, making room at the front and center for Alpopcorn, the one with curly white and yellow hair that looked like a pile of buttered popcorn on top of his head. She was sure someone would buy him.

Pretty soon, a guy paused at her table and looked at her wares. Emily jumped up and started chatting happily, telling him each alpacorn's name and detailed back stories. She had to leave her table for a moment to follow him since she hadn't finished explaining alpacorn culture. He almost ran the other way; maybe he had some emergency to rush off to.

When she got back to her table she found several more shoppers, but the more she talked to them, the faster they left. Emily was sure if she could share the joy of alpacorn ownership they wouldn't leave empty-handed. Who wouldn't want to own one of these adorable little guys?

Emily left her friend to watch her table while she grabbed lunch in the refreshment tent. As she ate, she pondered each encounter. What had happened when they came to her table, and more importantly, right before they left? Each time, the shoppers had been wandering around the fair looking at many different things before they got to her. They glanced at her alpacorns, and she immediately started talking, non-stop. Maybe that was too much pressure.

Emily decided to take a different approach. She got out a book to read, to keep herself occupied so she wouldn't come on so strong. She noticed that people seemed to stay at her table a little longer, but no one actually bought anything, either. Was she maybe too unapproachable, with her nose in a book? For the rest of the afternoon she put the book away and brought out her sewing basket. She worked on a new alpacorn, but each time someone came to her table she looked up, smiled, and said hello. She didn't push information on them, but she answered questions and let them see her project. She actually made a couple of sales! It was so exciting!

When she finished that alpacorn, she noticed sellers standing at their tables instead of sitting. It put them at eye level with customers She tried it. If they seemed to be pausing longer than most, she asked if they had any questions. She made five more sales!

While her day at the fair wasn't a huge success financially, Emily had learned a thing or two. Coming on too strong and following shoppers to talk scared people away. Reading a book and ignoring them flopped. Two things seemed to increase sales: working on an alpacorn so they could see the process, and standing by her table being open to questions or comments. Self-awareness of how other people saw her was a good skill for her to learn.

ZACH, 33

Zach read the email from the temple trustee. It said that the fire department would contact him for the annual fire extinguisher

CHAPTER 20

inspection. They wanted Zach to go with the inspector through all of the buildings, unlock each room, and wait while they inspected the fire extinguishers and attached certification tags. When they were all done, Zach should make sure all the rooms were locked again and notify the trustee that it had been completed.

No problem. When he got the call, Zach arranged it for the next day. He followed the inspector to each room, saw that each fire extinguisher had been tagged, and then locked up.

Then Zach went to the offices. The rabbi's door was open and he was reading scripture.

"Everything's all taken care of," Zach said from the doorway.

"Pardon?" The rabbi looked up and adjusted his glasses.

"All of the fire extinguishers have been inspected. All taken care of," Zach repeated.

"Well, that's nice, thank you." The rabbi returned to his reading.

Two weeks later, he was called into the office by the trustee. He looked stern and said, "Zach, I'm sorry, but this arrangement doesn't seem to be working out. We need a caretaker who can be responsible to take on assignments in a timely manner. When you ignored my email about the fire extinguisher inspection, you put us at legal risk for noncompliance."

"What do you mean? I didn't ignore it, I took care of it the next day." Zach was confused and concerned. It sounded like they were going to fire him, and he'd be homeless and jobless.

"I sent you an email request, and you never replied. I asked you to tell me when it was taken care of, and I have heard nothing."

"The day after you sent that email, they came and did all of the inspections, put on all of the tags. Then I came straight over to the office and told the rabbi it was taken care of."

"You told the rabbi? Why would you tell the rabbi about fire extinguishers?"

"Well, I came over to the office, and the rabbi was here. So I told him."

"You told the rabbi instead of telling me, as I had asked?" He seemed incredulous.

Zach looked down, embarrassed. It had made sense to him at the time, but now it seemed foolish. "I guess I thought he would tell you, since you all work together. I made a mistake. I should have told you, not the rabbi."

"That is correct. A rabbi is not a message boy. From now on, if I send you an email, please reply immediately that you have received it and will act on it. And if I ask you to get back to me, do not go through the rabbi. He has enough to do."

Zach was relieved he hadn't been fired. He thanked the trustee and promised to do better. Being the temple caretaker wasn't his long-term career goal, but he'd better improve his communication skills if he wanted to move up in the world.

MARIA, 45

Maria needed a job. She wouldn't get spousal support forever. Although her needs were simple and her overhead low, she needed an income of her own. The problem was, she hated the idea of working with other people. The thought of it made her anxious, and she had to watch her sloths. After she felt calmer, she asked the internet about jobs that could be done from home. There was telemarketing, but Maria didn't like talking on the phone. Finally, she found the ideal job for her: editing and proofreading from home. There was a small, local self-publishing company whose authors often needed help with editing and proofreading. The publishers would email the editor books to review, and correct grammar, punctuation, and word usage.

Maria thought she was perfect for this job: she had strong attention to detail and extensive knowledge of the rules of good writing. She was often bothered by errors she saw in online posts and wished she could correct them. Shouldn't everyone know the difference between your and you're, or there, their, and they're? She would be happy to share her knowledge and get paid for it, all while working at home. But was she good enough to be a professional? She wasn't sure. Maria went online and took several free proofreading tests. She discovered that she was, indeed, very good at this. She had the skills, now she would pay the bills.

ROBERT, 62

Time was not Robert's friend. There was too much of it since he retired. Often, he felt like he was wasting time, spinning his wheels and getting under his wife's feet. He missed having a job to go to. Maybe it was time to find one.

Robert looked online for television repairman opportunities, but nowadays they were calling themselves television technicians, not repairmen. He didn't see himself as a technician, and he hated those newfangled flat-screen liquid-crystal-display (LCD) thingies. He knew how to repair a good old cathode ray tube (CRT) set, but you could hardly find them anymore. Still, he figured there must be some people left who held onto their old sets, and they'd need to be repaired if they broke. How could he find them and put his skills to use?

He decided to do an online search. There were a lot of big store chains where you could buy a TV, but when it broke, they just wanted to sell you a new one. Finally he found a small, family operated repair store. Maybe they could use him part time. He was no good on the phone, so he decided to drive on over there and see what the store was like.

Robert felt at home as soon as he walked in. It was cramped and dusty with shelves of used TVs and radios, floor to ceiling. He looked around, then approached the guy at the counter.

"Do you do television repairs on old CRT sets?" he asked.

"Well, we don't get much call for that these days. I mostly see the LCDs. If you need one fixed it might take a while, because my guy that handles those is on a cross-country RV trip. He's mostly retired, but when he gets back I can have him take a look at it for you."

"No, I do repairs myself. I'm retired from it, but I guess retirement isn't my cup of tea. I was hoping you needed some help. I wouldn't charge much, whatever you think is fair. You'd be doing my wife a favor if you'd get me out from under her feet." Both men chuckled.

"Well, sir, I'll give you a shot. Got an old set in the back, see what you can do with it."

Robert took the old set apart, tightened what needed tightening, and fixed what needed fixing. When he put it back together and turned it on, it worked like a charm. The owner said he could put him to work if an old set came in. This worked for Robert, especially since the owner said he could come hang out between jobs if he liked. For Robert, having skills and finding a place that needed those skills got him back on the road to employment.

SPEAKING FOR OURSELVES

"When I first started thinking about selling my art at conventions, I feared my work wasn't good enough. I also worried about the social aspect. Then I realized that most of the people at these cons share interests with me, or they wouldn't be there. They'd be glad to see artwork of their favorite characters, even if it wasn't perfect. Also, a lot of them were shy and had difficulty communicating, too, so I shouldn't worry so much. I learned that actively socializing and using aggressive sales tactics with potential customers actually harms sales. Being visible, standing behind the table, and using relaxed body language, on the other hand, benefits sales."

— Noel, autistic artist

CHAPTER 21
INTERVIEW SKILLS

—————◆————

(Talk the Talk)

O ne of the first steps down the road toward employment is usually a job interview. Most people feel anxious about interviews, so if you're nervous, you're not alone. It's one thing to write your skills and experience in a resumé or application, but to talk about it face-to-face is different. There are things you can do to make a good first impression. These include paying attention to the five Ps: be Prepared, be Professional, be Punctual, be Positive, and provide a Portfolio.

Be Prepared

In his book, *Preparing for Life*, Dr. Jed Baker wrote, "it is crucial to develop a plan for having a successful interview." There are several important steps in the preparation process.

First, do your homework. Research the company you are interviewing with. What is their primary purpose? What is their mission statement? Can you get behind it? Coming in knowing what they're all about will give you an advantage.

Second, think about the questions they might ask you and how you'll answer. Most interviews include an open-ended invitation for you to talk about yourself. Stick to relevant, professional information, things that will help them to realize you'd be a good fit for their job. Don't go into detail about your family, pets, vacations, or hobbies. They'll probably also ask about your strengths and weaknesses. Again, only share things that would affect your ability to do this job. If you're an expert in Tae Kwon Do, it won't help you get a data processing job.

Third, practice interviewing. If you can find a mock interview class, coach, or online interview prep service, consider using it. Alternately, enlist friends and family to set up a mock interview experience for you. Remember to pretend that they're your real interviewers and behave as you would in the real thing. With practice comes familiarity. The more you practice, the more comfortable and less stressed you'll feel in your real interview.

Fourth, relax. Use breathing to reduce anxiety. Before you get called in, when you're alone, exhale fully through your mouth so that it makes a slight "whoosh." Then close your mouth and inhale gently through your nose while counting to four. Hold your breath while counting to seven. On the eighth count, whoosh your breath out through your mouth again. Repeat the process, keeping your shoulders relaxed. If you're alone while you wait, consider striking a power pose, hands on your hips, feet apart and planted firmly, chin up, shoulders down. You should feel like a super hero doing this pose. You are strong, capable, and ready for anything!

Be Professional

You want to be seen as a serious professional who is the best person for the job. This means your physical presentation, including

CHAPTER 21

hygiene and clothing choices, should be impeccable. This is the time to dress like a boss. Avoid hats, shirts or jewelry with words, or extreme clothing; opt for simplicity over flash. By dressing nicely, you show that you're serious and professional.

You also want to be professional in your attitude. Greet your interviewers with your head up, looking toward their eyes, and shake hands. The shake should be firm without being painful, accompanied by a single, unexaggerated, up-and-down movement. Don't make the mistake of shaking hands weakly, putting your fingertips into their offered hands, or too powerfully, crushing their hands in your grip. Also, release promptly so that the handshake does not become a lengthy ordeal. If you are extremely uncomfortable shaking hands and cannot do this in an interview, be brief in your refusal. You might put your hands together, incline your head towards them, and if they still put out their hand to shake, say, "I don't shake hands, but I am happy to meet you." Then move on without discussing it further unless specifically asked.

When seated, remain upright with your feet down or crossed neatly, close to your chair. Keep your back straight, shoulders down, head up, oriented toward your interviewers. Look at the person asking you a question, and then let your glance move from person to person when answering; don't focus on the one across from you, ignoring the others. Do not slouch, put your feet on any furniture, lean over sideways, stick your feet out in front of you, or hold your head down so that they see the top of your head rather than your face.

When speaking, modulate your volume, neither too loud nor too soft. Many autistic people don't realize that their normal voice is louder or quieter than everyone else's. Ask people who know you well if you need to fix the volume, and then practice hitting the right note.

Be Punctual

The last thing you want to do is to arrive at your interview late and have your potential boss waiting for you. They'll think that if they hired you, you'd be late for work, too. Plan how you will get there. Will you drive, get a ride, take public transportation? Consider making a practice run. How long should it take? How long might it take if there were extra traffic, or construction, or an accident? It's better to be early than late, so plan to be early enough that you wouldn't be late even if all of these things happen. Find a nearby coffee shop where you can relax, read a book, and enjoy a cup of soothing herbal tea if you get there way too early. If you do this, be sure to set an alarm or keep your watch visible so you don't miss your time.

Be Positive

This is the time to put your best foot forward. When they ask for your strengths, honestly tell them the things you are good at that apply to this job. If you are an outstanding Dungeon Master (DM) for your Dungeons & Dragons group, think about the skills that go in to being a good DM. Is it your ability to research and track information from various sources? Is it your attention to detail? Your respect for rules and standard operating procedures? Or is it your strength in focusing on the task at hand? These are all important strengths that could be important in many careers. These skills are what you want to talk about, not D&D.

CHAPTER 21

When employers ask about your weaknesses, don't disguise a brag as a fake weakness, like saying, "My weaknesses are that I work too hard and I give too much." This is not fooling anyone, and it can put them off. Instead, have a realistic idea of your actual weaknesses, and be prepared to share briefly. What the interviewer is looking for is to find out if you have the self-awareness to recognize your weaknesses and the strength to have dealt with or overcome them. You might consider saying something like, "Because of my strong attention to detail, I have sometimes missed social cues, and I may even come across as socially awkward. I've been working on this and I welcome feedback as I continue to develop my skills." Any time you share a weakness which does not affect the position you are interviewing for, and you describe how you have overcome it or turned it into a strength, this can work in your favor. Just be careful not to share a weakness that would make you wrong for this job; for example, don't say you hate talking on the phone when applying for a telemarketing position.

It's at this point in the interview that some people choose to disclose their disability. The decision to disclose is a personal one, with pros and cons on both sides, as we saw in Chapter Fifteen. Whether or not you disclose that you're on the autism spectrum, remember to stay positive and end on an uplifting note. Thank them for their time, smile, and shake hands again as you leave. Send a thank-you note or email later thanking them again for taking the time to interview you.

Provide a Portfolio

Let your work speak for you. Even if the job you want doesn't involve a physical product, a portfolio can still be a useful part of your interview process. Especially if talking about yourself is not a great strength of yours, your portfolio can give interviewers something tangible.

Make sure your portfolio is neat and easy to navigate. A binder with plastic page protectors, rather than a file with random papers sticking out of it, can set a professional tone. So, what should you include in your job interview portfolio?

Start with an introduction cover page, including your name, contact information, and the position you are seeking. This may change if you are applying for a range of different kinds of jobs, and it's important to change your portfolio to reflect the current interview. Some people add a picture of themselves to remind interviewers who you are when they make their decisions.

Next, include your updated resumé showing relevant training and experience.

Be sure to have three references, people they can ask about you. If you've had a job before and you left on positive terms, list your previous boss or bosses. If you had a professor or teacher in school whose course is relevant to this job, you can list that person. Someone else that you've known a long time and can speak to your character, who is not related to you, could also be listed here. Do not list your parents, spouse, siblings, other close relatives, or friends you've never worked with. Be sure to ask each of them if they're willing to be a reference and ask what contact information they want you to share. Include any formal letters of recommendation here.

CHAPTER 21

If the job you're looking for is in a field such as graphic art, writing, design, or photography, include your best work samples. You want to let your work shine. If you worked on a special project and you have photographs showing your participation, include them with a brief description of the project. Be aware of others in the photographs, however, and do not share recognizable images of others without their permission. If you did a project at a school and your photos have children in them, find one where the children's backs are to the camera, or find a way to crop them out. It's not okay to share other people's pictures without their permission. Finally, do not put in anything that is less than your best. This is where your work can make up for any awkwardness you may have felt in the face-to-face interview.

On the last page of your portfolio, repeat your contact information and thank them for the opportunity. If possible, make copies and leave a portfolio with your interviewers to read later.

Let's see how our five characters managed the five Ps of the interview process.

JACOB, 18

Finally, a class worth going to. Last semester of his senior year, Jacob had a class called IRL Prep: Survival Skills for Life After Graduation. It covered a lot of topics about how to do things for yourself and become independent, instead of expecting parents or teachers to do everything for you. Jacob thought that most kids would rather do things themselves, anyway.

The final project was all about getting a job. They created portfolios and practiced telling the class about them. They watched videos of mock interviews. The teacher even brought back a former student who talked about how she got her first job. Finally, they held mock interviews. Jacob had a love-hate relationship with them. He hated getting in front of the class and answering questions; it made him sweat and forget how to words put together. But the more he did it, the easier it got. Eventually he could do the interview without feeling sick, his mouth as dry as the Sahara. He just did it. He answered the questions without losing his train of thought. He made eye contact and smiled, but not too much. He shook hands without squeezing too hard or holding on too long. With repetition and feedback, the process was becoming natural to him. That's when he started loving the mock interviews. Unlike algebra, this was one class he'd use.

EMILY, 22

Everybody in Emily's group home had chores; they worked together to keep the house running smoothly. There were meal teams that took turns planning, shopping, cooking, and cleaning up after meals. There were upkeep teams that took turns vacuuming and mopping and cleaning the kitchen. Everybody cleaned their own bedroom and bathroom.

There were also rotating extra jobs. The front porch caretaker position was opening up at the end of the month, and Emily was interested. She could use the extra cash for materials to make more stuffed alpacorns.

Emily filled out the application carefully, using her best block printing, and she turned it in to the office before the deadline. The next step was an interview. She put on a nice dress and

CHAPTER 21

knocked on the office door at the time she had been told to come in. The house manager and another staff member interviewed her. They asked her questions about how long she'd lived there and what she liked best and least about the group home. Emily was a natural-born optimist, and she had plenty of good things to say. After a few minutes she caught herself going on and on, without letting them ask the next question. She quieted down and controlled her impulse to chat.

They showed her the employee binder with the job requirements and checklists to fill out. The front porch caretaker watered the hanging plants, swept the porch and steps, dusted the end tables, and shook the dust out of the chair pillows. There were daily tasks and weekly tasks, with boxes to write in the dates she did them. It looked pretty clear and easy to understand. When they asked if she thought she could handle the responsibility, she was sure she could. She smiled and shook their hands enthusiastically before she left. Emily had a really good feeling about this!

ZACH, 33

Zach liked living at the temple and being the caretaker. It was easy enough to unlock buildings and lock them back up at night, and to make rounds to make sure everything was fine. He knew someday he'd want a career, more than a part-time job for free rent, but he wasn't sure what he wanted to do. One of the guys he volunteered with worked for a nonprofit corporation that provided services for disabled adults. He seemed to like it, and Zach wondered what it would be like to do that kind of work. When he asked his friend, he learned that they had an opening for an assistant. It was part time and didn't pay much, but he could keep his job at the temple. A letter of recommendation was required, so Zach decided to ask his rabbi for one.

As he sat in the rabbi's office, Zach thought back to his interview for the job he held now, sitting in this very office. It wasn't a formal interview, more of a conversation about the job requirements, so Zach hadn't been particularly nervous. Interviewing with a stranger for the non-profit job was different, though. It made him anxious. He asked the rabbi why he had hired him in the first place. What had Zach said or done right that got him the job?

The rabbi told him it wasn't anything in particular, but that he'd known Zach since he was in Hebrew school and was glad to see him return to the temple as a young adult. He always saw potential in Zach, but he also knew that it wouldn't be easy for a shy, awkward man to get a job. The rabbi wanted to give him a boost with a job and a way to move out of his parents' home. Now, he wrote Zach a glowing recommendation, addressing his character and integrity as well as his capability. Zach thanked him, and admitted he was afraid of messing up the interview.

"Zach, Zach, Zach." The rabbi put his hand on his shoulder. "Al tira. Have no fear. Remember that the person across the desk is another child of God, as you are. Christians, Muslims, Jews, we all worship the same God. Remember that you are formed from the same dust, and you need not fear. But remember this as well, for this also is important," he added.

"What is it, rabbi?"

"Get a better haircut."

Zach smiled. "I will," he said, "and thank you."

CHAPTER 21

Maria was excited about a career as an at-home proofreader. The only problem was going to the office for the interview. It made her nervous, but she'd have to if she wanted this job.

On the day of her interview, Maria dressed carefully. Her dress was dark blue, with a high neck and a hemline that reached below her knees, and she wore simple black flats. She wanted to appear professional, and she didn't want anything she wore to call attention to itself or be distracting. She was hoping for, and achieved, anonymity of presentation.

She arrived a bit early for her appointment time and waited in the foyer to be called in to the office. It was a relief to be early rather than late. Maria hated being late for anything.

When she was called in, she saw the interviewers were dressed more casually than she was. The men wore slacks and polo shirts and the women wore tasteful trousers with brightly colored blouses and chunky jewelry. They made Maria feel at home and welcomed. She'd taken the editing test they sent her, and they were impressed with her skills. They hired her on the spot and told her she could work from home except for the required monthly staff meetings.

Maria was elated! It seemed like the perfect job for her. By being punctual, demonstrating her skills, and paying attention to her personal presentation, Maria showed herself to be professional and the best person for the job.

ROBERT, 62

After about a week of hanging out at the TV repair shop, the owner told Robert that his CRT guy wasn't coming back. He and his wife liked the RV life so much they were making it permanent. That left a part-time opening.

Robert was definitely interested. They scheduled an interview, and he even put on a tie for it. He felt silly, since they usually wore T-shirts and baseball caps around the store, but an interview was different, somehow. More formal.

The owner managed not to laugh when he saw Robert in a tie, but he said it showed gumption; he must really want the job if he was willing to wear that choker. The interview itself didn't take long. Because he'd already seen what Robert could do, the owner didn't have many questions and was willing to hire him based on his on-the-job performance. That was a huge relief to Robert, because he knew he wasn't so great with small talk. By demonstrating what he could do on the job and showing he was serious by dressing up for the interview, he was hired.

CHAPTER 22
YOU'RE HIRED! NOW WHAT?

(How to Succeed in Business)

You've got the job. Congratulations! Now what?

Well, the obvious answer is, do the job. This means putting into daily practice everything you've learned along the road.

Remember the five Ps of interviewing? You'll still need four of them: be Punctual, be Professional, be Prepared, and be Positive. Each of these four Ps is slightly different at work, as compared to the interview process.

Be Punctual on the Job

Being punctual is important in any career. You're being paid to be on the job on time. If getting out of bed in the morning is hard for you, there are things you can do. No, not asking a parent or spouse to get you out the door. Now that you're an adult, that responsibility is yours. Here are a few tips:

1. *Set multiple alarms.* If you're one of those people who find alarms jarring, find one that's calming but will still wake

you up. You may need to invest in another device or an app if there are no sound options on your phone that work for you. Some people prefer having light come on gradually in the room, or having the bed vibrate. Try putting an alarm clock across the room so you can't turn it off without getting up. If you know you need extra time to adjust to being awake, then plan that into your schedule. Set your first alarm early enough that you can hit snooze and still get out the door on time.

2. *Get plenty of sleep the night before.* This can be tricky if you struggle with sleep, as do many autistic people. Most adults need seven to nine hours of sleep a night, although your need may be slightly different. Document how you feel after a night of only five or six hours of sleep, or after sleeping ten to eleven hours.

   Once you know how much sleep you need, count backward from the time you need to get up to see what time you should go to sleep the night before. If you take an hour to wind down before you actually fall asleep, add that hour in. Once you know what time you need to go to bed, remind yourself to do it. This is another time when a phone alarm or app can help you. Research sleep hygiene and put into practice the tips that are most helpful for you.

3. *Make a rule for yourself.* If you are the kind of person who complies with rules, make one that serves you. The rule might be to only hit snooze twice.

4. *Reward yourself.* If getting a coffee on your way to work is in your budget, then plan to reward yourself with a cup of your favorite brew. Only do this when you have allowed plenty of time to pick it up on your way. If you're running late, make do with the coffee at work and plan to get up earlier the next day. Use whatever makes you happy as your reward. Keep track of every day that you arrive on time, and at the end of the week or month, if you arrived on time every workday, celebrate your success.

Don't expect your boss to notice when you're on time, or to be praised for what is a normal part of your job. However, if you arrive late to work, it will be noticed. Be ready to do what it takes to arrive on time every day.

Be Professional in the Workplace

For your interview, you probably dressed up. Once you have the job, the dress code may (or may not) be more relaxed. Notice how other people at your level of employment dress. Present yourself professionally at a level commensurate with or only slightly above your position. There are companies that specialize in making clothing that looks professional but feels comfortable. Find what's best for you.

You may have a strong preference for wearing the same outfit every day. Don't do it. Even if you have five identical shirts or dresses and are wearing a different, clean one every day, people might think you're wearing the same, unwashed outfit. If you've found a comfortable piece of clothing, buy it in every color rather than wearing the identical piece all week.

If your office has an established casual Friday, make sure you know what that means. You don't want to show up on your first Friday in yoga pants, a T-shirt, and flip flops only to find that everyone else is wearing dress slacks and jacket but no tie. Also, not every company even has casual Friday. If you work with customers or attend meetings with higher-ups all week, you probably won't have casual Friday. Don't assume Friday will be different from other days.

Be Prepared at Work

If you've been given a work assignment and it's time to present your results to your boss, make sure you've done your homework and prepared everything that is expected. Being prepared means knowing what's expected, and not being caught off guard.

Be Positive Around the Office

The optimistic employee whose glass is half full will be appreciated. The negative one who's overly critical may find people avoiding them, or even be passed over for promotions.

If you are anxious by nature, work on channeling your anxiety into positivity. When you start to feel fearful, think about what that's like for you. Is your heart pounding, your breathing faster? Can you feel increased blood flow or an adrenaline rush? All of these are your body trying to take care of you. If your body thinks you're in danger, it will rally to prepare you for battle. Tell yourself, "My body is working to support me. It's ready for anything, but I'm okay."

CHAPTER 22

Try reframing your emotions using different words to describe how you feel. Instead of thinking, "I'm nervous," tell yourself, "I'm excited." The physical response of excitement is almost identical to that of anxiety. Your attitude may imperceptibly change as you use more positive words or phrases to label what's going on inside of you.

When it's time to talk, ask yourself three questions. Is it kind? Is it true? Is it necessary? If your answer is yes to all three of these questions, then go ahead and speak up. People who say whatever comes into their heads without filtering their thoughts come across as rude. By choosing your words carefully, you can put a positive spin on what you share at work. You can always go home and vent to your dog or SO, but don't vent at work. Keep it positive and upbeat.

When you're punctual, professional, prepared, and positive, you're on the road to success in your new job. Let's see how our five fictional characters did.

JACOB, 18

Jacob was excited to get a part-time job at a local coffee drive-through. His work-study teacher helped him with the application process, and he was glad he'd done so many mock interviews. He was proud to wear his official work polo shirt when he showed up on his first day.

"You're late," his supervisor said as soon as he walked in.

Jacob was confused. "I don't think I'm late," he said.

"You start at 3:30, and it's 3:45 now. You're late."

"Oh, yeah, but it takes me fifteen minutes to get here from

school, so that's why." Jacob thought he had cleared that up.

"Your shift starts at 3:30. That means you are at the window ready to take your first order at 3:30. Arrive at least five minutes before that. We don't pay you to drive here."

Jacob felt his face go hot. He felt so stupid. After lunch he'd hung out with the guys, bragging about his job, and he left school at 3:30 sharp. Why had he assumed his work day started with leaving for work? Now that he thought about it, it made no sense. Would someone who worked an hour away get paid for driving an hour? Of course not. He felt mortified.

"It won't happen again," he mumbled, and he quickly got started.

"Good."

Jacob got off on the wrong foot because of his own misunderstanding. He promised himself he would never be late again. He knew plenty of other people would love to have his job, and he wouldn't let his boss down again. From then on, Jacob was fifteen minutes early to every shift. His workday started out better when he wasn't rushed. Being punctual was not only important to his boss, it was important to Jacob, too.

EMILY, 22

The first day Emily started her new job as front porch caretaker, she was so excited! She hummed as she watered plants and swept and dusted. She carefully filled in and initialed the form in her employee binder.

The next week, she almost forgot about it entirely. She just wasn't used to thinking about it, and the excitement of the first day had lessened. She'd make sure she didn't forget again.

In her cell phone she set reminder alarms, then she set more alarms in case she missed the first one. She knew she had a tendency to get distracted. Since there wasn't a set time that her job had to be done, it would be too easy for her to keep putting it off until she forgot about it. For the first alarm, a snippet from a favorite song would tell her to rise up. An hour after that, another song snippet would remind her not to throw away her shot. If she blew it, she could get fired.

She also found it helped to prepare by putting the watering can and the dust cloths in the same closet with the broom she'd use to sweep. When everything was together, it was easy.

For Emily, using prompts on her phone to keep her punctual and preparing her materials in advance made it easier for her to get the job done.

ZACH, 33

During his first week at the nonprofit, Zach noticed that every time he started talking on one of his topics, it would get quiet. He was giving in to the temptation to lecture about something he cared about, but maybe not everyone there shared his feelings. Also, it started to sound like he was complaining all the time. That wasn't the impression he wanted to give. He'd better change this habit so he wouldn't put people off with a lot of negative venting.

The next day, he wore three large rubber bands around his wrist. They weren't tight enough to hurt, but he was aware of them. The purpose was to remind himself to ask three questions before he said anything. Is it true? Is it kind? Is it necessary? If the answer to even one of those was no, he would keep it to himself. If he needed to vent, he could wait until he got home and talk about it in one of his online chat rooms where everyone shared his feelings.

Zach wanted to be careful not to let his tendency to talk about negative things affect his work environment. It didn't feel professional; he wanted to be upbeat so they wouldn't think he was a downer. The rubber band wrist reminders kept him on track with his new positive attitude.

MARIA, 45

Maria loved her new job, but she dreaded going to her first staff meeting. What should she wear? How should she act? Should she say anything, or be quiet the whole time? She wanted to be professional and also fit in. Attending meetings was something new for her, and that increased her anxiety. At least it would be in the same room where she had interviewed for the job, so the place would be familiar, and some of the people, too. She reminded herself of what would be familiar each time she started to feel nervous. She also brought a small key chain of a sloth and one of a robot. They would stay hidden in her purse, but knowing they were there reminded her to be calm like a sloth and strong like a giant robot.

On the day of the staff meeting, Maria took a long time choosing what to wear. She remembered how comfortable and casual the interviewers had been, and she felt that her wardrobe

CHAPTER 22

was stuffy and buttoned-up in comparison. She didn't own any clothes that were casual, except the kinds of things she would wear around the house or to pick up the newspaper and mail. Those things were far too informal and shabby. She finally chose a dark rose-colored dress and added a floral scarf her daughters had given her for her birthday. It seemed cheerful and in line with what she'd seen the others wear, but true to the simple style she was comfortable with.

When she got to the meeting, she found an empty chair as far as possible from the head of the table. She accepted an offer to help herself to the coffee and refreshments, because stirring coffee and holding a cup gave her something to do with her hands. She smiled vaguely to others as they came in, but didn't initiate conversation. It was hard enough to be in this place without trying to manage small talk, too. Once the meeting started, she relaxed a bit. She was surprised when the boss introduced her as their newest team member and she gave a little wave, blushing when they looked at her and clapped. They seemed glad to have her join their company.

Maria glanced at the other women in the room periodically to see what they were doing so she could imitate them. They sat oriented toward the person speaking, and occasionally nodded at a point they agreed on, or laughed at a joke. Maria was surprised at how often one or another of them spoke up and offered ideas or suggestions. They seemed so confident. Maria would not be doing that herself, preferring the sidelines, but she found it gratifying to work in a company that valued the women's ideas as much as the men's.

After the meeting was over, Maria was relieved to go back to working out of her home until the next month. She had effectively used her people skills to observe and imitate what others did in the meeting. She also tried to match her choice of outfit to what she had seen other women wearing, but without sacrificing her personal style. These skills helped her fit in rather than stand out, which was right for her. She felt like a real professional.

ROBERT, 62

Robert loved being back in the work force, even if it was part time. Retirement didn't sit well with him; he craved the familiarity of going to work and the satisfaction of doing a good job. His workplace was so casual he never felt uncomfortable, and his boss was easy-going and seemed to like him. If he noticed any social awkwardness or quirks, he never mentioned them. It was the ideal workplace for an old geezer like Robert.

What worked best for Robert in this new job was to be prepared for whatever job walked in the front door, or whatever task his boss tossed his way. He brought his own tools; he'd worked with them for so long that they fit his hand like an extension of his arm. Having the tools he needed helped him feel ready to take on anything.

SPEAKING FOR OURSELVES

"Two of the hardest things for me have been working for fools and holding my tongue when I saw injustice. If my boss had a stupid idea, it was difficult for me to filter how I responded to it.

CHAPTER 22

I had a tendency to be brutally honest, which never ended well. If I saw that a coworker was being bullied, I would just blurt out what a jerk the boss was and tell them they couldn't treat people that way. I lost a couple jobs because I didn't control those impulses. As I matured and understand more about myself and my autism, I'm learning to stop and think before I jump right in. I have to ask myself, is action required? Maybe holding my tongue for now and bringing it up later will let me do the right thing and still keep my job. The older I get, the more important this is. I may need a job, but I also know I can't ignore injustice. Taking the time to figure out the best way to address a problem and asking for advice from someone I trust is important for me."

~ *Scott, autistic adult*

PART VI

THE BIG PICTURE

———◆———

Bringing It All Together

"It isn't all over; everything has not been invented;
the human adventure is just beginning."
— *Gene Roddenberry, creator of* Star Trek

CHAPTER 23
ONE LAST PEP TALK

———⟨∘⟩———

(You're Ready!)

I hope this book has helped you further along your own trip through adulthood. We may be at the end of the book, but it's not the end. It's time to get on with rest of your road trip through life. Let's check in one last time on our five characters and see how they're doing in their journeys.

JACOB, 19

Jacob blew out the candles and his parents, grandparents, aunts, uncles, and cousins all cheered. He was nineteen years old, and about to graduate from high school. He'd had quite a year. He'd improved his relationship with his parents and people at school by learning more about his autism and how it affected his communication, social life, and sensory stuff. He'd been using his bicycle to get around town. He had eco-club at school with kids who shared his interests, guys to hang out with at lunch and meet up with on weekends. He'd gone to prom with Hannah and they planned to see each other over the summer. He even had a part-time job, which he would keep when he started at the community college in the fall. Jacob wasn't sure yet exactly where he was going in life, but he knew he was on the right path and that he could handle whatever life sent his way. It was going to be another great year!

EMILY, 23

Emily clutched the envelope to her chest, tears in her eyes. She couldn't believe it. Inside the birthday card from her parents was a ticket to see *Hamilton: An American Musical*. She was overwhelmed by their generosity. They really did know her and what she was passionate about.

As she thought back over the last year, she realized how far she'd come. She'd moved out of her parents' home and was getting along with her housemates. She could get around on her own by bus. She learned to stand up for herself and say no. She had a good friend, Ashley, to share her feelings with. She sold some of her stuffed alpacorns, and she even had a part-time job in the group home. She could hardly wait to see what the next year had in store!

ZACH, 34

"Mazel tov! Congratulations!" Zach's parents beamed, handing him a birthday card. "It's cash," his mother said. "I said we should get you something more personal, something nice, but your father disagreed. So, it's cash." She rolled her eyes at her husband.

CHAPTER 23

"He knows what he needs, and what he doesn't need is a lot of tchotchkes gathering dust." His father looked to him for agreement. "Am I right, Zach? Would you rather have something else? Maybe a subscription to the Fruit of the Month club? I understand it's going to be pineapples next month."

"He doesn't want the Fruit of the Month Club. Nobody wants the Fruit of the Month club! It just would've been nice to get him something personal, that's all I'm saying."

"Thank you! Cash is perfect, Dad. Mom, I promise to get myself something personal with it and think of you whenever I use it." Zach smiled at their bickering, knowing they adored each other. He remembered how it used to annoy him, but now he found it charming. That must be the difference between living under their roof versus visiting once a week. He appreciated them more as friends now.

Zach thought back over all the changes he'd seen this year. He finally moved out into his own place at the temple. He had his first job as caretaker, and now his second job at the non-profit. He had friends through volunteering and the temple young adult group. Then there was Crystal. She seemed to really like him. Even though his old car had given up the ghost, he was on his way toward saving up for another one. Wanting to take Crystal out on a real date fired up his motivation to save. He decided to deposit all of his birthday money into his savings account, putting him further along the road toward car ownership. Life had been good, and the future was looking even better.

"I want to make a toast," he said. "You've been so patient with me through the years, and I want you to know how much I appreciate you and love you. Mom, Dad, thank you. You're the best." He smiled at them, and they all raised their glasses.

MARIA, 46

Maria laughed until tears streamed down her cheeks. The birthday card from her daughters tickled her funny bone. They'd obviously made it themselves, which touched her, and it showed they really got her. On the front was a picture of two sloths wearing birthday hats, with word balloons above their heads. One said, "You might think this card is early ..." and the other one said, "...but it's really late from last year." Inside the card was a picture of a giant robot and the words, "Hope your birthday is transformative!"

As she wiped her eyes and found a place to display the card, Maria thought back over the past year. So many changes! She started going back to church, found a friend, joined a book club, and even had a job. She, and those closest to her, had come to accept her autism. She was learning to cope with her unique challenges so that she could get out and try new things, balancing her need for solitude and her desire to connect. More and more, she felt she could be as calm as a sloth and as fearless as a giant robot. It was a good place to be for Maria.

ROBERT, 63

"Happy birthday, Grandpa!" Bobby gave Robert a brief hug, then backed off and the two of them shared their special handshake. "Want me to help you blow out the candles?"

"You don't expect an old geezer like me to blow out all those candles by myself, do you? I'm no fire extinguisher!" They blew out the candles together, and the party laughed and clapped.

CHAPTER 23

"Did you make a wish, Grandpa? Don't tell what you wished for, or it won't come true!"

Robert thought about the last year, since being forced into early retirement. He'd learned about his grandson's autism and his own. He'd made great strides in improving his communication and relationships with his wife, his family, and his friends at the diner. He quit smoking, this time for good. He even got a part-time job so he wouldn't be underfoot all the time. What could be better?

"I guess you'd better make this wish, Bobby," he said with a smile. "I already have everything I want."

Like our fictional friends Jacob, Emily, Zach, Maria, and Robert, you may have experienced a year of growth and success. Like most people, you've probably also run into your share of detours and dead ends along the way. Don't be discouraged. A setback is not the end of the road. No matter what your dreams are, your autism is not an insurmountable obstacle to achieving them.

Do you wonder if you'll ever fall in love and have a family? It's not a guarantee for anyone, on or off the spectrum, but it's not out of reach, either. David felt like an alien on this planet, never quite understanding other people, never quite being understood. Dating was difficult and disappointing. He longed for a family but didn't know if he'd ever have one. In his late twenties he met, fell in love, and married his wife, who was his personal intense interest. They had three children and a life-long, loving relationship. Learning that he had autism as an adult, when two of their children were diagnosed, was a welcome revelation and answered many questions. David found meaning and fulfillment as a loving spouse and parent.

Perhaps you feel called to teach. So did Chris Bonello, also known as Captain Quirk (www.autisticnotweird.com). After a career as a teacher, he went on to become an autism writer, speaker, and advocate. This might be your calling, as well.

Do you have a talent for writing, a unique voice, and a lot to say? You could become a blogger like Morgan Marie. She started www.confessionsofanautisticfreak.wordpress.com as a way to express her personal feelings, struggles, passions and pride, and many people relate to what she shares online. Perhaps your perspectives can find a following on the internet, too.

Maybe your faith is an important part of your world, like Ron Sandison (www.spectruminclusion.com). Not only does he have a full-time career in the medical field, he is also a professor of theology, a writer, speaker, and an advisory board member of the Autism Society Faith Initiative. When it looked like his autism might get in the way of his future, Ron's faith, family support, and optimistic persistence helped him get where he is today.

Want to make it in the entertainment industry? Celebrities on the spectrum include singers Travis Meeks, James Durbin, and Susan Boyle. Dan Ackroyd, Daryl Hannah, and Courtney Love have acknowledged their autism. Obviously, not everyone with talent becomes rich and famous, but being autistic doesn't have to hold you back.

A number of historical figures who have made extraordinary contributions are now thought to have been on the autism spectrum. Norm Ledgin wrote *Diagnosing Jefferson: Evidence of a Condition that Guided His Beliefs, Behavior, and Personal*

CHAPTER 23

Associations using historical accounts to make a convincing case that Jefferson had Asperger's. He later wrote *Asperger's and Self Esteem: Insight and Hope Through Famous Role Models* to highlight more people who may have been on the spectrum, ranging from Mozart to Carl Sagan. If you search online for "famous people with autism" you will find many, many more examples.

Maybe you have an intense interest that doesn't lend itself to a career. Don't let that stop you from pursuing your passion as a side hustle. Anita Lesko didn't. Although she has a successful career as a nurse anesthesiologist and is a published author (www.anitalesko.com), her true passion is aviation. Anita's dream was to fly in an F-15 fighter jet, just like in the movie *Top Gun*. She learned all she could about her interest. Eventually, in addition to her medical career, she became a military aviation photojournalist, ultimately achieving her dream. Anita didn't let her autism, or anything else, get in the way of her dream, and neither should you.

Are you interested in a career in the medical field? Autism hasn't stopped others from that path. Consider Kim, a physician who was diagnosed with Asperger's syndrome at age fifty-seven. Her strong work ethic, her interest in the deeper meaning of life, and personal and spiritual mentors all contributed to her success.

Perhaps you love animals and have a strong desire to help them. You may be like veterinary surgeon Neil McRae. His sharp attention to details made him good at his job.

Do you dream of a career in the arts? So did dancer-choreographer Leonora Gregory-Collura. A highly sensitive person, she always knew she was different, but wasn't diagnosed until age thirty-seven. With support from teachers and mentors, she learned to use the power of movement and dance to express her emotions. Today, she has a loving marriage and is a dancer-choreographer and an autism outreach consultant.

If you loved college, you might feel right at home as a professor. You'd be in good company with autistic professors Temple Grandin and Stephen Shore, among many others. Universities are perfect workplaces for many autistic adults. Imagine getting paid to lecture about your intense interest! (Read more about Anita, Kim, Neil, Leonora, Temple and Stephen, and many more successful adults with autism, in Temple Grandin's book, *Different ... Not Less.*)

Whatever road you choose, go forth boldly. Follow your path with confidence and pursue your dreams with tenacity. Be ready to adjust to new routes and unexpected side trips, accepting change as part of the adventure that you find along your way. You are an intrepid traveler, a wonderfully-made wayfarer.

As DC Comics character The Flash said, "Life is locomotion ... Keep moving, even if your path isn't lit. Trust that you'll find your way."

You, too, will find your way.

Bon voyage!

Still 'round the corner there may wait
a new road or a secret gate ...

— *J. R. R. Tolkien, English author*

ATLAS

———⟫●⟪———

A Collection of Maps
to Show the Way.

American Psychiatric Association. (2013). *Diagnostic and Statistical Manual of Mental Disorders (5th ed.)*.

Baker, J. (2005). *Preparing for Life: The Complete Guide for Transitioning to Adulthood for Those With Autism and Asperger's Syndrome*. Arlington, TX: Future Horizons, Inc.

Bartness, E. (Ed.). (2018). *Knowing Why: Adult-Diagnosed Autistic People on Life and Autism*. Washington, DC: The Autistic Press.

Bonello, Chris. www.autisticnotweird.com

Brown, K. W. (2018). *Adulting: How to Become a Grownup in 535 Easy(ish) Steps (Updated Edition)*. New York, NY: Grand Central Life & Style, Hachette Book Group.

Brown, K. W. (2017). *Gracious*. New York, NY: Rodale Wellness.

Cooper, J. O., T.E. Heron, and W.L. Heward. (2007). *Applied Behavior Analysis, Second Edition*. London: Pearson.

Doubleclicks. www.thedoubleclicks.com

Evans, C. R. with Attwood, T. (2018). *Ask Dr. Tony: Answers From the World's Leading Authority on Asperger's Syndrome / High-Functioning Autism.* Arlington, TX: Future Horizons, Inc.

Grandin, T. (2012). *Different ... Not Less.* Arlington, TX: Future Horizons, Inc.

Grandin, T. (2006). *Thinking in Pictures: My Life with Autism.* New York: NY Vintage Books, a Division of Random House.

Grandin, T. & Barron, S. (2017). *Unwritten Rules of Social Relationships: Decoding Social Mysteries Through the Unique Perspectives of Autism.* V. Zysk (Ed.). Arlington, TX: Future Horizons, Inc.

Higashida, Naoki. (2007). *The Reason I Jump: The Inner Voice of a Thirteen-Year-Old Boy with Autism.* New York, NY: Random House, Inc.

Ledgin, N. (2013) *Asperger's and Self-Esteem: Insight and Hope Through Famous Role Models.* Arlington, TX: Future Horizons, Inc.

Ledgin, N. (2000) *Diagnosing Jefferson: Evidence of a Condition That Guided His Beliefs, Behavior, and Personal Associations.* Arlington, TX: Future Horizons, Inc.

Lesko, Anita. www.anitalesko.com

Marie, Morgan. www.confessionsofanautisticfreak.wordpress.com

Miltenberger, R. G. (2012). *Behavior Modification: Principles and Procedures, Fifth Edition.* Belmont, CA: Wadsworth Cengage Learning.

ATLAS

Newport, J. (2007). *Your Life is Not a Label: A Guide to Living Fully with Autism and Asperger's Syndrome for Parents, Professionals, and You!* Arlington, TX: Future Horizons, Inc.

Newport, J. & Newport, M. (2002). *Autism-Asperger's & Sexuality: Puberty and Beyond.* Arlington, TX: Future Horizons, Inc.

Sandison, Ron. www.spectruminclusion.com

Schaber, Amythest. www.conversationsthatmatter.com
@neurowonderful
https://www.youtube.com/user/neurowonderful

Shore, S. (ed.). (2004). *Ask and Tell: Self-Advocacy and Disclosure for People on the Autism Spectrum.* Shawnee Mission, KS: Autism Asperger Publishing Co.

Tammet, D. (2007). *Born on a Blue Day: A Memoir.* New York, NY: Free Press, A Division of Simon & Schuster, Inc.

Tew, L. & Zajac, D. (2018). *Autism and Employment: Raising Your Child with Foundational Skills for the Future.* Arlington, TX: Future Horizons, Inc.

ABOUT THE AUTHOR

 Dr. Wendela Whitcomb Marsh is a Board Certified Behavior Analyst®, counselor, and autism specialist. She was married for 27 years to an amazing man with Asperger's syndrome and has two autistic adult daughters. She loves working with neurodivergent adults, as well as their parents and family members, to help them achieve independence and solve life problems. Dr. Marsh lives in Salem, Oregon with her three children and two cats.